Lawrence J. Haas

Harry & Arthur

Truman, Vandenberg, *and the*
Partnership That Created
the Free World

Potomac Books

An imprint of the University of Nebraska Press

Library of Congress Cataloging-in-Publication Data
Names: Haas, Lawrence J.
Title: Harry and Arthur: Truman, Vandenberg, and the
partnership that created the free world / Lawrence J. Haas.
Description: Lincoln: Potomac Books, an imprint of the
University of Nebraska Press, 2016.
Includes bibliographical references and index.
Identifiers: LCCN 2015036855
ISBN 9781612348124 (cloth: alk. paper)
ISBN 9781612348322 (epub)
ISBN 9781612348339 (mobi)
ISBN 9781612348346 (pdf)
Subjects: LCSH: United States—Foreign relations—1945–1953. |
Truman, Harry S., 1884–1972. | Vandenberg, Arthur H.
(Arthur Hendrick), 1884–1951.
Classification: LCC E813 .H23 2016 | DDC 327.73009/04—dc23
LC record available at http://lccn.loc.gov/2015036855

Set in Garamond Premier Pro by L. Auten.

To Marjie and Samantha
My loves, my life

CONTENTS

ACKNOWLEDGMENTS

WRITING A BOOK IS one thing; writing it in a timely fashion is quite another. I never could have done the latter without the invaluable assistance of a dozen talented research interns from the American Foreign Policy Council (AFPC), the Washington think tank with which I'm affiliated: Joshua Truman, Megan Carey, James O'Bryant, Jared Swanson, Kayla Scott, Sarah Reynolds, Anabel Hallewell, Cameron Harris, Lauren Danen, Jason Czerwiec, Ben Schwartz, and Drew Jansen. These talented young professionals each spent a few months assisting me and, over the course of nearly three years, tracked down vital sources of information—newspaper and magazine accounts from the late 1940s, journal articles, government reports, and so on—and fact-checked the words I put to paper. I thank them for their work, and I thank AFPC President Herman Pirchner, Vice President Ilan Berman, and Director of Operations Richard Harrison for making them available.

I also thank Ilan Berman, Richard Cohen, Mark Fife, Marjorie Segel Haas, Ben Schwartz, and Drew Jansen for reading the manuscript, offering suggestions, catching typos and grammatical problems, and pinpointing factual errors that could have proved embarrassing. Any errors that still crept into this book are my fault alone.

Peter Bernstein, my agent and an accomplished author and editor, improved this book immensely with his suggestions for both my book proposal and the book itself. The structure and focus of *Harry and Arthur* owe much to our conversations. Whatever its deficiencies, this book is far better than it would have been without Peter's prodding. The book is also better due to the efforts of many wonderful people at Potomac Books, on both the editorial and marketing sides, who worked with great care to turn a raw manuscript into a finished product of which I could be proud.

No one has more patience than my wife, Marjie, and my daughter, Samantha. As much as possible, I try to research and write my books while they're asleep or busy with their own things, but my work invariably impinges on our family time. I appreciate their willingness to tolerate it more than I can ever express. The best I can do is dedicate this book to them as a heartfelt expression of my love.

PROLOGUE

April 1945

ON THE MORNING OF April 12, 1945, Harry Truman, the vice president of the United States, and Arthur Vandenberg, the top Republican on the Senate Foreign Relations Committee, awakened to a world in turmoil—a world that, with Franklin Roosevelt's death later that day, they would inherit.

World War II was fast approaching its end, with U.S. troops slicing through Germany from the west and Soviet troops advancing from the east. With the Nazi regime collapsing, more of its liberated victims— prisoners of war, slave laborers, and concentration camp survivors; mostly men but also women and children—were wandering the streets, desperate for food, clothing, shelter, or a way out of Germany. Gaunt, dirt-caked, lice-infested, and malodorous, their skin sagging from skeletal bodies, they relayed tales of almost unimaginable horror. In Britain's House of Commons, members merrily traded premature rumors that Hitler was dead. In France, the lights of Paris had returned recently for the first time since the war began to celebrate Allied victories on the western front, illuminating the Arc de Triomphe and Cathedral of Notre Dame, the Champs-Elysees and Place de la Concorde. In the Pacific, U.S. forces were progressing steadily against Imperial Japan, claiming land on nearby islands as Japanese citizens committed suicide in hordes rather than face capture.

For Truman and Vandenberg, however, the prospect of victory offered only limited satisfaction. As they could see, an America that was desperate for a reprieve from global tumult would not enjoy one. Already, the Soviet Union was presenting a huge new challenge for the United States, as the allies of war were fast becoming the rivals of an emerging postwar world. With misery and want plaguing vast stretches of Europe, the Mediterranean, the Middle East, and beyond, Moscow and its Communist minions were seeking to exploit the chaos and expand the Soviet Empire first across Eastern Europe and then elsewhere. Attitudes about the Soviets were hardening in Washington where opposition grew to more Lend-Lease aid for Moscow, and across the country where Catholic leaders and Polish Americans condemned Soviet activities in Eastern Europe.

If Truman and Vandenberg had read the cables between FDR and Joseph Stalin in the weeks before Roosevelt's death, they would have seen that U.S.-Soviet relations had deteriorated even more than they knew. In his final days, FDR complained bitterly that, in establishing puppet regimes in Eastern Europe, Stalin was breaking his promises at the Yalta Conference of February to allow for free elections in Poland and elsewhere. He also protested that, in Soviet-held territories, Soviet soldiers were preventing American soldiers from helping U.S. prisoners of war, some of whom were ill or wounded. The day before his death, FDR advised the State Department that it had higher priorities than the Soviet request for a $6 billion loan. Stalin, meanwhile, accused FDR and Britain's Winston Churchill of seeking a separate peace with Germany to spare the lives of U.S. and British soldiers while allowing Russian soldiers to continue dying. Suspicious of U.S. and British motives, Stalin expressed his irritation by announcing that his foreign minister, Vyacheslav Molotov, would not attend the organizing conference of the United Nations, a top Roosevelt priority, which was scheduled to begin in San Francisco on April 25.

So when Roosevelt died later that day of a cerebral hemorrhage, Truman and Vandenberg inherited a world in flux, its future very much in doubt.

. . .

Peace would bring no return of the old order. With a dormant economy and a flattened infrastructure, Britain, France, and the other traditional stalwarts of Europe were struggling merely to survive.

Across the continent, where forty million people had perished through six years of war, millions of newly "displaced persons," including lost or orphaned children, fled their war-torn cities and towns in search of new lives—or were forcibly moved by new governments or invading armies. More than half of the housing in Europe's major cities was "reduced to rubble," along with hundreds of ships, thousands of bridges, and tens of thousands of miles of rail. (In Germany alone, 3.6 million "dwelling units" were destroyed or heavily damaged, leaving 7.5 million people homeless, while cities were "largely reduced to hollow walls and piles of rubble."[1]) With farms destroyed, mined, or lying fallow, their equipment wrecked and their horses gone, nations could not grow the food to feed their people. Many were starving, many more scraping by on little, with most Europeans consuming just half to two-thirds of their prewar calories.[2] In the former German city of Konigsberg, which the Soviets annexed, people were eating offal and selling human flesh as fried meatballs.[3]

"It is hard for Americans to picture the devastation, the disruption and dislocation of life and the awful crippling shortages that this war has left as a heritage to those who survived it," the *New York Times'* Raymond Daniell wrote from Berlin in mid-1945, predicting a "hard and hungry winter in all of Europe . . . These people are short of everything—of food and clothing, of shelter, of transportation, of medicine, and even of time and faith and hope. Theirs is a grisly past of terror, persecution and death, a present of dire urgency and woe, and a future of grim uncertainty."[4] By November, tuberculosis was "rife," with "the very young and the very old especially . . . beginning to die in droves as the autumn leaves fall."[5] As historian Margaret MacMillan put it, "The four horsemen of the apocalypse—pestilence, war, famine, and death—so familiar during the middle ages, appeared again in the modern world."[6]

Clearly, neither Britain nor France nor Italy nor Belgium nor Holland nor Austria nor any other European nation was in any position to maintain order on the continent, to rebuff the designs of a new Soviet aggressor.

. . .

If the old order could not be restored, what would take its place? What would prevent the Soviets from conquering not just Eastern Europe but Western Europe, the Mediterranean, and the Middle East?

As World War II was ending, the United States stood tall. Unlike the other major combatants, its mainland was untouched by war. No armies had crossed its borders; no bombs had leveled its cities. Free from such dangers, Americans built the planes and ships that carried its troops to battle thousands of miles from home, tipping the balance to the Allies. After the war, America strode the world like an economic colossus, producing almost as much in goods and services as the rest of the world combined.[7]

A Western Europe that was engulfed in hunger and homelessness, misery and despair, was looking to what it hoped was a new savior. "One of the most infuriating but also one of the most persistent questions which an American encounters in Paris," a *New York Times* correspondent wrote from the continent in June of 1945, "is, 'Well, when is America going to fight the Russians?'"[8]

Whether America was willing to "fight the Russians" or do anything else of note around the world, however, was an open question.

. . .

Up to that point, the United States had been a steadily rising, but stubbornly reluctant, giant on the world stage.

For 150 years, the nation had taken its guidance on foreign affairs largely from George Washington's warning, in his Farewell Address of 1796, to "steer clear of permanent alliances." America lived largely alone—with vast oceans to its east and west, friendly neighbors to its north and south, no desire to meddle in Europe, and no real interests beyond its borders. It had no permanent military establishment to speak of and no military commitment to any other nation. Not even its entry into World War I altered that reality. After the armistice in November 1918, America rejected U.S. participation in the League of Nations, dramatically reduced its military, erected huge trade barriers to wall off foreign competition, and largely maintained its isolationist stance for two decades until Pearl Harbor.

Not surprisingly, then, as America approached victory in the spring of 1945, isolationist sentiments were returning. A war-weary public anticipated the return of husbands, fathers, and sons, and Truman faced growing calls to "bring the boys home" as fast as possible. Wives wrote to lawmakers to urge the speedy return of their husbands, often sending baby pictures and even baby shoes with their letters. Tightfisted Republicans and influential columnists like Drew Pearson argued that America's resources were better spent at home. When Truman proposed universal military training in October 1945 to ensure the nation's readiness for future conflict, Congress ignored the request.

In November Assistant Secretary of State Dean Acheson told the Maryland Historical Society, "I can state in three sentences what the 'popular' attitude is toward foreign policy today: 1. Bring the boys home; 2. Don't be a Santa Claus; 3. Don't be pushed around." Around that time, the influential U.S. diplomat Averell Harriman said Americans wanted to "go to the movies and drink Coke."[9]

Historian Eric F. Goldman, who lived through the period, wrote a few years later of his countrymen of that day,

> For the first time during an American era of peace, it was next to impossible to discuss domestic problems coherently without having the points become entangled in foreign affairs. To millions this was an intensely irritating fact. They felt, as generations of Americans had felt before them, that concern over international matters was to be confined to unfortunate periods of war. Foreign policy was something you had, like measles, and got over with as quickly as possible.[10]

Thus, a new U.S. approach to the world was hardly inevitable. Someone would have to bring it to fruition.

. . .

It was Harry Truman and Arthur Vandenberg who would build the architecture of a dramatic new foreign policy through which, for the first time, the United States stepped up boldly to protect its friends, confront its enemies, and promote freedom. The change was more sudden than gradual, more revolutionary than evolutionary.

Under their leadership from the spring of 1945 to the summer of 1949, the United States would spearhead the birth of a United Nations to replace the ineffective League of Nations that it had spurned; pledge through the Truman Doctrine to defend freedom from Communist threat virtually anywhere in the world; rescue Western Europe's economy from the devastation of war through the Marshall Plan; and commit itself through the North Atlantic Treaty (which established NATO) to defend Western Europe if the Soviets attacked.

It was, as an influential diplomat of that period, Charles Bohlen, wrote later, "the transition from total protected isolationism, as the most secure—and non-military—country in the world, to the greatest responsibility that any single country has ever borne in the history of the world."[11]

Together, Truman and Vandenberg transformed the United States from a reluctant giant on the world stage to a self-confident leader; from a nation that traditionally turned inward after war to one that remained engaged to shape the postwar landscape; and from a nation with no real military establishment to one that, today, spends more on defense than the next dozen nations combined. They crafted the philosophy, built the machinery, and secured the funds for America's new role that has endured to this day.

. . .

To be sure, Truman and Vandenberg did not work alone. They had lots of help as they crafted America's new foreign policy.

From the administration, they were assisted by Secretary of State Edward Stettinius, whom Truman and Vandenberg both disparaged but who nevertheless effectively led the U.S. delegation (on which Vandenberg sat) to the UN organizing conference in San Francisco in 1945;

Jimmy Byrnes, the wily ex-senator whom Truman chose to replace Stettinius and who built a sturdy partnership with Vandenberg; George C. Marshall, the stern, driven, iconic figure who succeeded Byrnes, was worshipped by Truman, and worked closely with Vandenberg on the Marshall Plan; Dean Acheson, the Groton, Yale, and Harvard Law graduate who held top State Department posts and who, despite his aristocratic airs and condescending ways, formed strong partnerships with the plainspoken Truman and the egotistical Vandenberg; Averell Harriman, the tall, lanky, square-jawed diplomat who counseled Truman to harden U.S. policy toward the Soviets; and such other important figures as Robert Lovett, George Kennan, Will Clayton, and Leo Pasvolsky, all of whom served in key positions and significantly influenced Truman and Vandenberg.

On Capitol Hill they were assisted by, among others, Tom Connally, Vandenberg's Democratic counterpart on the Senate Foreign Relations Committee, who spoke with a deep Texan drawl, displayed a flair for histrionics, and sometimes felt ignored by an administration that lavished so much attention on Vandenberg; and by Charles Eaton, the top Republican on the House Foreign Affairs Committee, who was born in Canada, became an American citizen in his late twenties, first made his mark in the clergy and journalism, and teamed with Vandenberg to fight isolationists within Republican circles.

. . .

More striking than the help Truman and Vandenberg received, however, were the obstacles they were forced to overcome. For as the two men worked together from 1945 to 1949, their parties confronted one another in bitter political battles that make today's partisanship seem dainty by comparison.

These were years of both real danger to U.S. national security from Soviet spying as well as reckless demagoguery that laid the groundwork for the McCarthyism that arrived a few years later. Congress held hearings on "un-American" activities; Republicans accused Truman, his top aides, and congressional Democrats of "softness" on Communism;

Truman sought to inoculate himself politically by creating a "loyalty program" for federal workers; business and religious groups launched anti-Communist campaigns; and civil servants, professors, and others who came under suspicion lost their jobs.

In this period Republicans were angry over FDR's four straight presidential victories and determined to bring a long era of Democratic rule to an end. In the 1946 congressional elections and 1948 presidential election, Republicans and Democrats attacked one another in vicious, searing, personal language that far exceeded the acceptable rhetoric of our day. Republicans questioned not just the judgment of Democrats but their patriotism. By early 1946 influential Senate Republican Robert Taft and his colleagues were routinely calling Truman's domestic initiatives "Communist."[12] A young House Republican candidate named Richard Nixon won his race that year by labeling Democratic incumbent Jerry Voorhis a Communist, while Republican National Committee Chairman B. Carroll Reece, a Tennessee House Republican, called the congressional elections a "fight basically between communism and Republicanism."[13]

As elected officials, Truman and Vandenberg could not remove themselves from the politics of the day, nor did they want to. Vandenberg won reelection overwhelmingly as expected in 1946, while Truman shocked everybody but himself by winning reelection in 1948. When they weren't running for office, each naturally sought to do whatever he could to help his party and its candidates at election time.

On foreign affairs, however, the Democratic president and Republican senator never lost sight of the big picture. They never sidestepped the monumental challenge of Soviet aggression and the awesome role that only America could assume. They never forgot that, to reach their goals, they needed each other. They never let the bitter politics swirling around them affect their relationship.

. . .

Today, in Washington and across the country, many of our leaders and citizens are questioning America's global role, doubting our continued capacity to address big challenges at home and abroad, and lamenting the pettiness of our political dialogue.

Nearly three-quarters of a century ago, the leaders and citizens of that day had the same questions, the same doubts, and the same laments. As the nation emerged from World War II, they struggled to define America's new role in a world in which long-standing power structures had been torn asunder, leaving a vacuum on the world stage that, if left unfilled, could have proved hazardous to freedom. They came to understand that their traditional isolationism would no longer do if they hoped to ensure peace and prosperity. Consequently, under the leadership of Truman and Vandenberg, they created the architecture and provided the funds for a revolutionary new foreign policy that served the United States well through the decades that followed—and that can continue to do so.

Thus, the landmark partnership of Truman and Vandenberg offers a timely, inspiring, and instructive history lesson.

. . .

Who were these men?

HARRY & ARTHUR

Introduction

Harry and Arthur

IN MARCH OF 1951 Arthur Vandenberg was a month from death. He was still the senior senator from Michigan but, with his body ravaged by the cancer that had spread along his spine, he hadn't attended a Senate session in ten months. At home in Grand Rapids, pale and haggard, in excruciating pain and a shell of his former imposing self, he was left to reading the get-well wishes of former colleagues like Secretary of Defense George C. Marshall and Senator Henry Cabot Lodge, a Massachusetts Republican.

From Key West, where he had taken the presidential yacht for a few days of poker with his pals, Harry Truman sent Vandenberg a telegram. "All of your friends are disturbed by reports that you have not been getting on so well lately," he wrote. "This is just a line to let you know that I am thinking of you and hope you will be back in your old place soon. The country needs you. Best of luck always."

Vandenberg replied by letter the next day, addressing the president as "My dear Harry" for the first time. "I am deeply touched by your telegram of March 6," he wrote. "I know it is inspired by a long-time personal friendship which you and I enjoy. It moves me to greet you in this personal way. Your message is good for my morale. I hope you enjoy your Key West outing and that it will reinvigorate you for the heavy burdens which you carry. I have abiding faith in the future of our good old U.S.A."[1]

The poignant exchange between Truman and Vandenberg evoked

memories of grander times, of the days when they had worked in close collaboration. From the spring of 1945 through the summer of 1949, the Democratic president and Republican senator had done great things. Indeed, no two leaders had ever done more in such a bipartisan way and at such a perilous time. But, while Vandenberg was "deeply touched" by "My dear Harry," this mushy exchange did not reflect their historic partnership. During their collaboration, they did not exude great warmth toward one another. They were less personal friends than professional colleagues. Each had many qualities that the other found off-putting. Truman could be harsh in his judgments and crass in his language, sometimes offending Vandenberg along the way, and he whitewashed history to put himself in the best possible light. Vandenberg was frequently the kind of self-important bigwig for whom Truman had no patience, protecting his senatorial prerogatives zealously and reminding everyone of his importance. That two such leaders of different parties could form a working partnership at all, much less one of monumental consequence, was no small miracle.

Despite their differences in personal style and political philosophy, however, Truman and Vandenberg shared important traits, some nurtured in their youth, others developed in their later years. They were both products of America's Midwest, and they inherited from their parents the same down-home values of right and wrong, honesty and integrity, that later shaped their thinking about global affairs. From a young age, they developed a seriousness of purpose and a commitment to hard work. Most of all, as America emerged from World War II, they came to share the same perspective about the nation's security challenges and about the need for both parties to work together to address them.

. . .

They were born just forty-seven days apart in the spring of 1884, in an era of rising incomes and expanding opportunities but also of great risks, with the economy of the late nineteenth century plagued by depressions that bankrupted businesses and threw millions out of work. Truman and Vandenberg exploited the opportunities but also fell victim to the risks, and their economic highs and lows shaped their personal outlooks, professional choices, and political philosophies for decades to come.

Arthur Hendrick Vandenberg arrived first, on March 22 in Grand Rapids, a major lumbering center of 42,000 people in western Michigan. He was the son of Aaron Vandenberg, a harness maker, and his second wife, Alpha Hendrick, who came from a prominent family in Clyde, New York. In Arthur's earliest years, his family lived a solid middle-class life in the "River City." Harry S. Truman was born on May 8 in Lamar, an isolated farm village of just 700 people in southwestern Missouri. He was the first of three children of John Anderson Truman, an ill-tempered farmer and mule trader, and the more cultured Martha Ellen Young. In Harry's early years, his father moved the family from one farm to the next in and around Lamar before settling everyone in more cosmopolitan Independence, a town of 6,000 to the southeast of Kansas City, in 1890.

The Civil War was still fresh in the minds of many in late nineteenth-century America, and it left profoundly different marks on Truman and Vandenberg, shaping their partnership many decades later. Missouri had entered the Union as a slave state and, though it was neutral during the war, pro-South sentiments ran high in its southern tier, which included Independence. Union irregulars stormed the farm of Truman's maternal grandparents, forced his grandmother to "bake biscuits until her fingers blistered," killed all four hundred hogs, stole the hams, and set the barns on fire. Harry's mother and grandmother carried grudges about it forever after. When, years later, Truman showed his grandmother his new uniform as a member of the National Guard, she said, "Harry, this is the first time since 1863 that a blue uniform has been in this house. Don't bring it here again."[2] Truman's mother even refused to sleep in the White House's "Lincoln Bedroom" when Truman was president.

Truman inherited a long memory from his mother and grandmother. As an adult, he held grudges against those who slighted him personally or offended him from a distance, be they foreign leaders, political opponents, corporate chieftains, labor rabble-rousers, pollsters, or "gutter snipe columnists." Within weeks of his reelection in 1948, he fired the

Secret Service's chief, who had visited Republican candidate Thomas Dewey's campaign headquarters on election night, and the National Security Resources Board's chairman, whose wife had suggested that the wives of administration officials wear black to her election night party so they were dressed appropriately for Truman's certain defeat. Nor, like many thin-skinned politicians, did time dim his bitterness. After Britain's foreign minister, Ernest Bevin, suggested in 1947 that Truman backed the creation of a new state of Israel merely to attract Jewish support at home, Truman disparaged him to aides a full two years later as he prepared to meet with him in Washington around the signing of the North Atlantic Treaty.

While Independence wallowed in southern bitterness after the Civil War, Grand Rapids reveled in northern pride over its men who had fought valiantly for the Union. With no grudges to pass on, the Vandenbergs instilled in Arthur a graciousness, a generosity, and a forgiving spirit that he tapped years later at awkward political moments. At a White House reception for Britain's King George VI in June of 1939, FDR insulted Vandenberg badly as the two met on the receiving line. Referring to Vandenberg's presidential ambitions, an unsmiling FDR told the King, "Here's a chap who thinks he is going to succeed me in the White House; but he isn't." FDR neglected even to mention Vandenberg's name, leaving the senator angry as the two Roosevelt sons standing nearby laughed heartily.[3] Nevertheless, when FDR and Vandenberg spoke ten months later at the annual dinner of the Gridiron Club, the nation's oldest club for journalists, Vandenberg set aside any lingering bitterness and offered the president an extraordinary tribute for persevering in the face of paralysis and addressing America's needs.

"However much we may quarrel over policy," Vandenberg said of FDR, "there is *one* point at which I can join his loudest psalm-singers. Speaking of the *man* himself, I do not hesitate to say that I never knew a more gallant soul who has laughed triumphantly at the handicaps of life and given his country a superb example of *personal* courage and a *personal* challenge to 'carry on' to victory, no matter what the burden, no matter what the odds. His example to us in this regard has never been equaled and it will never be excelled." Moreover, Vandenberg added, "history will accord him credit for making America *social-minded* . . . And it was high-time this phenomenon should come to pass because our best defense of democracy—in a sodden, saddened world of dictators—is to make democracy consciously and intimately advantageous to our whole people. These are adequate achievements for any man."[4]

Vandenberg's grace would prove crucial to his collaboration with Truman, for he chose mostly to seethe quietly, rather than fight publicly, when Truman lambasted Republicans in the harshest and most unfair ways.

. . .

Truman and Vandenberg came from stable families, and their mothers nourished their self-confidence by doting on them, teaching them right from wrong, and cultivating their minds, all of which gave them strong personal foundations on which to build their careers.

Truman, his mother liked to say, was "intended for a girl,"[5] and from a young age she taught him to cook, clean house, and care for his younger sister. In those years, Truman said later, he was a "sissy." He made eggs, oatmeal, and biscuits for the farmhands, watched over his mother's garden, and milked the cows. But Mrs. Truman, who had high hopes for the elder of her two sons, also taught him to read before age five and play piano a few years later. Harry's parents moved the family to Independence so he and his siblings could attend the town's well-regarded schools.

Truman later recalled a happy childhood, and it instilled in him an optimism about the future, a belief that tomorrow would be better than today, that he brought first to his business ventures and then to his public career. He vividly remembered laughing uproariously as he chased a frog at age two. In the next few years, he frolicked in the pasture behind his house with his younger brother, John Vivian, and a few neighborhood boys; rode the black Shetland pony that his father bought him; played checkers, chess, and poker with his uncle; and attended the county fair with his grandfather.

But childhood nurtured his serious side as well, for young Harry was confined to watch sports rather than participate due to his thick glasses (and to endure the teasing that came with life as a "four eyes"). He became a voracious reader, mostly of history but also of biography, and he came to appreciate the great role that a single individual can play. He later bragged that, by age fourteen, he had read all three thousand books in the local library, however unlikely that seems. He "most admired Alexander the Great, Hannibal, Charles Martel, Cincinnatus, and Robert E. Lee," and he "read Caesar, Cicero, Plutarch, Marcus Aurelius, Ralph Waldo Emerson, and Mark Twain."[6] As president, he often cited history when pondering great issues, astonishing his most sophisticated advisers with his knowledge. "There's nothing new in human nature," Truman said later. "The only thing that changes are the names we give things. If you want to understand the twentieth century, read the lives of the Roman emperors, all the way from Claudius to Constantine . . . Those people had the same troubles as we have now. Men don't change. The only thing new in the world is the history you don't know."[7]

Like Mrs. Truman, Mrs. Vandenberg had high hopes for her son, nurturing his serious side and teaching him to play piano. Like Harry, young Arthur was preternaturally serious, and it showed in his leisure-time activities. Unlike Harry, however, Arthur also loved the sound of his own voice, and he sought praise for what he said. Thus, while Harry read books, Arthur and a neighbor, Edward Perkins, played a game called "lectures" in which "the boys would choose speech topics and invite adults to listen to their talks."[8] The boy of "lectures" would later become the man of grand Senate oratory.

A good student like Harry—though, ironically, more in the hard sciences than English—Arthur pursued journalism and public speaking in high school; he liked to see his name in print and hear his voice on a stage, both of which fed his emerging ego. He worked for three years on the school yearbook and then assumed its editorship as a senior. He also served as vice president of the Literary Society and won a silver medal at the State Oratorical Contest for his speech on the First Hague Conference of 1899 (at which the world's leading powers sought ways to reduce arms and avoid war).

Not surprisingly, Vandenberg's speech making subjected him to high school derision. The yearbook of his junior year asked, "When will Vandenberg stop talking?" while that of his senior year stated amusingly, "A is for Arthur, the man with a voice." But if the teasing about his public speaking bothered him, he never showed it. In fact, at a very young age, "the man with a voice" was also the man with a plan. While in high school, he began reading the *Congressional Record*, the daily digest of congressional proceedings, and he had already decided to become a senator. In that role, as he recognized, he could speak to larger audiences on matters of great consequence. It would be nearly three decades before he turned that dream into a reality.

. . .

If family life was stable, childhood was hardly idyllic for either Harry or Arthur. They both saw their fathers fail at business, giving them striking lessons about life's hard edges. They were forced to grow up early, to work hard as youngsters to help pay the family bills, to defer their dreams, to set aside their passions in the interest of practicality. The day-to-day demands that were thrust upon Truman and Vandenberg gave them both a doggedness and sense of purpose that served them well in later years.

While in grade school, Truman worked both before and after classes at a local drugstore, dusting the bottles, sweeping the floor, and emptying the trash. After graduating high school in 1901, he hoped to attend West Point for its free education and the possibility that he could "perhaps imitate" one of the generals about whom he had read, be it Napoleon, Hannibal, Alexander, Caesar, or Lee. But West Point rejected him for his poor eyesight, and his father lacked the funds to send him to college for any sustained period. He attended Spalding's Commercial College in Kansas City for a year before his finances ran out. His father then went broke in 1902 after speculating in grain futures, costing the family its farm, $40,000 in cash, and other personal property and leaving Harry the family's lone breadwinner at eighteen. In the coming years, the dutiful son worked as, among other things, a night watchman, a timekeeper, and a bank clerk. Together, his simple roots, uncertain finances, and modest jobs nurtured his affinity for working people over moneyed interests.

By 1903 Truman was living on his own in a Kansas City boarding house, attending theater, piano recitals, light opera, and a Baptist church and serving in the National Guard. He was happy about the present and hopeful for the future. Once more, though, his family's finances forced his hand. His father summoned him home in 1906 to help with the next family farm, most of it owned by his maternal grandmother, and he stayed there for the next decade. Five years into his tenure, his father made him a partner, but it was a mixed blessing. When his father died in 1914, Truman found himself with debts to settle.

For Truman, the world of business proved no more successful. While still farming, he sought his fortune by investing with two associates in a zinc and lead mine near Commerce, Oklahoma. The venture flopped, leaving him with more debt and forcing him to lay off some workers before the mine closed altogether. Then it was on to the oil business, this time as a partner in a brokerage company that bought oil leases. That, too, failed when drilling on the land came up dry. So, too, did a haberdashery that he opened with his army buddy, Eddie Jacobson, in 1919. The failures took their toll on Truman, who also married his high school sweetheart, Bess, in 1919. He worried about how he would support her, and by then he considered himself a loser. When local Democratic leaders asked him to run for county office in 1922, he figured that he had nothing else to do anyway.

Vandenberg was just nine when his father went bankrupt, and it proved a searing experience. Now recognizing the value of a dollar, he went to work at a shoe company and, over the next year or so, sold vegetables, ran flower and lemonade stands, ushered at a theater, and sold newspapers. "I had one passion—," he recalled, "to be certain that when I grew old I would not be in the position my father was."[9] Vandenberg chose journalism not only because he followed public affairs and loved writing, but because he thought it would give him the financial security later to pursue his ultimate goal—a life in politics.

Like Truman, Vandenberg wanted to attend college but faced the same hurdle of low finances. After graduating high school in 1900, he worked to earn money for the University of Michigan. But he was fired from his job as a billing clerk when, denied time off, he nevertheless disappeared for two hours to watch Teddy Roosevelt, who was nearby campaigning for vice president, deliver a speech. After working a short time for the *Grand Rapids Herald*, whose editor and publisher knew him from his high school journalism, he left in the fall of 1900 for the University of Michigan's law department, completing a year of study before his money ran out. He returned to the newspaper in June 1901, stayed for two years until *Collier's* magazine lured him to New York for a job in its art department, and returned again in 1904 after a dismal time at *Collier's* and in New York. He assumed the perch of editor at age twenty-two in 1906, the same year he married his high school sweetheart, Elizabeth Watson.

. . .

Truman and Vandenberg came to their political affiliations as youngsters, inheriting them from their parents rather than choosing them through careful deliberation. But neither Truman, a New Deal Democrat, nor Vandenberg, a Main Street Republican, ever regretted it. They were comfortable in the mainstreams of their parties, even as each party tilted right or left through the course of their careers.

Truman tasted politics early. At age eight, he came to school one day in a white hat emblazoned with the words "Cleveland and Stevenson," the Democratic presidential ticket of 1892 that his father favored. Some bigger boys who backed the Republican ticket stole his hat and tore it up (and, Truman liked to say later, "the Republican boys have been trying to do that to me ever since"). At sixteen, a friend of Truman's father secured Harry a job as a page at the 1900 Democratic National Convention in Kansas City, where Democrats nominated William Jennings Bryan for president a second time. As a teenager, Harry accompanied his father to local political meetings. He maintained his involvement in local Democratic politics, worked as a clerk in the local precinct at election time, and secured appointments as a town postmaster and, as his father had been, an overseer of county highways. He was a Democrat through and through, and he never looked back to reconsider.

Vandenberg, too, was steered early. His father was wiped out in the "Panic of '93" and blamed President Grover Cleveland and the Democrats. Lying on his deathbed, embittered by his financial fate, he forced young Arthur to pledge a lifelong commitment to Republicanism. The boy never resisted and, in fact, seemed as proud a Republican as Harry was a Democrat. He often bragged that his maternal grandfather, who was a delegate to the 1860 Republican convention in Chicago, had helped nominate Lincoln for president.

In their later years, Democrat Truman and Republican Vandenberg were both tough partisans. At election time, they campaigned not just for themselves but for their parties. Nevertheless, between elections, when it was time to govern, they were pragmatic enough to work with their colleagues across the political aisle to orchestrate hearings, draft bills, and enact laws—to nourish bipartisan support for policy. Their pragmatism and bipartisan inclinations laid the groundwork for their later landmark achievements.

. . .

World War I was a defining event for Truman and Vandenberg, shaping their views about the world in ways that proved important decades later. Both were captivated by President Wilson's call of early 1917 for America to help make the world "safe for democracy," and both supported his successful effort to create a League of Nations and his unsuccessful push to bring America into it. Truman remained consistent thereafter in his view that America must engage with the world, while Vandenberg turned to isolationism in the 1930s before returning to global engagement after Pearl Harbor and, even more, after World War II.

"My whole political career," Truman once said, "is based upon my war service and war associates."[10] By the time Truman answered Wilson's call by enlisting in the army—viewing himself as a "Galahad after the Grail"—he was already disciplined, hardworking, and organized.

The army then taught him how to manage others, a skill he later put to good use in the White House. As an artilleryman, clerk, and first lieutenant, and then on a tour at Oklahoma's Camp Doniphon where he ran a canteen, he was forceful, demanding, diligent, and unimpeachably honest, while also popular with the men. After training in France, he took command of the 129th Field Artillery Regiment's Battery D in July 1918, displaying the no-nonsense decisiveness that marked his early days as president. In less than two weeks, "Captain Harry" seized full control of the once-unruly outfit, moving one soldier to reflect, "He not only commanded the outfit, he owned it."[11] Truman led his regiment into harrowing battles in rain and sleet, muck and mud. During the battle of Meuse-Argonne from late September 1918 until the war's end in November, he marched his men for twenty-two nights, went sixty hours without sleep at one point, and shrunk from 175 to 135 pounds.

Nurtured in the fires of war, Truman's bond with his men remained strong for the rest of their lives. After the fighting ended, the men gave him a loving cup with the words, "Captain Harry S. Truman. Presented by the members of Battery D in appreciation of his justice, ability and leadership." Three decades later, a reelected President Truman invited the men of Battery D to his inauguration and, when one of them called out "Mr. President," Truman replied, "We'll have none of that here. I'm Captain Harry."[12]

Vandenberg had no comparable wartime bonding experience; he followed the fighting from the comfort of his desk in Grand Rapids. At the time, he was amid an intellectual journey that began before World War I and continued for decades thereafter. Before the war, he promoted a strong, Teddy Roosevelt-like U.S. presence in the world. America, he wrote in a 1907 editorial for the *Herald*, should join other nations "to fight if need be and [to be] able to fight well, if for no other purpose than to serve as policeman to keep the unruly in order and the peaceful from being imposed upon."[13] Vandenberg advanced such notions as "manifest destiny" (that America had both a right and an obligation to expand its borders) and the "white man's burden" (that America should civilize people of different races by exporting its ideals of freedom, democracy, and so on). In the run-up to World War I, he supported Wilson's efforts to confront Germany about its submarine warfare and urged America to defend the "cause of righteousness." Once the United States joined the war, he supported Wilson with wild enthusiasm, calling the effort "the greatest revival the world has ever known since Christ came upon the earth."[14]

As a senator in 1934, however, Vandenberg helped North Dakota's senator Gerald Nye create an investigating committee on the munitions industry and then served on it. As wholeheartedly as he had supported U.S. entry into World War I, he just as wholeheartedly came to believe that it had been a mistake driven by profit-hungry weapon makers. As war clouds gathered overseas again through the 1930s, he became a strident isolationist, determined to keep America out of the tumult. As war erupted in Europe in late 1939, he told the American Legion, "This so-called war is nothing but about 25 people and propaganda . . . They want our money and men."[15] Vandenberg strongly backed the Neutrality Acts of the 1930s, which Congress passed against FDR's wishes, to impose U.S. neutrality toward the growing tensions in Europe. He railed against FDR's interventionism, particularly his efforts to assist Great Britain early in World War II. He fought unsuccessfully against Roosevelt's push in early 1941 for Lend-Lease, through which the United States sent Britain (and later the Soviet Union and other allies) ships, aircraft, land vehicles, food, and other vital supplies before and after America entered the war.

"When [Lend-Lease] passed the Senate, and thus negotiated its final hurdle," Vandenberg wrote after the Senate's 60–31 vote in March of 1941,

> we did vastly more than to "aid Britain." I doubt if *all* those who supported it realized its implications. I hope I am wholly wrong when I say I fear they will live to regret their votes beyond anything else they ever did. I had the feeling, as the result of the ballot was announced [*sic*], that I was witnessing the suicide of the Republic . . . We have torn up 150 years of traditional American foreign policy. We have tossed Washington's Farewell Address [counseling the nation to "steer clear of permanent alliances"] into the discard. We

have thrown ourselves squarely into the power politics and the power wars of Europe, Asia and Africa. We have taken the first step upon a course from which we can never hereafter retreat.[16]

It took Pearl Harbor to force Vandenberg to rethink the isolationism with which he had grown so comfortable.

. . .

Truman was as daring in his political pursuits as he was in his business ventures, reflecting the optimism of his youth and the reckless example of his father. He sought office even when he seemed to have little chance of victory. Vandenberg, by contrast, was cautious to the point of paralysis. His ego could not bear the possibility of a loss. Accordingly, the two men pursued starkly different paths to power.

Truman lost a race for township committeeman in 1916 but, six years later, accepted a request from Mike Pendergast—the uncle of his army buddy Jim Pendergast and brother of famed Jackson County Democratic boss Tom Pendergast—to run for eastern judge on the Jackson County Court. He won a two-year term, lost his reelection bid in 1924, but returned in 1926 to win a race for presiding judge, a more powerful position that he held for eight years. Rather than hear cases, the judgeships required that he allocate funds for roads, bridges, and other public works projects. By all accounts, he served with honor and distinction while avoiding the stain of corruption that tended to plant itself on anyone linked to the Pendergast machine. As eastern judge, he helped reduce the county debt and improve its credit rating. As presiding judge, he launched a massive roads project, pushing through two bond issues that put Jackson behind only Michigan's Wayne County and New York's Westchester County in the sophistication of its roads system. Proud of his accomplishments, he sponsored a booklet about the road improvements he spearheaded and sent it to every county in the state. He also served as chairman of the Missouri State Planning Association and as a board member of the National Conference on City Planning.

In 1934 Truman set his sights on a U.S. House seat, but Boss Pendergast startled him by rejecting the idea. Then, after consulting with Jackson County Democratic chairman James Aylward, the boss returned with what later proved a far more consequential idea—that Truman run for Senate. He did so, winning the seat that would catapult him to national fame and FDR's presidential ticket in 1944. Despite a laudable Senate record in his first term, Truman bore the brunt of Democratic Party disarray in Missouri, and he was forced to win an uphill battle for reelection in 1940.

While Truman was decisive, Vandenberg was Hamlet-like in pondering public office. He knew where he wanted to be, just not how to get there. When, in 1913, he received lavish praise from Vice President Thomas R. Marshall after delivering a speech to dedicate a statue of Michigan's distinguished political leader Zachariah Chandler at the U.S. Capitol, the twenty-nine-year-old Vandenberg replied, "Some day I hope again to make a speech in Washington on the floor of the United States Senate—as a Senator from the State of Michigan."[17] He repeatedly questioned, however, whether he could afford to run for public office and, if so, whether he'd win. So, he dismissed a series of entreaties from state Republican leaders from 1914 to the late 1920s to run for seats ranging from mayor to governor. Through the 1920s he engaged in partisan politics of a different kind, writing editorials and delivering speeches for some Republican candidates at the expense of others. When Republicans won office, he monitored their commitment to GOP values while they served. He was influential but dissatisfied, eyeing the Senate but too fearful to take the plunge and risk losing.

As the 1928 election approach, Vandenberg concluded that, for him, it was decision time. His *Herald* stock brought him $549,000 when the paper was sold that year,[18] securing his finances, but he continued to agonize over his political prospects. "I have at least come to this conclusion," he wrote, "if I am *ever* going to do this, it ought to be in 1928 . . . But I certainly am *not* prepared to say that I will in '28 or ever."[19] He wavered through 1927 and early 1928, still relishing a run for Senate but fearful he might not win. Then, political lightning struck in the spring of 1928 as incumbent Democrat Woodbridge Ferris died of pneumonia. After considerable pressure from Vandenberg's supporters, Michigan's Republican governor, Fred Green, appointed him to the seat. That gave him a much more assured path to win a full term that November because he ran as an incumbent. A year later, he joined the Senate's prestigious Foreign Relations Committee, ascending the ranks of committee seniority in subsequent years until he became its chairman in 1947.

. . .

Truman and Vandenberg tried on their Senate roles very differently as well. Truman was insecure about his abilities until he had mastered the task before him, whether that was commanding troops, building roads, serving in the Senate, or inheriting the presidency; the stresses gave him headaches, stomach pains, and other such maladies. Thus, he was shy and tentative as he assumed his Senate seat. By contrast, with his enormous ego, Vandenberg was supremely self-confident as he took office.

Arriving in Washington in early 1935, Truman was, as he put it, "as timid as a country boy arriving on the campus of a great university for his first year."[20] He rented an apartment rather than buy a house, fearing he wouldn't win a second term. The pols and the press did nothing to boost his ego. FDR took his vote for granted and ignored him, Senate party leaders gave him a desk in the last row of the chamber, most senators barely noticed him, and the *New York Times* called him a "rube from Pendergast land." Watching him in his early months, a Kansas City journalist wrote, "His is the conventional way. He ruffles no oldsters' feathers, treads on no toes."[21]

But as he worked hard—arriving so early in the morning that he secured the first key to the Senate Office Building ever given to a senator[22]—his confidence grew and he carved out a name for himself in Washington and beyond. "It just takes work and more work to accomplish anything—," he wrote to his daughter, "and your dad knows it better than anyone . . . It takes work to do anything well."[23]

Vandenberg suffered no such painful self-doubt. As his son, Arthur Hendrick Jr., later wrote, he was "self-confident . . . probably a little cocky."[24] That was an understatement, for the new senator began his work in Washington "with all the grace and energy of an unbroken steer . . .

and he was put down as vain and brash. He came to be regarded in the Senate as an able, energetic, somewhat cocky lone wolf."[25]

. . .

War was coming as the 1940s beckoned, and it profoundly affected both men—Truman from well before Pearl Harbor, Vandenberg from immediately after.

As America prepared for war, Truman heard reports of favoritism in defense contracting, which offended his sense of right and wrong. Curious and angry, he drove himself on a 3,000-mile tour of defense plants across the country—first south from Maryland to Florida, then west to Texas, north to Nebraska, and east to Michigan—during which he found disturbing evidence of war profiteering. Unsure of what to do, he enthusiastically seized the advice of a Missouri journalist that he propose a new Senate committee, which he'd chair, in order to investigate. He convinced a reluctant White House to let him launch an investigation—in essence, to probe the administration—if only because White House officials thought that would forestall an investigation by a less supportive House committee. Lacking much by way of funds or staff, Truman's committee started slowly. But as the panel of five Democrats and two Republicans attracted favorable notice, other senators sought its limelight. The Special Committee to Investigate the National Defense Program, soon known as the Truman Committee, grew to ten with one more Democrat and two Republicans.

From early 1941 through Truman's resignation in 1944 (when FDR asked him to run as his vice president), the panel investigated a wide range of issues related to war preparation, including aluminum production, defense housing, government contracting, and the aviation program. It held scores of hearings, interviewed hundreds of witnesses, issued thirty-two reports, identified billions of potentially wasted dollars, and convinced the Roosevelt administration to replace its Office of Production Management with a streamlined War Production Board. Truman's careful but aggressive work attracted notice not just on Capitol Hill but across the country, landing him on *Time*'s cover in March of 1943. In the cover sketch, he wears a light suit, striped shirt, polka-dot tie, and his trademark steel-rimmed glasses, and he looks skyward, as if seeking divine inspiration.

"The Truman Committee this week celebrated its second successful birthday as one of the most useful Government agencies of World War II," *Time* wrote. "Its members had heard hundreds of witnesses, taken 4,000,000 words of testimony. With battle-royal impartiality, they had given thick ears and red faces to Cabinet members, war agency heads, generals, admirals, big businessmen, little businessmen, labor leaders." Of Truman, it wrote, "For a Congressional committee to be considered the first line of defense—especially in a nation which does not tend to admire its representatives, in Congress assembled—is encouraging to believers in democracy. So is the sudden emergence of Harry Truman, whose presence in the Senate is a queer accident of democracy, as the committee's energetic generalissimo."

Time quoted a "Washingtonian" who declared: "There's only one thing that worries me more than the present state of the war effort. That's to think what it would be like by now without Truman."[26]

. . .

As Truman was climbing new political heights, Vandenberg was rethinking his views about America's place in the world.

"My convictions regarding international cooperation and collective security for peace," he wrote later, "took firm form on the afternoon of the Pearl Harbor attack. That day ended isolationism for any realist."[27] In reality, Vandenberg's shift had been more evolutionary. In the years before Pearl Harbor, the foundation of his thinking was already evolving due to his frequent conversations with his nephew, Air Force general Hoyt Vandenberg, and influential Republican foreign policy adviser John Foster Dulles.

After Pearl Harbor, Vandenberg sought an opportunity to help FDR win the war. He wanted an active partnership, however, one in which the administration brought him into its trust in exchange for his support at crucial moments. Driven, as usual, by both high-mindedness and ego, he wanted not just to help but to matter. He sought the inner circle, demanded a role in the action, and grew petulant when left out. A week after Pearl Harbor, Vandenberg wrote FDR to propose a "Joint Congressional Committee on War Cooperation"—with six senators and six House members, evenly split between the parties—to work with the administration. The idea went nowhere, but Vandenberg was pleased to learn a month later that the Senate Foreign Relations Committee's Democratic chairman, Tom Connally, had secured a commitment for a State Department official to meet with the panel once a week to provide what Vandenberg called the "inside dope."

Vandenberg also launched his own efforts to put a Senate stamp on U.S. war efforts. In late 1943 he and Connally crafted a bipartisan Senate resolution to express the Senate's war goals. Their resolution, which passed on an 85–5 vote, culminated months of work and came amid questions in Europe about whether the United States would leave the international stage after the war (just as, European officials bitterly recalled, it did after World War I). The resolution called for "complete victory," U.S. cooperation with its allies to achieve a "just and honorable peace," and Senate support for an international organization (i.e., a United Nations) to maintain "peace and security." After the Connally Resolution came more bipartisan efforts by Vandenberg to influence U.S. policy—whether welcomed by the White House or otherwise. When, in 1943, FDR planned to ratify U.S. participation in a new United Nations Relief and Rehabilitation Administration by executive fiat, Vandenberg rallied his Senate colleagues to force the administration to submit it for congressional approval. When, in 1944, FDR's team was sketching its vision for the United Nations in hopes of securing Allied support and Senate acquiescence, Vandenberg convinced Connally to create a Senate "Committee of Eight" to work with the White House.

Vandenberg also pushed his own party toward a more enlightened foreign policy, advising that it "end the miserable notion (so effectively used against us in many quarters) that the Republican Party will retire to its foxhole when the last shot is fired."[28] Largely at his direction, leading Republicans from around the country drafted the "Mackinac Charter" in late 1943, expressing support for U.S. participation in a peacekeeping organization. Named for the picturesque Michigan island on which it was drafted, the charter was largely adopted in the 1944 Republican platform. "The Mackinac Charter," Vandenberg told the Senate,

> has done one basic, superlatively important thing—which is sadly needed if we are to have any sort of common national vision in foreign policy. For the first time, it has plainly been put down in black and white the indispensable doctrine that Americans can be faithful to the primary institutions and interests of our own United States and still be equally loyal to the essential post-war international cooperations [*sic*] which are required to end military aggression for keeps and to create a post-war world in which organized justice shall protect freemen. By the same token, it has put down in black and white the basic truth that Americans can constructively contemplate their world duties without sacrificing their American allegiance.[29]

On January 10, 1945, with the end of World War II in sight, Vandenberg rose in the Senate, said he needed no more than a half hour of its time, and asked his colleagues to let him speak without interruption. "I have always been frankly one of those who has believed in our own self-reliance," he reflected in the key passage of his speech. "I still believe that we can never again—regardless of collaborations—allow our national defense to deteriorate to anything like a point of impotence. But I do not believe that any nation hereafter can immunize itself by its own exclusive action. Since Pearl Harbor, World War II has put the gory science of mass murder into new and sinister perspective. Our oceans have ceased to be moats which automatically protect our ramparts. Flesh and blood now compete unequally with winged steel. War has become an all-consuming juggernaut."

It's known as the "speech heard 'round the world," for it supposedly marked Vandenberg's public conversion from prewar isolationism to postwar engagement. The speech, however, was more confirmation than revelation because, as we have seen, Vandenberg's conversion had begun well before.

. . .

In the summer of 1944, Harry Truman was happy as a senator. He had long since overcome his insecurities, and he was doing high-profile work that was making a difference and attracting national attention. He later called his Senate tenure "the happiest ten years of my life." He didn't long for higher office, and he feared that the public scrutiny of a national campaign might reveal that Bess's father had committed suicide—a topic about which, naturally for that era, she was quite sensitive.

Nor, despite his coast-to-coast profile, was he anyone's first choice for vice president for FDR's fourth ticket. But FDR, his top advisers, and key supporters, including union chiefs and southern leaders, were split over who he should pick. The unions wanted him to stick with Vice President Henry Wallace, but southern Democrats found him too liberal and—with FDR's physical decline raising concerns that he wouldn't survive a fourth term—other party leaders worried that the odd, mystical, remote Wallace simply wasn't fit to be president. Southerners backed Jimmy Byrnes, the former South Carolina senator who had guided much of FDR's New Deal through the Senate. At various points, FDR's aides suggested to Byrnes that the president had settled on him, and Byrnes grew so confident that he secured Truman's commitment to nominate him at the Democratic Party's convention that summer in Chicago. Truman, however, remained in the mix within FDR's inner circle.

Truman repeatedly insisted he didn't want to be vice president, but FDR and his aides were coming to see the problems with choosing anyone else, most notably Byrnes—a lapsed Catholic with a poor record on labor and race issues. FDR told his aides more than once that, of his options, Byrnes was probably the best qualified to be president. But, his risks as a candidate threatened FDR's reelection. Not until Truman arrived in Chicago did he learn from the Democratic National Committee chairman, Bob Hannegan, that FDR—by then browbeaten by some advisers and labor leaders—no longer wanted Byrnes. He wanted Truman. When Truman resisted, Hannegan called him to a meeting with party leaders at which he phoned FDR. Hearing from Hannegan that Truman was reluctant to run, Roosevelt yelled loudly enough for everyone in the room to hear, "Well, you tell the Senator that if he wants to break up the Democratic Party in the middle of the war, that's his responsibility," and slammed down the phone. "Oh, shit." Truman replied. "Well, if that's the situation, I'll have to say yes. But why the hell didn't he tell me in the first place?"[30]

After FDR tapped Truman, his insecurities returned with a vengeance. With FDR fading fast physically, Truman recognized that if they won, he would soon inherit the presidency. In late August Roosevelt and Truman lunched at the White House where, Truman recalled, FDR's "hands were shaking and he talks with considerable difficulty ... It doesn't seem to be any mental lapse of any kind but physically he's just going to pieces." When, a month later, Truman's pal Eddie McKim told him that he'd soon be president, Truman replied, "I'm afraid you're right, Eddie, and it scares the hell out of me." Roosevelt and Truman met in late February 1945 after FDR returned from the Yalta Conference with Churchill and Stalin, and Truman was "shocked by [FDR's] appearance. His eyes were sunken. His magnificent smile was missing from his cakeworn face. He seemed a spent man. I had a hollow feeling within me, for I saw that the journey to Yalta must have been a terrible ordeal."

FDR's death scared him even more. "I feel like I have been struck by a bolt of lightning," he told his best friend, Saint Louis banker John W. Snyder, by phone after returning to his apartment on his first evening as president. "I'm not big enough. I'm not big enough for this job," he told another friend, Senator George Aiken of Vermont, the next day at a Capitol Hill luncheon. "Boys," he told reporters after lunch, "if you ever pray, pray for me now. I don't know whether you fellows ever had a load of hay fall on you, but when they told me yesterday what had happened, I felt like the moon, the stars, and all the planets had fallen on me. I've got the most terribly responsible job a man ever had."[31]

. . .

Vandenberg must have witnessed the earthshaking political developments of early 1945 with a touch of envy.

He had long relished the chance to serve as president, and leading Republicans and pundits put him at or near the top of their lists of preferred candidates in 1936 and 1940. But, Vandenberg being Vandenberg, he refused to run. He wasn't sure that he'd win the nomination or election, and he feared that a loss of either would diminish his power in Washington and threaten his reelection as a senator. Influenced if not blinded by ego, he wanted—remarkably—to be *anointed* as the party's nominee in a year in which a Republican could win the presidency. In his mind, party leaders would choose him at a deadlocked convention, or Republicans would vote for him in state primaries even if he didn't campaign. In either of these highly unlikely scenarios, he would avoid the messy process of running for the nomination.

Key Republicans touted Vandenberg in 1936 as an effective opponent of FDR's New Deal, but he rejected a run that year because he lacked a sufficient national profile and predicted (correctly) that FDR would win reelection easily (though he always left the door open to accept a draft nomination). Heading into 1940, he was widely considered the Republican front-runner, and he was now clearly more interested in the party's nomination. He still refused to run, however, arguing that a public declaration of interest would hurt his effectiveness as a senator and fearing that his failure to win the nomination would imperil his Senate reelection that year.

In the spring of 1940, Vandenberg put his name on the ballot for primaries in Wisconsin and Nebraska, assuming naively that he'd win without campaigning and that, from there, the nomination would be his. His losses in both states effectively doomed his candidacy, though he still hoped to seize the nomination at the GOP convention in June. He didn't seek the nomination at all in 1944, promoted General Douglas MacArthur before he flamed out, and then rallied behind nominee Thomas Dewey, New York's governor. He didn't seek it in 1948, either, though he came to that year's Republican National Convention in Philadelphia with an acceptance speech all prepared, just in case a deadlocked convention turned to him.

Truman, who never wanted the presidency, now had it. Vandenberg, who relished the presidency but refused to go for it wholeheartedly, was left to work with Truman and make his foreign policy a success.

. . .

In his early days on the job, Truman received many supportive messages. One, however, stood out in his mind.

"Good luck and God bless you," Vandenberg wrote to him. "Let me help you whenever I can. America marches on."[32]

At the time, Vandenberg also took to his diary, writing more somberly, "The gravest question-mark in every American heart is about Truman. Can he swing the job? Despite his limited capacities, I believe he can."[33]

The two men began to work together immediately, but not out of any sense of friendship. Theirs was a relationship of mutual respect and professional courtesy. They did not reach out to one another to touch base, exchange pleasantries, and share gossip. They did so almost solely when business demanded it. Reflecting the formalism of their relationship, Truman wrote later that "Senator Vandenberg was thoroughly familiar with the workings of the Senate and knew how to get results. He could take ideas conceived by others . . . and then include an element or two that would add his legislative trademark without changing anything basic. From then on he would fight for the ideas without letting up. When Vandenberg died, nobody in the Republican ranks was able to step into his shoes."[34]

In the spring of 1945, both men turned sixty-one. Harry Truman was short and powerfully built like his father. He had a round face, thin lips, blue eyes, and thinning gray hair that he parted neatly on the left. He wore steel-rimmed glasses and a gold Masonic ring on his left pinkie, and he favored polka-dot ties. Arthur Vandenberg (or "Van," as he was widely known) was tall and paunchy. He wore wire-rimmed glasses and parted his thinning gray hair low on the left as he fought a losing battle with his receding hairline. He wore custom-made blue or gray suits for which his wife chose the cloth, and his double chin rested on his trademark bow tie.

Alike in their values, united in their goals for the postwar world, they were oh so different in their personalities and styles.

. . .

Truman and Vandenberg both worked extremely hard, but they approached work very differently.

Burdened by work, Truman was prone to self-pity, complaining about long hours, missed meals, mounting decisions, piles of nightly reading, and, when his wife and daughter were in Missouri as they often were, aching loneliness. "I am getting ready to go see Stalin & Churchill, and it is a chore," he wrote before the Potsdam Conference in July of 1945. "Wish I didn't have to go, but I do and it can't be stopped now."[35] On his way aboard the presidential ship *Augusta*, he wrote, "I wish this trip was over. I hate it. But it has to be done."[36] He called the White House the "great white jail," making him its embattled prisoner. He even called it the "great white sepulcher," suggesting he was entombed there. After firing Commerce Secretary Henry Wallace in September 1946 for criticizing his foreign policy in a high-profile speech at New York's Madison Square Garden, Truman wrote, "[Press Secretary] Charlie Ross said I'd shown I'd rather be right than President and I told him I'd rather be anything than President."[37]

The stress gave Truman continual bouts of stomach pain, and he sought to relax most often over a game of poker, Kentucky bourbon, bawdy stories, and colorful language. Poker usually unfolded on the presidential yacht (the *Williamsburg*), setting sail on Friday afternoon and returning on Sunday morning, with regulars at the poker table who included White House Counsel Clark Clifford, Commerce Secretary Averell Harriman, Treasury Secretary Fred Vinson, Agriculture Secretary Clinton Anderson, Air Force Secretary Stuart Symington, Democratic operative George Allen, and a young Texas senator by the name of Lyndon Johnson. For Truman, work was work and fun was fun, and one finished the former as quickly as possible to resume the latter.

Vandenberg, by contrast, knew no such distinction. For him, work was fun. As a senator, he came early, stayed late, and worked fanatically. Every morning, after reading the *Washington Post* and two New York newspapers over breakfast, he arrived by government-chauffeured black Cadillac at his office at eight thirty. After clearing away correspondence, he often visited the offices of the Senate Foreign Relations Committee, plopped his feet on the desk of Chief of Staff Francis Wilcox, and tested out his ideas about foreign policy, the Senate, or the State Department. He was always ready for one more conversation, one more hearing, to convert a strong committee majority for a proposal to a unanimous one, figuring that would speed its approval by the full Senate. "We will kill the opposition with kindness," he liked to say. He did his "homework," allotting two nights a week to his wife and reserving all others for study. On weekday evenings at their apartment at Washington's Wardman Park Hotel, he slipped into comfortable slacks before beginning his reading, which usually included a scan of Washington's evening newspapers along with papers from Grand Rapids and Detroit.

He even held Saturday seminars, which he called "school's in session," for top journalists who included the Associated Press' Jack Bell, the International New Service's William Theis, United Press' John L. Steele, the *Washington Post*'s Ferdinand Kuhn, and the *Baltimore Sun*'s William Knighton and Philip Porter. He spoke to them at great length, providing his most intimate thinking, though much of it "off the record." He rehearsed his speeches for, and solicited reactions from, the *New York Times*' James Reston, the *New York Herald Tribune*'s Bert Andrews, the *Detroit News*' Blair Moody and Jay Hayden, and columnist Marquis Childs. All told for Vandenberg, "senator" was less an honorific than a life.[38]

Reston, Washington's top reporter, was especially close to Vandenberg, as much a confidante as a source. Vandenberg leaked confidential information to him and passed along his broader insights, helping to shape the analytical pieces about Washington's mood for which Reston was well-known—and which were read closely in key capitals around the world. Reflecting their closeness, Vandenberg showed Reston a draft of his January 10, 1945, speech, and Reston suggested adding the proposal that the major powers come together to prevent any resumption of German aggression.

Vandenberg was more practical than visionary, more a master of politics and procedure than a crafter of grand doctrines. As Reston wrote for a cover piece on him for *Life* in May 1948, "He tends to be indifferent to anything that he feels cannot be translated into action."[39] Feeling the Senate's pulse, he loved to devise strategies to move tough issues through the unwieldy body. Once he backed a proposal, he worked hard to gather the votes, such as by adding amendments to legislation or tweaking its language. He often affixed his name to key measures and savored the acclaim for his speeches that promoted them.

. . .

Truman and Vandenberg were different as well in how they communicated with people publicly and interacted with them privately.

Truman was direct, straightforward, and down to earth. Despite his insecurities as he assumed the presidency, he seized the role aggressively, issuing directives with a clarity and crispness that delighted those who had served under the secretive, meandering Roosevelt. "You could go into his office with a question," Averell Harriman, Truman's ambassador to Moscow and London and then commerce secretary, beamed, "and come out with a decision from him more swiftly than from any man I have ever known."[40] He was the president as army captain, this time taking his troops into political battle.

Truman favored declarative sentences and simple words whether filling his diary, writing his memoirs, or delivering a speech. Indeed, Clark Clifford, who served as his chief wordsmith, used to "Trumanize" the drafts that his speechwriters would produce by shortening sentences and replacing polysyllabic words with shorter ones. For an elected official, he was strangely uncomfortable with public speaking to begin with, and he didn't deliver his first speech in the Senate until his third year there. His voice was tinny, his delivery awkward, his connection with an audience poor. He was no worthy successor to the stirring FDR and he knew it. Consequently, he much preferred speaking off the cuff, whether on the campaign trail or at news conferences, through which he could unload his thoughts with a straightforwardness that better reflected his simple upbringing.

Truman was modest about himself (often writing "Ain't that sompin" when an honor came his way), and he was impatient with phonies; a life-long fan of William Jennings Bryan, "the Great Commoner," he identified with the "ordinary man," not "greedy men" and "special-interest groups." He called General Douglas MacArthur, with whom he clashed mightily, "Mr. Prima Donna, Brass Hat, Five Star MacArthur," adding, "He's worse than the Cabots and the Lodges—they at least talked to one another before they told God what to do. Mac tells God right off."[41] He mused that the power of high office could go to the head of its occupant, and he fretted about those who sought proximity to power. "Some of my boys who came in with me are having trouble with their dignity and their prerogatives," he wrote less than two months after becoming president. "It's hell when a man gets in close association with the President. Something happens to him."[42]

Truman usually didn't second-guess himself after making a decision—what's done is done, he believed—but he despaired when the public didn't appreciate what he was trying to do. Exhausted by work, he blew off steam when things didn't go well, writing letters he didn't send and speeches he didn't deliver in which he insulted his critics and chastised Americans for not rallying behind him. In the best example, he drafted a speech in response to a railroad and coal strike in early 1946, complaining that his opponents had "flouted, vilified and misrepresented" his positions, lambasting Congress as "weak-kneed" and filled with "Russian Senators and Representatives," and closing this way: "Let's put transportation and production back to work, hang a few traitors, make our own country safe for democracy, tell the Russians where to get off and make the United Nations work."[43] When Truman calmed down, aides convinced him to deliver a more moderate address.

. . .

Vandenberg suffered from no such flights of fury; he was far more deliberative and controlled, driven far more by ego than rage.

When Senator Robert Taft, the Republican with whom Vandenberg
battled for years, asked his wife to "butter Van up" at a dinner party that
Taft threw for Vandenberg, the witty Martha later reflected, "I tried
manfully, but he buttered himself so thoroughly that I really couldn't
find a single ungreased spot."[44] When the Senate rushed to formally
declare war on Japan after Pearl Harbor and the White House sought a
speedy vote without speeches, Vandenberg insisted on speaking anyway.

Vandenberg demanded the respect he thought he deserved, and he
responded to presidential initiatives based largely on whether he had
received it. That is, he sought early notification of presidential proposals and continuous opportunity to reshape them as his price for supporting them and convincing his Republican colleagues to do the same.
The notification and opportunity were his prerequisites for nourishing
"bipartisan foreign policy" (or, as he sometimes put it, "nonpartisan" or
"unpartisan" foreign policy). "I don't care to be involved in the crash-
landing," he liked to say in a line from Harold Stassen, Minnesota's former Republican governor, "unless I can be in on the take-off." He chafed
when he wasn't "in the know," steaming about "executive dictatorship."

Truman responded accordingly. A day after assuming the presidency,
he directed his military aide, Harry Vaughan, to send Vandenberg the
last box of cigars from his vice presidential office, delighting the senator.
In the ensuing years, Truman's aides spent countless hours with Vandenberg, sharing their thoughts, revealing their plans, and showing him
secret cables from foreign governments. They lavished so much attention on him that Francis Wilcox, the Senate Foreign Relations Committee's chief of staff, had to remind them not to neglect the panel's top
Democrat, Tom Connally.

For the most part, Truman solicited Vandenberg's support early and
often on the signature elements of his foreign policy—the United Nations,
the Truman Doctrine, the Marshall Plan, and the North Atlantic Treaty.
His ego stroked, Vandenberg offered his support on every one of those
items and his counsel about how best to secure their congressional pas-

sage. Thus, these four measures became the central features of the "bipartisan foreign policy" of which Vandenberg was so proud.

Truman, however, did not reach out to Vandenberg with such care on some other high-profile foreign policy crises, and Vandenberg responded accordingly. Out of personal pique and wounded ego, he would not lend his hand—no matter how big the issue, how dire the circumstances, how important the outcome. He did not, for instance, support Truman's policy toward China (then in the midst of civil war) or his approach to nuclear arms. He would not bear the burden of nourishing a bipartisan consensus for those initiatives or, in the case of China, "be involved in the crash-landing."

. . .

Unlike Truman, Vandenberg viewed himself as a man of words. He honed his writing as a journalist and penned three scholarly books as well as more than a hundred short stories (though none of his stories were ever published). Filling his diary in fits and starts, he wrote hundreds of letters in response to those from constituents and from admirers and critics across the country. Some were short answers; others, long essays. He kept scrapbooks of his speeches and hundreds of articles on issues that interested him. But, with an individuality that reflected his vanity, Vandenberg spelled carelessly and "scatter[ed] superfluous quotation marks, underlinings, capital letters, and asterisks with wild abandon through letters and diary entries," as his son put it.[45] "Business" became "bizness," "although" became "altho." He invented words on occasion, preferring "insulation" to the more common "isolation."

While Truman struggled with public speaking, Vandenberg relished it, laboring for hours to prepare his addresses, often rewriting the important ones multiple times on the manual typewriter on his rolltop desk at home in Grand Rapids. He delivered them in dramatic fashion to a Senate chamber that was often crowded when he spoke. He was the orator as performer, drawing strength from the nodding and clapping of his attentive colleagues. "His one oratorical trick," an observer wrote, "is to draw a deep breath, then roar into his first paragraph until his breath is gone. His gestures are patterned around a sweeping sidearm swish, something like Pitcher Carl Hubbell."[46]

Vandenberg could mix it up with the best of them, but he was offended when attacked in personal terms, as he was by the isolationist *Chicago Tribune* of Colonel Robert McCormick. After, in late 1946, the *Tribune* attacked his foreign policy bipartisanship as a "partnership in iniquity" and its cartoons portrayed him as Benedict Arnold, Vandenberg wrote, "I do not know why honest men cannot honorably disagree without resort to bitter personalities which generate 'heat' instead of 'light.'"[47] He later complained about the newspaper's "personal vendetta" against him.

"Was Arthur Vandenberg a likeable man?" Dean Acheson, the former secretary of state, asked years later, fighting perceptions to the contrary. "Yes, he was. He had humor and warmth and occasional bursts of self-revealing candor. He was not among the 'popular' Senators. His ego was too strong for that. Some regarded him, as Mr. James B. Reston of the *New York Times* concedes that he did for a time, as the 'most pompous and prejudiced man in the United States Senate.' But this was wrong. He was not that; but he took a bit of knowing."[48]

. . .

How did two such different men as Harry Truman and Arthur Vandenberg work together to such great effect?

This Democratic president and this Republican senator succeeded on a grand scale because, for starters, they shared a guiding vision for what the United States must do on the world stage at a perilous time. They recognized that America must shed its isolationist tendencies, assume global leadership, help rebuild Europe's economy, and lead the fight against aggressive Soviet expansionism. While others hesitated, they crafted the doctrines and created the architecture to revolutionize U.S. foreign policy.

Though surely imperfect, surely flawed in both personality and temperament, Truman and Vandenberg also exuded a high-mindedness about public affairs that drove their "better angels" at crucial moments. Beyond that, Vandenberg enjoyed a national stature and following as his party's undisputed leader on foreign policy that any modern-day senator would envy. With that stature and following, he exerted enormous influence over his Republican colleagues who, in turn, were willing to collaborate with Truman on foreign policy while battling him bitterly on domestic matters.

Simply put, Truman and Vandenberg would not let their differences in personality and style, or the swirling politics around them, jeopardize the tasks at hand. If Vandenberg needed stroking before he would cooperate, Truman provided it. If Truman became mean and petty, Vandenberg's grace saved the day. If the two men needed to communicate privately during times of brutal interparty combat, they did so.

If Truman and Vandenberg were leaders of different political parties in a bitterly partisan environment, they were smart enough not to let the partisanship around them destroy their partnership.

. . .

As Truman took over for FDR, the U.S. delegation to the United Nations organizing conference, which was scheduled to begin on April 25 in San Francisco, was finalizing its positions on outstanding issues.

America's spearheading of this conference, and its eventual membership in the United Nations, would mark a dramatic turn away from its traditional isolationism and toward a new posture of global engagement. In mid-April, however, Washington and Moscow were battling over what the new organization would do, and nobody could guarantee that the San Francisco gathering would prove successful.

Truman had some big decisions to make about San Francisco—and they would quickly put him in close contact with Vandenberg.

PART I

"A Victory against War Itself"

IT WAS THE EVENING of April 12, 1945, and Harry Truman, who had just taken the oath as America's new president, was holding an emergency meeting with the cabinet he had inherited from FDR. Earlier in the day, Senator Tom Connally, chairman of the Senate Foreign Relations Committee, had issued a statement predicting that, in light of FDR's death that afternoon, the United Nations organizing conference that was scheduled to begin in San Francisco in two weeks could be delayed. That Connally was not just the Senate's top Democrat on foreign affairs but also a member of the U.S. delegation to San Francisco made his prediction particularly newsworthy. Reporters wanted to know what Truman would do, and they were asking Steve Early, who had been FDR's press secretary.

As the cabinet meeting was starting, Early walked in to ask Truman what he should tell the reporters. In his first major decision as president, Truman said firmly that the San Francisco conference would start on schedule. He wanted no ambiguity about it. Concerned after the meeting that his response to reporters wouldn't reach U.S. allies and other foreign audiences, he ordered White House aides to issue a statement in his name to that effect that evening. He also directed Secretary of State Edward Stettinius more than once over the next day to reinforce the point publicly.

"I wanted to make it clear," Truman recalled, "that I attached the greatest importance to the establishment of international machinery for the prevention of war and the maintenance of peace. I knew many of the pitfalls and stumbling blocks we could encounter in setting up such an organization, but I also knew that in a world without such machinery we would be forever doomed to the fear of destruction. It was important for us to make a start, no matter how imperfect."[1]

Arthur Vandenberg, who was also a member of the U.S. delegation to San Francisco, was relieved to hear the news. "I liked the *first* decision Truman made—namely that Frisco should *go on*," he wrote in his diary the next day. Of Connally's suggestion, he added, "Truman promptly stopped *that* mistake (which would have confessed to the world that there *is an* 'indispensable' man who was bigger than America)."[2]

Truman shared Vandenberg's concern about how the nation and the world would react to FDR's death. He knew that he needed to seize the role of president quickly and leave no doubt that he was now in charge. That was no small challenge, for the notion of anyone besides FDR serving as president was hard for many people to swallow. (On Truman's second full day on the job, he called Jesse Jones, who ran the Reconstruction Finance Corporation, to tell him "the President" had appointed his friend, John W. Snyder, to serve as a federal loan official. When Jones asked if "the President" had made that decision before he died, Truman snapped, "No. He made it just now."[3])

Truman and Vandenberg wanted the San Francisco conference to start on time for other reasons as well. They were both longtime UN enthusiasts who carried high hopes for what the new body could accomplish, and they were eager to see it established as soon as possible. They also recognized the symbolism behind San Francisco—that in hosting the conference and driving the proceedings, the United States was reassuring a nervous world that it did not intend to repeat its disastrous posture of the 1920s and 1930s when it refused to join the League of Nations, erected huge new trade barriers, slashed its military, ignored emerging threats in Europe and Asia, and retreated to its traditional isolationism. Instead, America now planned to actively participate in global affairs on a sustained basis.

. . .

"Victory against War"

In their successful efforts, Truman and Vandenberg brought to fruition the first piece of their revolutionary new foreign policy, transforming the United States from a reluctant global presence to a proud global leader.

With Truman in Washington and Vandenberg in San Francisco, the two coordinated their actions largely through Stettinius—who chaired the U.S. delegation effectively even though neither Truman nor Vandenberg thought much of him. Complicating matters further, the San Francisco meeting ensued in the midst of growing U.S.-Soviet conflict, with the Soviets breaking their promise to allow for democratic governments in Eastern Europe and more top U.S. officials abandoning hopes of postwar collaboration with Moscow.

As Truman set overall policy for the U.S. delegation from Washington and Vandenberg tweaked the details in San Francisco, U.S. and Soviet officials clashed over key features of the emerging United Nations. They struggled over the relationship between the General Assembly of all UN nations and the Security Council, which would include five permanent members (including the United States and Soviet Union) and six rotating members. They also struggled over the power of the veto that the five permanent Security Council members would wield as well as the extent to which nations around the world could establish regional defense pacts that would operate outside the Security Council. Backed by Truman, encouraged by Vandenberg, and steered by Stettinius, the U.S. delegation dug in for its major priorities and, in the end, secured virtually everything it had sought.

Unlike the other pieces of their revolutionary new foreign policy (the Truman Doctrine, Marshall Plan, and North Atlantic Treaty), which Truman and Vandenberg created largely out of whole cloth, the United Nations was years in the making. Its roots lay in the utopian visions of monarchs and philosophers of centuries earlier, in the forlorn efforts of Woodrow Wilson to convince America to join the league, and in a half decade of spadework by FDR and his top aides in the early 1940s.

Its roots lay as well in the dreamy hopes for global peace that Truman harbored since his teens, and in Vandenberg's pivot from isolationism to global engagement. Thus, the story of their collaboration to create the United Nations begins not in 1945 but years earlier—in the days when, separately, Truman and Vandenberg were developing their views about America and its place in the world.

I

"President Wilson Tried to Work Out a Way"

EVER SINCE HIS SENIOR year of high school, Harry Truman had carried part of his favorite poem, Tennyson's "Locksley Hall," in his pocket. Written in 1835, it portrayed a utopian future when war would end, men would resolve their disputes peacefully, and the rule of law would prevail. That Truman carried this snippet from the thousands of books, stories, and poems he had read, and that he always recopied it when the paper frayed, spoke to his optimism about the future that dated back to his happy childhood.

A peaceful utopia, Tennyson envisioned in the words that Truman carried with him, would emerge through a "Parliament of Man," a "Federation of the World."

> For I dipt into the future, far as human eye could see,
> Saw the Vision of the world, and all the wonders that would be;
> Saw the heavens fill with commerce, argosies of magic sails,
> Pilots of the purple twilight, dropping down with costly bales;
> Heard the heavens fill with shouting, and there rained a ghastly dew
> From the nations' airy navies grappling in the central blue;
> Far along the world-wide whisper of the south-wind rushing warm,
> With the standards of the people plunging thro' the thunderstorm;
> Till the war-drum throbb'd no longer, and the battle-flags were furl'd
> In the Parliament of Man, the Federation of the World.
> There the common sense of most shall hold a fretful realm in awe,
> And the kindly earth shall slumber, lapt in universal law.[1]

As Truman well knew, monarchs and philosophers had been searching for a global arrangement to keep the peace from well before Tennyson's time. "I had made a study of the 'Grand Design' of King Henry IV of France," Truman wrote of the man who ruled France in the late sixteenth and early seventeenth centuries. "This plan called for a kind of federation of sovereign states in Europe to act in concert to prevent wars. This, as far as I know, was the first practicable international organization ever suggested."[2] The "Grand Design" was followed by other plans for international collaboration. Philosopher Immanuel Kant in 1795 envisioned "perpetual peace," a utopia in which no state would dominate another, none would meddle with the government of another, standing armies would disappear, and "the laws of nations shall be founded on a federation of free states." In Tennyson's time, Europe's great powers crafted an informal alliance to keep the peace. Led by Austria's Prince Klemens Wenzel von Metternich, they gathered at the Congress of Vienna in 1814 to redraw national boundaries after the Napoleonic Wars and establish "spheres of influence." Austria, Britain, France, and Russia would help settle local disputes and maintain peace—a task at which they largely succeeded until World War I.

As young men, Truman and Vandenberg had high hopes for long-term peace, and they were captivated by President Wilson's efforts to secure it. As they both turned thirty-three in the spring of 1917, Wilson argued that the United States should enter World War I to help make the world "safe for democracy" and that the world should create an international body to keep the peace. "Our object," Wilson said, "is to vindicate the principles of peace and justice in the life of the world as against selfish and autocratic power and to set up among the really free and self-governed peoples of the world such a concert of purpose and of action as will henceforth ensure the observance of those principles."

Wilson couldn't convince the Senate to ratify America's entry into the league and, partly for that reason alone, it proved a colossal failure. For Truman and Vandenberg, Wilson's epic defeat hovered like a ghost over their efforts to create the United Nations.

. . .

"Victory against War"

"President Wilson tried to work out a way to prevent another world war," Truman wrote later. "He was the most popular man in the history of the country at the time he went to Europe [in 1918] and when he came back [in 1919]. But unfortunately there were men in Congress who, jealous of Wilson's popularity, began to undermine his efforts."

That was but half of the story, however, as Truman acknowledged. If the jealous "men in Congress" wanted to hang Wilson politically, he gave them more than enough rope. He invited no Senate Republican leader to accompany him to Europe, even though Republicans controlled the Senate and had more than enough votes to derail his foreign policy dreams. Nor would Wilson consider any suggestions from Republicans on how to modify the postwar Treaty of Versailles, which included the league, in ways that would address their concerns.

"In a way, [Wilson] aided his opponents," Truman wrote, "for he took none of the leaders in the Senate into his confidence. Instead, he waited until he came back with the treaty and then, with too little regard for the feeling on Capitol Hill, presented it to the Congress. It was my opinion that if President Wilson had had the leaders of the Congress in his confidence all the time and had trusted them he would not have been defeated on the League of Nations. The fact was that he did not like many of them, and very few were his close personal friends."[3]

Truman had watched Wilson's failure mostly from Europe, where the army captain toured in early 1919. For him, it served as a cautionary tale. A quarter century later, as the San Francisco meeting beckoned, he was determined not to make the same mistake of ignoring Republicans. Instead, he consulted with Vandenberg regularly, listening to his concerns and addressing his needs. He wanted to ensure that Vandenberg was happy enough in San Francisco that, when he returned to Washington, he would gather the Senate votes to ratify the UN Charter.

Vandenberg had observed Wilson's failure from Grand Rapids. For him, it presented an opportunity. A quarter century later, he was the most powerful Senate Republican on foreign policy—the successor to Henry Cabot Lodge, the Senate Foreign Relations Committee chairman of Wilson's day—so he held the cards when it came to Truman's fate with the Senate over the United Nations. He used that leverage to force the U.S. delegation in San Francisco to tilt his way at moments of disagreement. The U.S. delegation, in turn, pressured other nations' delegations to take America's side in disputes in San Francisco under the threat that an unhappy United States might again choose not to participate in a new global organization.

Truman and Vandenberg thought often about Wilson's failure until fate gave them a chance to rectify it.

. . .

As senators in the years leading up to 1945, Truman and Vandenberg worked both separately and together to nourish support in Washington and across the country for a successor to the league.

Vandenberg was a leading isolationist until Pearl Harbor shook him to his core in December of 1941. But as war clouds gathered in the late 1930s, he began to rethink his outlook. As the Senate Foreign Relations Committee debated the Neutrality Act of 1939, Vandenberg raised the prospect of creating "international machinery to secure international peace." Writing to a constituent four months before Pearl Harbor, he expressed the need for "some rational formula under which the next peace agreement can be underwritten by *all* the major powers of the world, including the United States."[4]

In 1943 Truman and Vandenberg both supported Senator Connally's resolution that urged FDR to endorse the concept of a global peacekeeping body. (The House passed a similar resolution that year.) Also in 1943, Truman joined other senators on a speaking tour of twenty-six states that proponents of a global body had arranged. Vandenberg, meanwhile, worked to build support for the idea among his fellow Republicans. In July 1943 he teamed with Senator Wallace H. White of Maine on an all-Republican foreign policy resolution that included a call for "postwar cooperation among sovereign nations."[5] Two months later, the Mackinac Conference of leading Republicans from around the country—the gathering over which Vandenberg exerted great influence—expressed support for U.S. participation in a postwar global organization. "*It was my position,*" he wrote in his diary that year, "*that the United States obviously must be a far greater international co-operator after this war than ever before.*"[6]

Vandenberg's "speech heard 'round the world" of January 10, 1945, supposedly marked his conversion from isolationism to global engagement. At the time, however, his comments about international cooperation to maintain peace received far more attention. He called on America to "appeal to our allies" to "frankly face the post-war alternatives which are available to them and to us" to keep the peace. "There are two ways to do it," he declared. "One way is by exclusive individual action in which each of us tries to look out for himself. The other way is by joint action in which we undertake to look out for each other. The first way is the old way which has twice taken us to Europe's interminable battlefields within a quarter century. The second way is the new way in which our present fraternity of war becomes a new fraternity of peace."

In that speech and later, Vandenberg described his hopes for a global body in words that echoed Tennyson and Kant. The United Nations must be, he said in late March of 1945, "tomorrow's free and untrammeled 'town meeting of the world'"[7]—a phrase that he would repeat often in the months ahead. Committed to stamping his "concept of justice" onto the UN Charter, the senator pledged on his way to San Francisco "to give this new International Organization a 'soul.'"[8]

2

"We May Perfect This Charter of Peace and Justice"

ON FEBRUARY 13, 1945, Vandenberg learned that President Roosevelt—
who had served as Wilson's assistant secretary of the navy and witnessed
up close his mistake in ignoring the Senate Republicans of his day—had
chosen him for the seven-member U.S. delegation for San Francisco.

In San Francisco Vandenberg and the other delegates would final-
ize a UN Charter from the draft that U.S., British, Soviet, and Chinese
officials had written from August to October of 1944 at Dumbarton
Oaks, an estate in the Georgetown section of Washington. The Dumbarton Oaks document contained the basic UN elements that survived
San Francisco and have endured ever since—a General Assembly of all
nations; a Security Council of five permanent members (the United
States, Soviet Union, China, Great Britain, and France) and six others
that the General Assembly would select for rotating terms; a secretary-
general to run the organization on a daily basis; an International Court
of Justice; and other agencies that the General Assembly would create
as necessary.

The significance of U.S. leadership at Dumbarton Oaks was not lost
on America's savviest observers. As that meeting was just underway in
late August of 1944, the *New York Times'* James Reston wrote, "Four
great decisions mark the foreign policy of the United States: the pur-
chase of the Territory of Louisiana from France, the pronouncement of
the Monroe Doctrine, the extension of our obligations to the Asiatic
waters of the Western Pacific after the Spanish-American War, and our

rejection of the League of Nations. This week it became evident that the Republic was moving toward a fifth, toward a decision on whether or not to join with its allies in creating a world security organization that would have the authority, under certain specific conditions, to 'direct' the forces of the United States and other nations against any future potential aggressor."[1]

But however consequential the work in San Francisco would be, and however much he craved a seat at the table where decisions were made, Vandenberg did not accept FDR's offer immediately. Instead, for reasons of both policy and ego, he reacted cagily, refusing to take the post until FDR accepted his conditions. Vandenberg worried that, by serving on FDR's delegation, he'd be forced to support all the decisions about the new body that FDR had already made and privately relayed to Soviet leader Joseph Stalin and British leader Winston Churchill. He had long distrusted FDR, finding him imperial and secretive with Congress and far too accommodating to Stalin. He had opposed Roosevelt's establishment of diplomatic relations with the Soviet Union in 1933, voted against confirming any U.S. ambassador to Moscow, and objected when FDR wouldn't sever ties with the Soviets after they occupied Poland and invaded Finland in 1939.[2] He wanted unfettered freedom to express his views and put his imprint on what would emerge from San Francisco.

More crassly, Vandenberg knew that by withholding his acceptance, he would generate a series of "will he or won't he" newspaper stories, particularly back in Michigan, that would only raise his profile. Craving the limelight, he reveled in the predictable attention; asked by reporters a day after the State Department's announcement of his impending selection whether he would accept if he received the official request from FDR, Vandenberg replied mischievously, "As the President would say, that is an 'iffy' question."[3]

. . .

At the time, Vandenberg was disturbed by what FDR, Stalin, and Churchill (the "Big Three") had decided for Poland.

At the Yalta conference in early February, FDR and Churchill had sought a democratic government in Warsaw, but Stalin demanded a pro-Soviet government as a buffer against any hostile forces to the west. As Vandenberg later learned, the Big Three had decided that Poland's "Lublin" government, which the Soviets established after liberating Poland from the Nazis, would remain in place but expand to include Polish democratic leaders from abroad, such as those in the West-backed government-in-exile in London. Vandenberg didn't think the Lublin government deserved recognition, and his skepticism that the Soviets would democratize it in any real way proved prophetic. In fact, while FDR and Churchill were pushing Stalin to expand that government to include democratic elements, Soviet forces on the ground in Poland were exchanging gunfire with the Polish Home Army, which was loyal to the democratic government-in-exile.

To Vandenberg's further dismay, he learned that FDR and Churchill had agreed to Stalin's request to set Poland's eastern border essentially at the "Curzon Line," to which Soviet forces had occupied Poland during the war. That allowed the Soviet Union to annex hundreds of miles of eastern Poland. To compensate Poland, the Big Three agreed to shift its western border a considerable distance to the west, enabling it to absorb former German territory. (Vandenberg didn't know that FDR and Churchill had essentially accepted Stalin's territorial demands two years earlier at the Tehran Conference.) By early 1945 FDR and Churchill didn't have much leverage to do otherwise anyway because Soviet troops were well positioned on the ground to enforce Stalin's dictates.

Vandenberg was now in a tough spot. In his "speech heard 'round the world" just a month earlier, he had warned about Stalin's designs for Eastern Europe; encouraged all of the allies to not "seek aggrandizement, territorial or otherwise," when the war ended; urged Moscow to rely on "collective security" to protect itself rather than establish "a surrounding circle of buffer [i.e., puppet] states"; and announced that he was not "prepared to guarantee permanently the spoils of an unjust peace."

Just as the State Department was unveiling Vandenberg's selection for San Francisco, the Big Three revealed their decision about the "Curzon Line." "It was announced," columnist David Lawrence wrote, "that

President Roosevelt had agreed at the Yalta conference . . . to do the exact opposite regarding Poland of that which the Michigan Senator had urged . . . Now to cap the climax President Roosevelt has asked Senator Vandenberg to serve as a member of the delegation to the coming conference of the United Nations where a peace organization is to be set up, presumably to underwrite the very kind of thing against which Mr. Vandenberg inveighed in his speech . . . Where does this leave the Michigan Senator? Must he turn a somersault?"[4]

The "Michigan Senator" was wondering the same thing.

. . .

Vandenberg recognized the enormous hurdles to overturning Big Three decisions, but he wasn't ready to give up. In writing its charter, he wanted to empower the United Nations to view such decisions as tentative, subject to change.

In a February 15 letter to Roosevelt, Vandenberg expressed his "deepest gratitude" for his selection and reiterated his "profound conviction that we *must* organize the post-war world on the basis of effective, collective security." But, he asked, "what specific commitments, if any, would be implicit in my acceptance of this designation" and "whether I might feel that it will not violate your commission or your expectations if I freely present my own points of view to our Delegation and if I reserve the right of final judgment upon the ultimate results of the Conference."[5]

Awaiting FDR's response, Vandenberg put the issue more bluntly two days later in a letter to John Foster Dulles, who advised Vandenberg on all major foreign policy challenges in the late 1940s (and later served as President Eisenhower's secretary of state). "I cannot go to this conference as a stooge," he wrote, explaining that, at the very least, he needed the freedom to improve the Dumbarton Oaks draft. "I should have preferred not to have been named," he said—unconvincingly, in light of his hunger for the action. "At best, it represents an equivocal role. On the other hand, I do not think the Republican Party can make a graver blunder than to decline Senatorial cooperation (under appropriate circumstances) when it is tendered by the President in a critical case of this nature and at such a critical moment . . . If I am assured untrammeled freedom to present this point of view (and to render my own independent judgment upon the final results at San Francisco) I think I am called upon to put my head in the noose and take my chances."[6]

For Vandenberg, Poland's status was politically sensitive. Michigan was home to a large Polish constituency, one that chafed at prospects that the United States would leave Poland in the clutches of a brutal regime in Moscow. But Vandenberg refused to see himself as a mere politician who sought public popularity and feared voter disdain. He viewed himself only as a higher-minded leader. Consequently, he could not admit the obvious, insisting that his perspective on Yalta was untainted by politics.

"The speculation in the [newspapers] about the relationship between my decision and the Polish question was without foundation," he wrote in another letter. "There are no political considerations (except freedom of action) involved in my attitude." The "Polish question," he insisted, "is not a question of 'popular votes' for me; it is a question whether the American people will ever sanction a Peace League which permanently stratifies the palpably unjust decisions made at Yalta." While expecting to accept FDR's invitation, he warned vaguely that if he could not, "I shall have 'to tell the world.'"[7] What he planned to "tell the world," however, was anyone's guess.

Vandenberg received a "Dear Arthur" letter of February 26 from FDR and, whether due to a White House snafu or Roosevelt's legendary shiftiness, the president ignored Vandenberg's questions about the "commitments" to which he would have to abide in San Francisco, instead thanking him for agreeing to serve. Only after Vandenberg reiterated his request in a March 1 letter to "freely present my own points of view" did FDR agree in his reply two days later. "We shall need such free expression in the delegation, and in America before and after the conference," FDR wrote. "I am counting, indeed, on the wisdom I know you can add to our entire effort to secure a program for permanent peace. Always sincerely, Franklin D. Roosevelt."[8]

. . .

By that point, Truman had been vice president for about six weeks. He was a heartbeat away from the presidency, and anyone who had seen Roosevelt around that time (his staff, lawmakers, foreign leaders, and, of course, Truman himself) recognized quickly that FDR didn't have long to live. Unfortunately for Truman, Vandenberg knew far more about U.S. preparations for San Francisco than he did.

That's because FDR, who didn't know Truman well before tapping him as his running mate in 1944, had kept him out of his foreign policy meetings. In fact, Truman met with FDR only twice during his eighty-two days as vice president, leaving him strikingly ignorant about foreign policy. He didn't know what FDR had promised Churchill and Stalin at Yalta, and he didn't even know about the Manhattan Project that would later produce the atomic bomb. "They didn't tell me anything about what was going on," he complained later to Commerce Secretary Henry Wallace.[9] That made Truman's early days as president, whether pondering the United Nations or other foreign challenges, that much harder.

Vandenberg, by contrast, had been well briefed by administration officials on discussions both within the State Department and among the Big Three about a new global body. FDR's longtime secretary of state, Cordell Hull, also had recognized Wilson's mistake in ignoring the Senate Republicans of his day. Consequently, when he met with the Senate Foreign Relations Committee in early 1944, he suggested that the committee create a smaller bipartisan panel of its members with whom he could confer regularly. In response, the Foreign Relations Committee established the "Committee of Eight," which met privately with Hull in the ensuing months and learned the most intimate details of U.S. efforts to create a global body.

Whether in the Senate in 1944 or the White House starting in early 1945, Truman was privy to none of it.

. . .

Upon accepting FDR's appointment to the U.S. delegation, Vandenberg began his preparations for San Francisco.

Along with Vandenberg, the delegation included its chairman, Secretary of State Edward Stettinius; Senator Connally; the House Foreign Affairs Committee's Democratic chairman, Rep. Sol Bloom; that committee's top Republican, Rep. Charles A. Eaton; Minnesota's former Republican governor, Harold Stassen, who was then considering a run for president; and Barnard College dean Virginia C. Gildersleeve. On March 13 they met as a group for the first time and also met briefly with FDR at the White House.

When they met again with FDR on March 23—a meeting for which, Vandenberg later noted snippily, Roosevelt kept them waiting for an hour—Vandenberg didn't like what he heard. FDR revealed that he had promised Stalin three Soviet votes in the General Assembly (to account for the Soviet Union and its republics of Ukraine and Belarus) and, in return, the United States would have three. Stalin had first asked for six, to match the British votes for its dominions, and FDR offered three each for Moscow and Washington as a compromise. FDR then complicated matters further by trying to make everyone happy. On one hand, he told the delegates that were he one of them, he would support the compromise. On the other, he told them that they were free to accept or reject it.

The episode proved important, for it reinforced Vandenberg's fears about FDR's appeasement of the Soviets, upset his sense of right and wrong, threatened to explode as a major concern for virtually every other nation in San Francisco, and foreshadowed the tough negotiations with the Soviets that would occur out west. For several days Vandenberg steamed privately about FDR's acquiescence to Soviet bluster. He was unhappy that Britain had more votes than the United States, and that the United States and Soviet Union each had three when neither deserved more than one.

"This will *raise hell*," Vandenberg predicted in his diary on the day he learned the news. A few days later, he reflected, "The more I have thought about the President's amazing tentative deal with Stalin to get extra votes in the Assembly, the more deadly it has become (1) to American public opinion and (2) to any further pretense of 'sovereign equality' among the lesser nations of the earth." (The Dumbarton Oaks draft referred to the "sovereign equality" of all peace-loving nations as one of its guiding principles, and, as such, it provided that each would have one vote in the General Assembly.) Determined to relay his concerns to a top administration official, Vandenberg sought unsuccessfully to reach Stettinius, who was in Florida, and Undersecretary of State Joseph Grew, who was home sick, before spending an hour with Assistant Secretary Jimmy Dunn.[10]

That's where things stood until the *New York Herald Tribune* broke the story of the secret deal on March 29, prompting Vandenberg to break publicly with FDR on the issue. Previously assured by FDR, per their exchange of letters, that he could speak his mind on any matter, Vandenberg declared, "I would deeply disagree with any voting proposal, if made, which would destroy the promised 'sovereign equality of nations' in the Peace League's [General] Assembly as previously proposed at Dumbarton Oaks. This applies just as much to extra votes for us as for any other nation. This Assembly must continue to be tomorrow's free and untrammeled 'town meeting of the world.' The voice of the Great Powers will be amply protected in the [Security] Council."[11]

The story forced two weeks of scrambling by FDR, Stettinius, Vandenberg, and the delegation to decide what it all meant and whether delegates were bound to support the three votes for Moscow, three for Washington, both, or neither. After Stettinius refused to clarify things at a press conference and days of further deliberation between administration officials and the delegation, the issue remained unresolved, leaving it to San Francisco. In the meantime the Soviets made clear that they did not plan to drop what they considered this promise from FDR. Throughout April, in Washington and then San Francisco, Vyacheslav Molotov, the Soviet foreign minister, and Andrei Gromyko, the Soviet ambassador to the United States, pushed for the three votes and threatened to block the business of San Francisco if they didn't get them.

The issue even prompted an awkward exchange between Truman and Vandenberg that confused each. Truman called Vandenberg on April 2 to relay FDR's assurance that U.S. delegates could do whatever they wanted about U.S. and Soviet votes. Vandenberg then told Truman about FDR's comment that, were he a delegate, he would vote for the compromise. Truman, Vandenberg recalled, was left "completely flabbergasted."

. . .

As the issue of U.S., Soviet, and British votes was about to explode publicly, Vandenberg received a visit from Dr. Leo Pasvolsky, the longtime assistant to Secretary of State Hull who was now the key behind-the-scenes staffer on all UN-related issues for Stettinius and the delegation. He had led State Department planning for a new global peacekeeping body all the way back to 1939.

Born in Pavlograd, Russia, in 1893, Pasvolsky had immigrated to the United States with his parents in 1905. After night school at the City College of New York and graduate study in political science at Columbia University, he covered the Paris peace talks in 1919 for the *New York Tribune* and other newspapers and attended League of Nations sessions. Pasvolsky, who later became a PhD economist, was an odd-looking man, as he himself acknowledged. He was short, round, bald, and bespectacled, sported a narrow mustache, and smoked a pipe. His appearance and legendary doggedness evoked numerous colorful descriptions—"Friar Tuck," "the brain that walked like a man," and "the third little pig in Disney's version of that fairy tale—the one whose house could not be blown down."[12] Vandenberg said he "has a face as round as the moon but a head 'as long as necessary.'"[13] Years later, U.S. diplomat Richard Holbrooke called him "one of those figures peculiar to Washington—a tenacious bureaucrat who, fixed on a single goal, left behind a huge legacy while virtually disappearing from history."[14]

Pasvolsky came to discuss Vandenberg's proposed amendments to the UN Charter, but the senator had something else on his mind. Two weeks earlier, he had said in a Senate speech that the United States should confront the Soviet-dominated Lublin government about its harsh treatment of Poles who were loyal to Poland's government-in-exile in London, and that Poland was a test case that "will have a large effect upon the success of our ultimate plans for collective security and organized peace."

When the Communist press in Moscow and New York reacted bitterly and attacked Vandenberg personally, the senator visited FDR at the White House and offered to resign from the delegation so that he wouldn't complicate U.S.-Soviet negotiations in San Francisco. "I can conveniently arrange to break a leg—if you wish," Vandenberg said. FDR firmly rejected the idea, telling the senator, "Just between us, Arthur, I am coming to know the Russians better, and if I could name only one delegate to the San Francisco conference, you would be that delegate."

Vandenberg remained worried, however, and he now raised the issue with Pasvolsky. This key staffer, too, reassured Vandenberg. To Vandenberg's concern that he'd be "persona non grata" with the Soviets, complicating U.S. efforts to work with Moscow, Pasvolsky replied, "Not at all—they respect a fighter—they like to 'be told.'" In fact, he said, Vandenberg would be the delegation's key member.

"The big question mark in every foreign delegate's mind," Pasvolsky told Vandenberg, referring to Wilson's failure over the league, "will still be the same one that has plagued them in past experience, namely, What will the Senate do?" "Well—," Pasvolsky went on, "when we are pressing for something we don't seem able to get, we'll send you in to tell 'em that it has to be done if they expect to get their Treaty past the Senate."[15]

. . .

On April 16, Truman's fourth full day as president, he sought to rally the nation behind efforts to create a United Nations.

"The task of creating a sound international organization is complicated and difficult," Truman told a joint session of Congress in a speech that the major radio networks carried live. "Yet without such organization, the rights of man on earth cannot be protected. Machinery for the just settlement of international differences must be found. Without such machinery, the entire world will have to remain an armed camp. The world will be doomed to deadly conflict, devoid of hope for real peace."

The reaction was telling. Lawmakers interrupted Truman seventeen times to applaud, suggesting that his call for the United States to help create, and participate in, a "sound international organization" would prove far less controversial on Capitol Hill than Wilson's call of nearly three decades earlier. Letters of support from around the country poured into the White House in the ensuing days.

That reaction reflected months of effort by public officials and private groups to nurture support for a new global body. In late 1944 the State Department launched a public relations campaign, collaborating with scores of groups. FDR tapped Archibald MacLeish, the librarian of Congress, to lead it, and the department deployed speakers around the country; distributed over 200,000 copies of the Dumbarton Oaks proposal and an eight-page question-and-answer packet to influential parties; sent a pamphlet on Dumbarton Oaks to more than a million other people; distributed a film about it to key organizations; and briefed other groups. In early 1945 MacLeish hosted a weekly radio program on NBC, and, in one segment, Undersecretary of State Joseph Grew said the world's choice in San Francisco was between "an organization of the type proposed at Dumbarton Oaks and international anarchy."[16] The National League of Women Voters, Woodrow Wilson Foundation, American Legion, and others sent material to hundreds of thousands of other people.

Such efforts paid huge dividends. Public recognition of Dumbarton Oaks rose from 43 percent in December of 1944 to 60 percent in March of 1945. Support for the San Francisco conference rose from 60 to 80 percent between January and February, while 94 percent of all Americans had heard about the conference on the eve of its start in late April.[17] In addition, the nation's leaders were far more broadly predisposed to U.S. participation in a global peacekeeping organization than those of Wilson's day. The House and Senate, as noted above, passed resolutions to that effect in 1943, and, a year later, FDR and Republican presidential candidate Thomas Dewey both praised the Dumbarton Oaks draft.

Just as telling was Vandenberg's experience a few days after Truman spoke.

. . .

On April 20, as they prepared to leave for San Francisco, Vandenberg and Connally addressed a crowded and attentive Senate chamber. Connally went first, expressing his hopes of improving the Dumbarton Oaks draft and helping to create a mechanism to secure a durable peace. After Connally sat down, tears filling his eyes, Vandenberg rose to speak.

"I have no illusions that the . . . conference can chart the Millennium," Vandenberg told his colleagues. "Please do not expect it of us . . . But I have faith that we may perfect this charter of peace and justice so that reasonable men of good will shall find in it so much good . . . that all lesser doubts and disagreements may be resolved in its favor . . . Once more I am asking that your prayers for this great enterprise shall fail neither it nor us."[18]

When Vandenberg finished, a wave of emotion overcame the normally staid body. Senators of both parties rose, clapped enthusiastically, and rushed to shake the hands and pat the backs of Vandenberg and Connally. In their honor, Senate Majority Leader Alben Barkley adjourned the Senate for the day.

To be sure, Stettinius, Connally, and the rest of the U.S. delegates all would play important roles in San Francisco. As the key Republican who was headed out west, however, all eyes focused on Vandenberg.

"As the conference opened this week," *Time* wrote in an April 30 cover piece about him, "Arthur Vandenberg was unquestionably the most important U.S. delegate present, and perhaps the single most important man . . . By & large the success of a world security organization would stand or fall on the question of U.S. adherence. And the answer to that question lay with Senator Vandenberg."[19]

"Victory against War"

3

"As Dumb as They Come"

As San Francisco beckoned, Vandenberg heard something about Truman's plans that worried him.

It happened on Truman's first full day as president as Truman ate lunch on Capitol Hill with Vandenberg and more than a dozen other key lawmakers. "He told me," Vandenberg wrote later, "he is *not* going to Frisco personally (as F.D.R. had intended to do) and that he expects to 'leave Frisco to our Delegation.' Unquestionably we will have greater freedom—but also greater responsibility.

"I am puzzled," Vandenberg continued. "Stettinius is now Secretary of State in *fact*. Up to now he has been only the presidential messenger. He does *not* have the background and experience for such a job at such a critical time—altho [sic] he is a *grand person* with every good intention and high honesty of purpose. *Now* we have *both* an inexperienced President *and* an inexperienced Secretary (in re foreign affairs.)"[1]

Truman judged the secretary even more harshly. "Stettinius was as dumb as they come," the plainspoken president said in one of his less charitable moments.[2] Others close to the U.S. delegation felt similarly. Dean Acheson, then assistant secretary of state, recalled later that Stettinius had "gone far with comparatively modest equipment." Archibald MacLeish called him "Snow White." Ralph Bunche, an outside adviser to the delegation, labeled him a "complete dud . . . He is simply in a job for which he has utterly no qualifications and about which he knows nothing." The press, led by the *New York Times*' James Reston, trashed him in similar fashion.[3]

Ironically, Edward Reilly Stettinius Jr. looked the part and, at least on paper, seemed credentialed for it. At forty-four, he cast a striking pose: blue eyes, white hair, dark eyebrows, and a sharp smile. He enjoyed a meteoric rise at General Motors and, at thirty-seven, was chairing the board of U.S. Steel and earning a then-whopping $100,000 a year. At the urging of FDR's closest aide, Harry Hopkins, he came to Washington in the late 1930s and built an impressive resume on foreign affairs, serving as chair of the War Resources Board, director of the Office of Production Management, administrator of Lend-Lease, and undersecretary of state. As undersecretary, he headed the U.S. delegation to Dumbarton Oaks. FDR appointed him secretary of state in late 1944 to replace the ailing Cordell Hull. Stettinius accompanied FDR to Yalta, and he was the one who suggested that San Francisco host the UN conference after FDR rejected other alternatives.

Truman, however, was never wowed by fancy titles and, while calling Stettinius "a fine man, amiable, good-looking, cooperative," Truman added that he "never had an idea new or old."[4] In fact, on the same day as his lunch with lawmakers, Truman privately asked Jimmy Byrnes, the former influential senator, to serve as secretary of state. But after Byrnes eagerly accepted, the two agreed that Truman shouldn't announce his plans or make the change until Stettinius finished his work in San Francisco.[5] (Not only did Truman think much more of Byrnes than Stettinius, he also believed that, since the secretary of state was next in line of presidential succession at the time, someone with serious political experience should hold the job. A former longtime senator and House member like Byrnes fit the bill.)

Truman and Vandenberg never fully lost their disdain for Stettinius. Truman kept him on a tight leash in San Francisco, ensuring that he followed his instructions with precision. Vandenberg pushed him to lead the delegation more forcefully and gave him tangible help at key moments. In the end, however, they both came to acknowledge that, for all his faults, the secretary had skillfully steered the conference to a positive conclusion, kept the delegation united, and made sure that the president and the senator—though three thousand miles from one another—worked in lockstep.

. . .

Stettinius coordinated U.S. preparations for San Francisco, scheduling delegation meetings in April while bringing Truman into the process. Vandenberg, though, was the driving force in crystallizing the U.S. position on outstanding issues and proposing improvements to the Dumbarton Oaks draft.

More than anything, the senator wanted to ensure that the United Nations would seek "justice" as one of its top priorities. He felt strongly that the Dumbarton Oaks draft was severely inadequate on that score, and, with that in mind, he put together a package of eight amendments to the draft that he wanted the delegation to endorse. He wanted to empower the United Nations not only to address threats to justice (e.g., foreign invasion, ethnic cleansing) that would emerge in the years to come but also to rectify conditions of injustice (e.g., foreign domination of sovereign states) that were already in place in 1945. That way, the United Nations would be free to revisit, for instance, the Big Three's decisions at Yalta that facilitated Soviet efforts to dominate Poland.

Meeting on April 16, the delegation discussed and endorsed Vandenberg's amendments, leaving Vandenberg "well satisfied."[6] The next morning, Truman welcomed the delegation to the White House for his first meeting with them, and Vandenberg found him "modest, unassuming and cordial—as usual." With rumors swirling about Truman's plans for foreign policy, Vandenberg said the president "told us there would be *no changes in the Delegation*—to set at rest reports that Stettinius would be replaced with Jimmy Byrnes and that Eleanor Roosevelt might want to go along."[7]

Truman also met separately with individual delegates before they left for the West Coast. "We were agreed," he recalled, "that we ought to strive for an organization to which all nations would delegate enough powers to prevent another world war. This was not going to be easy."

The notion that America would cede some power to a global organization raised the specter of Wilson's failure, for it was on this very issue that Senate Republicans of Wilson's day revolted against the league. That history was uppermost in Truman's mind. "We knew the Charter of the proposed organization had to be acceptable to the United States Senate," he recalled. "We did not want to run the risk of another League of Nations tragedy, with the United States standing in isolation on the side lines."

Truman was doing his best to keep Vandenberg happy. In a meeting with Stettinius on April 19, he signed off on Vandenberg's eight amendments, putting the president and senator on the same page in the days before San Francisco. Truman also outlined a strict modus operandi for Stettinius that put Truman and Vandenberg in closer coordination. He directed Stettinius to call him after every session in San Francisco, day or night, and whenever else he needed him, whatever the hour. He further ordered Stettinius to consult with Vandenberg and Connally "on every move" he made "in order to get full agreement." If Stettinius could not bring them along, Truman said that he'd step in and speak to the two by phone. Truman later recalled that he wanted to give Vandenberg and Connally "direct access" to him "at all times," and he wanted "the benefit of their counsel and experience."[8]

· · ·

Truman and Vandenberg recognized that, however overwhelmingly influential the United States would be in San Francisco, it could not unilaterally impose its will on the conference. Instead, America needed to work with its allies and other countries to build a global consensus for what it sought for a UN Charter. The two men, however, approached that challenge from different vantage points.

In their April 19 meeting, Truman recalled later, he told Stettinius,

It would be best for us to reserve our final position on all questions until we learned the views of other governments. We did not want to confront our neighbor governments in Central and South America and Canada with a *fait accompli*. It was a case of giving them a chance to say, "We don't like this

"Victory against War"

or that." We were particularly anxious to be sure that the Western Hemisphere nations and the British Commonwealth were in agreement. We felt that if we had that sort of backing we would get almost anything we wanted to build an international organization that would work.[9]

Where Truman counseled deference, however, Vandenberg anticipated leverage. Knowing he was the key to Senate ratification, he sought to exploit his power by nourishing support for his amendments beyond the U.S. delegation. On the evening of April 17, he visited Anthony Eden, Britain's foreign minister, and Lord Halifax, Britain's ambassador to the United States, at the British embassy in Washington. After describing Eden as "somewhat small physically, but handsome and affable and very brilliant," he relayed in his diary,

> I told him my story: that if I am going to be held responsible for Republican votes in the Senate for the new League Treaty, I must (as Churchill once put it) "be given the tools." I read him my Amendments as approved by our Delegation; and told him I would have to insist upon three "musts." (1) The distinct and specific inclusion of justice as an objective; (2) the identification of the pledges in the Atlantic Charter among our purposes; (3) enough "elastic" so the League can look *back* as well as *forward* in correcting injustice and curing potential war festers.

"I suppose you have Poland in mind," Halifax observed.

"Yes," Vandenberg replied.

Three days later, Australia's minister of external affairs, Dr. H. V. Evatt, visited Vandenberg and confirmed that his country's "demands" for San Francisco essentially mirrored Vandenberg's and said that its delegation would cooperate with him "from start to finish." The two then commiserated about Stettinius and Eden, agreeing that neither understood the Soviet threat adequately.[10]

. . .

Beyond his concern over Stettinius's limitations and his desire to keep Vandenberg happy, Truman had other reasons to insist on a buttoned-up operation for San Francisco.

U.S.-Soviet relations were deteriorating badly, raising doubts about whether the two superpowers would reach agreement on the most basic issues at the conference. Truman, Vandenberg, and other U.S. officials were questioning how much they should compromise with Moscow to assure its participation in the United Nations—and at what point they should dig in their heels, let the Soviets walk, and create a global body that lacked Soviet participation. With so much at stake, and with U.S.-Soviet conflicts growing, the United States could not afford a miscommunication that left its president thinking one way in Washington and its delegation acting another in San Francisco.

That the new president was making decisions about foreign policy largely on the fly raised the stakes of a miscue even higher. Because FDR had revealed virtually nothing to him about foreign affairs, Truman was forced to study up immediately. It proved an eye-opening experience, affecting his approach to San Francisco.

On April 13, his first full day as president, Truman asked Stettinius to give him a written overview of U.S. foreign policy challenges. When the secretary delivered it that afternoon, the section on the Soviets was particularly sobering. "Since the Yalta Conference," it began, "the Soviet Government has taken a firm and uncompromising position on nearly every major question that has arisen in our relations."[11] The document highlighted Soviet interference in other countries, such as Poland, Rumania, and Bulgaria, making clear that Moscow was methodically extending its empire beyond its borders. Moreover, in his first days as president, Truman read the final cables between FDR and Stalin, and he was struck by Stalin's dismissiveness and FDR's indignation as the two leaders bared their growing differences.[12]

Truman's research stiffened his spine about the Soviets, reflecting an emerging consensus in U.S. foreign policy circles. Notwithstanding U.S.-Soviet collaboration during the war, Truman's foreign policy team now increasingly believed that Washington must treat Moscow as an adversary, and that the two would not work out their fundamental differences through dialogue. Instead, they would compete fiercely around the world, with Moscow imposing its will wherever it could.

"Victory against War"

Churchill shared that view, and, in cables to Truman in mid-April, he recommended that the president rush U.S. forces to Eastern Europe and the Balkans before the Soviets could impose their will there. Truman rejected Churchill's approach, deferring to Supreme Allied Commander Dwight Eisenhower's view that the move was militarily unjustified as the Allies continued to battle the Axis powers. Nevertheless, briefed by his increasingly hard-line advisers, Truman moved toward blunt confrontation with Moscow.

Thus, Truman's views moved closer to those of Vandenberg, who had long complained that FDR was appeasing the Soviets. U.S.-Soviet maneuvering in the days leading up to San Francisco prompted the first overt manifestation of Truman's blunt new approach. More than anything else, it symbolized the turn in big-power relations from wartime warmth to emerging chill—and it thrilled Vandenberg to no end.

. . .

"The Soviet Government," Stettinius wrote in his April 13 overview for Truman, "appears to desire to proceed with the San Francisco Conference but was unwilling to send their Foreign Minister." Stalin's refusal to send Molotov not only irritated Truman (as it had FDR before his death), it also raised U.S. concerns about likely Soviet cooperation in San Francisco. It prompted as well a clever maneuver by Averell Harriman, the U.S. ambassador to Moscow, who desperately wanted to travel to Washington in order to shape Truman's thinking about Moscow. At the time, nobody was recommending a harder U.S. line toward the Soviets than Harriman.

Then fifty-three, Harriman was the quintessential U.S. diplomat by way of background, appearance, and demeanor. Born on November 15, 1891, he attended Groton and Yale, inherited a fortune, and grew it larger, giving him the financial freedom to serve in various top government posts from the 1940s through the 1960s. He was tall and lanky, "with deeply intent brown eyes, a square jaw and a demeanor of seriousness that made his sudden broad smile all the more disarming."[13] As U.S. ambassador to Moscow and London, secretary of commerce, special representative in Europe for the Marshall Plan—all for Truman—

and later as a roving ambassador for Presidents Kennedy and Johnson, Harriman sought the action and craved a proximity to power, sometimes aggravating his immediate superiors by working around them. He ran unsuccessfully for the Democratic nomination for president in 1952 and then served a term as New York's governor. Through it all, he displayed the patience and persistence that effective diplomacy requires.

After FDR died, Harriman sought to brief Truman in person about the Soviet challenge. He viewed the new president as a foreign policy novice who would benefit from Harriman's deep knowledge and sophisticated insights. But Stettinius, who resented Harriman's frequent efforts to bypass him, rejected his repeated requests to travel to Washington. So Harriman went to see Stalin at the Kremlin, encouraged him to reverse course and send Molotov to San Francisco as a goodwill gesture to Truman, and suggested that Molotov stop on the way in Washington to see the new president. He even offered a U.S. plane for Molotov's travel. Stalin agreed to send Molotov (though he didn't bite on the offer of air travel), and Harriman relayed the news to Truman. With Stettinius now forced to let him travel home and help prepare Truman for Molotov's visit, Harriman raced to Washington to arrive before the foreign minister, completing the trip in a then-record forty-nine hours and eighteen minutes.

Harriman landed on April 18, "the anniversary of Paul Revere's ride,"[14] and he brought a message of similar urgency first to his administration colleagues and then, in briefings that began on April 19, to Truman. The Soviets, he advised, were determined to dominate the governments on their border and push their influence far beyond; they would deploy secret police and use terrorist tactics to assert their control; and they represented an ideological opponent that was every bit as dangerous as the fascists of World War II. The United States and its allies faced a "barbarian invasion of Europe," he said, repeating a dramatic phrase that he had been using for weeks in cables from Moscow. Washington, he said, could find a way to work with Moscow but, to do so, U.S. officials needed to abandon fuzzy notions that the two sides viewed the world similarly.

. . .

"Victory against War"

Truman absorbed Harriman's message enthusiastically, telling him at one point, "The Russians need us more than we need them."

Truman wanted the Soviets to fulfill their commitment at Yalta to permit democratic government in Poland, and, he said, "I intend to tell Molotov that in words of one syllable." U.S.-Soviet agreements were "so far a one-way street," he added, and if the Soviets wanted to cause trouble in San Francisco, "they could go to hell." Heightening tensions just hours before the first of Truman's two meetings with Molotov, Moscow gave official diplomatic recognition to Poland's Lublin government in a ceremony that Stalin attended. Truman worried that without a reasonable solution to the Poland issue, the Senate might reject U.S. participation in the United Nations on the grounds that, at such a perilous time, the United States could not cede power to a global entity.

The story of Truman's confrontation with Molotov at the White House, which occurred in the late afternoon of April 23, is well-known. Truman lectured him about Poland and dismissed him unceremoniously, saying, "That will be all, Mr. Molotov. I would appreciate it if you would transmit my views to Marshal Stalin." When Molotov complained that "I've never been talked to like that in my life," Truman replied, "Carry out your agreements and you won't get talked to like that."[15] Truman was clearly proud of himself, later telling the dovish former U.S. ambassador to Moscow, Joseph Davies, "I gave him the one-two, right to the jaw."[16] But his language was so direct that even Harriman—who attended the Truman-Molotov meeting along with Stettinius and Charles Bohlen, a top State Department Soviet expert—was "a little taken aback."

Less well-known is Vandenberg's reaction to the confrontation, which showed just how aligned the new Democratic president now was with the seasoned Republican senator. When Vandenberg, then in San Francisco, learned the next day from Stettinius what had happened, he took to his diary gleefully, writing "This is the best news in months. F.D.R.'s appeasement of Russia is over. We will 'play-ball' gladly with the Russians and 'give and take' because we must have unity for the sake of peace *but* it is no longer going to be all 'give' and no 'take' so far as we are concerned."

Stettinius apparently raised the possibility with Vandenberg that, due to U.S. steadfastness, the Soviets might withdraw from San Francisco. The senator made clear that, if so, he would not be disappointed: "Stettinius does not know what the result [of the Truman-Molotov confrontation] will be. Molotov had to report to Stalin . . . But the crisis will come when Stalin's answer arrives. Russia may withdraw. If it does, the conference *will proceed without Russia*. Now we are getting somewhere!"

As the conference was about to open on April 25, Vandenberg mused ominously, "I don't know whether this is Frisco or Munich."[17]

"Victory against War"

4

"Sensible Machinery for the Settlement of Disputes"

AT FOUR THIRTY IN the afternoon of April 25, Arthur Vanden-berg sat among three thousand delegates, advisers, staff, other dignitaries, and media at San Francisco's opera house. Edward Stettinius ascended the stage, accompanied by California's governor, Earl Warren, San Francisco's mayor, Roger Lapham, and UN Acting Secretary-General Alger Hiss.

For the opening session of the long-awaited conference, the grand auditorium was bedecked in appropriate splendor. On the stage were "four golden pillars tied together with olive branch wreaths." Each represented one of the "Four Freedoms"—of speech and worship, and from want and fear—that FDR had envisioned for a postwar world. Ringing the stage and bathed in floodlights were the flags of all forty-six nations that sent delegations to San Francisco (a number that grew to fifty with four later invitees).

Stettinius occupied the penthouse apartment of San Francisco's Fairmont Hotel, a ten-minute car ride to the opera house, and that's where the secretary hosted meetings each morning of the U.S. delegation. When the delegation arrived in San Francisco, Stettinius announced that he'd appointed Vandenberg and Connally as its vice chairmen. So when the delegates met around a rectangular table in Stettinius's suite, he placed himself in the middle, with Vandenberg next to him on one side and Connally on the other. Stettinius's suite was also where he hosted meetings each evening of the "Big Five" major powers—the United States,

Soviet Union, Britain, and China, and, after the first few weeks, France; they would agree on major policies among themselves before selling them to the conference. Vandenberg and the rest of America's delegates took roomy suites on the Fairmont's fourth floor. For those who arrived from the far-flung corners of a war-torn world, the lavish amenities at the conference and the beauty of its host city were eye-popping sights.

The setting was ideal for round-the-clock work—as Stettinius, Vandenberg, and their colleagues would experience—and the spirited partying that others would enjoy. On hand for the plenary sessions at the opera house and smaller meetings next door at the War Memorial Veterans Building were journalists like Alistair Cooke, Eric Sevareid, and William Shirer; gossip columnists like Elsa Maxwell, Earl Wilson, Hedda Hopper, and Louella Parson; and movie stars like Lana Turner, Orson Welles, and Rita Hayworth.[1]

Stettinius called the opening session to order and, after a short prayer, directed attention to a voice coming through from Washington.

. . .

"Delegates to the United Nations Conference on International Organization," Truman told the gathering via radio hookup. "The world has experienced a revival of an old faith in the everlasting moral force of justice."

That Truman began his ten-minute welcome by mentioning "justice" was intriguing. He didn't say later that he was purposely trying to please Vandenberg. But, by then, he knew that Vandenberg thought a focus on justice was the most glaring omission from the Dumbarton Oaks draft, and he knew the pursuit of justice was the driving force behind Vandenberg's package of amendments.

While expressing the idealistic hopes for the United Nations that he shared with Vandenberg, Truman focused his remarks on a more practical hardheadedness—a belief that the new global body was the only thing that stood between international tranquility and more ghastly mayhem. "We who have lived through the torture and the tragedy of two world conflicts must realize the magnitude of the problem before us," he declared. "We do not need far-sighted vision to understand the trend

"Victory against War"

in recent history. Its significance is all too clear. With ever-increasing brutality and destruction, modern warfare, if unchecked, would ultimately crush all civilization. We still have a choice between the alternatives: The continuation of international chaos, or the establishment of a world organization for the enforcement of peace . . . The essence of our problem here is to provide sensible machinery for the settlement of disputes among nations. Without this, peace cannot exist."

Vandenberg felt similarly. Explaining why he wouldn't undermine the San Francisco conference over Soviet behavior in Poland, he told his friend Frank Januszewski, who owned Detroit's *Polish Daily News*, "It would be a relatively simple matter to dynamite the new Peace League . . . Then there would be no League. What would *that* do for Poland? It would simply leave Russia in complete possession of everything she wants . . . There would be no hope left of justice except through World War Number Three immediately."[2]

. . .

Truman and Vandenberg stood fairly firm against the Soviets in the first few days in San Francisco as Molotov tested U.S. resolve on several fronts. They did not, however, agree on the U.S. approach to each test.

Molotov first challenged the U.S. assumption that Stettinius would chair the conference, even though international protocol would have him do so as the top official from the host country. Molotov proposed that the top U.S., Soviet, British, and Chinese officials rotate as chairmen. After Truman and Stettinius spoke by phone on April 26, Vandenberg and his colleagues agreed to strongly oppose the idea. Stettinius invited Vandenberg and Connally to accompany him to meet with Molotov and Eden the next morning and, with the dispute still unresolved, to then go with him to the Steering Committee (which included the head of every delegation and was the conference's formal decision-making body). At the latter meeting, Molotov sidestepped defeat by accepting a British effort at compromise that left the Americans blindsided and Vandenberg temporarily suspicious of British motives—rotating chairmen, but with Stettinius serving as chairman of the chairmen; chairman of the

Steering Committee; chairman of the Executive Committee (of fourteen delegations, including the Big Five, that would make recommendations to the Steering Committee); and chairman of the conference itself.

Molotov next pushed for Ukraine and Belarus's admission not only to the United Nations—as FDR and Stalin had discussed—but, now, immediately to the San Francisco conference. That was, Vandenberg mused, "another example of the typical Russian technique—always crowding for more." Ukraine and Belarus remained a thorn in Vandenberg's side, for he saw no reason to approve Moscow's request for either UN or conference membership. He lacked the leverage to prevent a Soviet victory on the former. Truman had given Stettinius a letter directing the U.S. delegation to uphold FDR's promise to admit the two Soviet republics to the United Nations. At the April 27 Steering Committee meeting, Vandenberg went along, seething quietly. But when Molotov then pushed for conference membership as well, the Steering Committee set the issue aside.

Next, Molotov insisted on the Lublin government's admission to both the United Nations and the conference as Poland's legitimate government. At Soviet direction, the Czech foreign minister, Jan Masaryk, proposed that the Steering Committee admit the Lublin government to the conference, prompting Vandenberg to spring into action. Sitting behind Stettinius and fearing that realistic hopes of U.S.-Soviet collaboration in San Francisco hung in the balance, he told the secretary that he must kill the proposal, quickly drafted some remarks for him, and handed them to him. "I remind the Conference that we have just honored our Yalta engagements in behalf of Russia," Stettinius told the committee in reference to the two Soviet republics, reading Vandenberg's words verbatim. "I also remind the Conference that there are other Yalta obligations which equally require allegiance. One of them calls for a new and representative Polish Provisional Government. Until this happens, this Conference cannot, in good conscience, recognize the Lublin Government. It would be a sordid exhibition of bad faith." Eden backed Stettinius and, sensing defeat, Molotov backed off. "To Stettinius' credit," Vandenberg wrote later, "*he never hesitated an instant.* He took the floor and read exactly what I had written—and with great emphasis."[3]

It was just days after Truman's confrontation with Molotov in Washington, and now Vandenberg had tangled with him for the first time. "[Molotov] is a powerful fellow though not large—greeted me with a very genial smile and said he 'knew all about me,'" the senator recalled, undoubtedly pleased by his notoriety in Moscow. "It is evident that these Russians have an obsession about the necessity of preserving every semblance of their 'equality' with every other nation even in parliamentary forms."[4]

After Stettinius relayed the day's events to Truman by phone, noting that Vandenberg and Connally had worked in lockstep with him, a pleased Truman said, "I am going to take a drink and really sleep tonight."[5]

. . .

"The Conference Bulletin embarrassed me tonight," Vandenberg wrote unconvincingly in his diary on April 30, referring to an official publication of the conference, "by printing a quote from the Washington Times-Herald—'Molotov and Vandenberg are dominating figures of Conference—It looks as if entire history of Conference may revolve around a battle of wits between these two men—it is the hand of Vandenberg that is generally discerned in U.S. moves on Conference chess board. [*sic*]' This isn't true. But I *have* had my part in it—and I am very grateful for the prompt and whole-hearted consideration which Stettinius gives me upon all occasions."[6]

Vandenberg would have many more such moments as the conference shifted gears. With attention now focused on turning the Dumbarton Oaks draft into a UN Charter, the major powers met to consider pending amendments and reach consensus. The first issue, which revolved around one of Vandenberg's amendments, was whether the General Assembly could examine "situations arising out of any treaties or international engagements." That is, could the United Nations look backward, as Vandenberg desired, or just forward? Could it examine the status quo, including growing Soviet domination of Poland and, more broadly, Eastern Europe?

Not surprisingly, when they met on the evening of May 2, Molotov rejected Vandenberg's notion of reexamining treaties. Eden proposed substitute language, to which Vandenberg and China's foreign minister, Dr. T. V. Soong, agreed, but Molotov dug in. Vandenberg next played the Senate card. He insisted to Molotov, as he wrote later, that "I needed this explicit language (which everyone agrees to be implicit in Dumbarton Oaks) in order to win adequate Senate support." Molotov replied that it would weaken all treaties. Vandenberg then made his case for addressing past injustice. To each Vandenberg argument, Molotov replied simply in his broken English, "No O.K."

Vandenberg and Molotov later met separately and agreed to replace "treaties or international engagements" with a general reference to situations "regardless of origin." On the evening of May 4, after what Vandenberg called "two terrific days of constant consultation" among the major powers over amendments, they agreed on language stating, "The General Assembly should be empowered to recommend measures for the peaceful adjustment of any situations, regardless of origin, which it deems likely to impair the general welfare or friendly relations among nations." That provision was among twenty-seven amendments that the major powers agreed to push through the conference, including all references to "justice," "human rights," and "fundamental freedoms" that Vandenberg had sought. "It is an amazing achievement," the senator wrote euphorically, "and ought to substantially shorten the work of the Conference." He added—incorrectly as it turned out—that "the biggest hurdles are behind us." Vandenberg also came to admire Molotov, "an earnest, able man for whom I have come to have a profound respect—despite our disagreements."[7]

Vandenberg was thrilled with the "regardless of origin" language, which he believed strengthened the provision. But, if the truth be told, he was on a fool's errand, expending lots of energy on a matter that would not bear fruit. Truman mentioned the issue only in passing in the UN write-up in his memoirs. That's probably because he knew that even with this language, the United Nations had no realistic prospect of reversing Soviet domination of Poland or other Soviet efforts to fortify its border. Even if the General Assembly brought the Security Council a backward-looking proposal to reverse the status quo, Moscow could veto any tangible action—which is probably why Molotov relented.

What proved far more consequential, and what dominated the next two months in San Francisco, were two other issues. The first, on the veto power of the five permanent Security Council members, would help determine whether the United Nations would be Vandenberg's "free and untrammeled 'town meeting of the world'" and whether the Senate would ratify its charter. The second, on whether nations could form regional defense pacts, would determine whether the United States could later establish such regional agreements as the North Atlantic Alliance, which created NATO.

As attention turned to those issues in early May, U.S. officials received a stark reminder about their Soviet adversary. Weeks earlier, sixteen Poles from London's government-in-exile had disappeared while visiting Poland and worried U.S. and British officials had been peppering Soviet officials with questions about their status. On May 3 Molotov told Stettinius that, as U.S. officials had feared, Soviet armed forces had arrested them for "diversionist acts against the Red Army." Most were later tried, convicted, and sentenced to prison.

5

"America Wins!"

BY NOW, THE U.S. delegation had settled into a fairly effective routine. Truman and Stettinius were in close and constant touch with one another, and the secretary executed the president's wishes without a glitch, leaving Truman to conclude that the delegation was doing "an excellent job."[1] Stettinius was working closely with Vandenberg in particular as he sought to maintain the delegation's unity on outstanding issues.

Vandenberg, however, retained his doubts about both men. Though he believed Truman's instincts about the Soviets were much savvier than FDR's, he worried that the new president lacked the foreign policy background and knowledge to make the best decisions. As for Stettinius, Vandenberg's doubts went far beyond the secretary's ignorance on foreign affairs. They extended to his style of leadership and the gravitas (or lack thereof) that he brought to his role. Vandenberg was not alone in assessing Stettinius's performance that way, which he noted with a touch of sympathy.

"There is much underground chatter about Stettinius," Vandenberg wrote on May 13. "Unfortunately he pretty generally has the press against him. There is increasing gossip about a successor, when this Conference is ended. I agree that there is no longer any strong hand on our foreign policy rudder—neither Truman nor Stettinius nor [Undersecretary] Grew. I agree that it is a tragic situation in these difficult times. Stettinius does *not* have a seasoned grasp of foreign affairs. He rarely contributes to our policy decisions. We improvise as we go along. Stettinius is not *really* Secretary of State. He is *really* 'General Manager' of the State Department (which is a totally different thing).

"Incidentally," Vandenberg volunteered, Stettinius "is the *best* 'General Manager' I ever saw. He *gets things done*. But I am afraid that is his chief idea—just to 'get things done.' He does *not* take the same firm stand in respect to *policy* that he does in 'getting things done.' President Truman sadly needs a real Secretary of State in the realm of *policy*. But until someone shows me someone whom the President would appoint who is a real improvement in this direction, I am opposed to changing Stettinius."[2]

Consequently, Vandenberg schooled Stettinius as best he could, pushing and prodding him to step forward, seize the reins of leadership, confront the Soviets more boldly, and pursue the U.S. position more aggressively. He came away frustrated on some occasions and pleasantly surprised on others.

. . .

By mid-May, as Truman later wrote, "The question of the veto power in the [Security] Council was emerging as the single outstanding issue of the conference."[3]

Everyone agreed that each of the five permanent Security Council members should be able to veto what Vandenberg called "enforcement action" against an aggressor. The United States needed that provision as much as any other nation because, without it, fears would arise in Washington that the United Nations could order the United States to join a UN military effort against another nation. That would threaten U.S. sovereignty by undercutting the president's role as commander in chief and Congress's power to declare war, and it would raise prospects that the Senate would reject U.S. participation in the United Nations itself. Everyone also agreed (though Vandenberg went along only reluctantly) that each of the permanent members should be able to veto more general Security Council efforts "to bring about a peaceful settlement of a dispute."

The Soviets, however, wanted the power to veto even a Security Council *discussion* of a dispute, saying that's what FDR, Stalin, and Churchill

"Victory against War"

had envisioned at Yalta. If, then, any UN member brought a dispute to the Security Council, any of its five permanent members could keep it off the agenda. Truman and Vandenberg agreed that such a veto would violate basic tenets of free speech. Complicating matters, however, was that, according to Vandenberg, some State Department officials agreed with Moscow's interpretation of what the Big Three had envisioned at Yalta. "*We* are in the unfortunate position of being bound by our own State Department interpretation that Yalta includes this *total* 'veto' (which, of course, is the Russian position)," Vandenberg wrote. "It means, in plain language that the Russians can raise Hell all over the world, through satellites and fifth columns, and stop the new League from even inquiring into it. It is the *worst* of our legacies from Roosevelt."[4]

Nevertheless, Truman operated on the assumption that FDR and Churchill had agreed to no such thing. Around May 20 Vandenberg asked Stettinius to recommend that Truman discuss the matter directly with Stalin, "lest our stubborn adherence to this repugnant thing [Moscow's interpretation] may either wreck the Conference or ultimately shock the moral conscience of the country and the world."[5] On May 22 Truman ordered Stettinius to fly to Washington to discuss all remaining conference issues with him in person. When they met the next day, the president directed Stettinius to hang tough and reject the Soviet veto proposal. Meanwhile, the dispute was extending far beyond Washington and Moscow. Led by Australia, smaller nations were increasingly voicing their opposition to Moscow's interpretation, fearing it would leave them powerless to appeal any injustice (e.g., a foreign invasion) to the council. But they also raised questions about why the Big Power veto should be even as strong as Washington desired, forcing Stettinius to quell a small-nation uprising.

As the dispute dragged into late May, Vandenberg was conflicted. He had grown increasingly frustrated that negotiations over the veto were proving fruitless, largely because Soviet officials were forced to check with Stalin on their every move and that process could last for days each time. "Once more the whole thing hangs on Gromyko who is 'awaiting instruction' from Moscow," Vandenberg wrote on May 26 about the Soviet ambassador who, with Molotov's return to Moscow, was now directing Soviet negotiations in San Francisco. "He says he is 'inclined to go along'—but has to hear from home. It *might* be argued that when all the rest of us agree on an interpretation of Yalta, *our* view ought to govern rather than Russia's. That is *my* position. On the other hand there is much to be said for *not* giving the Russians *any* excuse for running out on Yalta itself. (Of course [Russia] *has* run out; but the rest of us are demanding that it make good—and so we go to painful extremes to 'make good' ourselves.)"

As for the veto itself, Vandenberg didn't want to give the Soviets what they were seeking, but he also didn't want to give them an excuse to abandon the other commitments they had made at Yalta. He also understood that a stronger veto for all five permanent Security Council members (including the United States) would make it easier for him to gather the Senate votes for UN ratification. "The irony of the situation," he mused, "is that the greater the extent of the 'veto,' the more impossible it becomes for the new League to involve America in *anything* against our own will. Therefore, the greater the 'veto' the easier it becomes to fight off our critics in Congress, in the country and in the press when the new Treaty faces its ratification battle. (Every cloud has a silver lining.)"[6]

. . .

On June 1 Gromyko relayed his instructions from Moscow, telling the Big Five in Stettinius's suite that the Soviets would insist on a veto of even a discussion at the Security Council.

"It is 'Yalta' carried to the final, absurd extreme," Vandenberg thought at the time. "We all knew that we had reached the 'zero hour' of this great adventure."[7] When Stettinius phoned Truman on June 2, he suggested that Stalin might not know what his underlings were doing in San Francisco. On previous occasions, he said, Molotov had issued instructions from Moscow without first informing Stalin, so this might be another such case. As Vandenberg had proposed in late May, Stettinius now suggested that someone ask Stalin directly.

At the time, Harry Hopkins, FDR's former top aide, was in Moscow at Truman's request. With Truman concerned about rapidly deteriorating U.S.-Soviet relations, Harriman and Bohlen had suggested sending Hopkins to clear the air with Stalin over the mounting issues separating the superpowers. They thought Hopkins, who represented FDR with Stalin during the war, would symbolize to Stalin the happier days of U.S.-Soviet collaboration. Truman thought well of Hopkins, who had helped him while he was in the Senate and prepped him for lunch with Roosevelt after FDR put him on the 1944 ticket, so he contacted Hopkins to ask whether he'd visit Stalin. Hopkins was suffering mightily from the cancer that would claim his life early the next year, looking ghastly and resting at home in bed. Nevertheless, he gathered his strength and, in late May, journeyed to Moscow after receiving Truman's instructions that, in talking to Stalin, "he was free to use diplomatic language or a baseball bat if he thought that was the proper approach."[8]

Truman then told Stettinius "to send a message to Ambassador Harriman and Hopkins, asking them to place the matter of the voting procedure of the Security Council before the Russian Premier."[9] Stettinius sent the message, but Hopkins didn't raise the issue with Stalin for a few days. In the meantime, tensions mounted in San Francisco, where progress among the major powers came to a standstill, and Vandenberg mulled a public break with Truman if the president didn't hold firm on the issue. Complicating matters further was a *New York Times* story that revealed Washington's plans to appeal to Stalin, turning a private U.S. strategy into a public test for everyone involved.[10]

At Stettinius's request a day later, Vandenberg met in the penthouse with Stettinius, Assistant Secretary of State Jimmy Dunn, and Senator Connally. The State Department was asking whether, in case Stalin wouldn't back down, the United States could sidestep the dispute by agreeing to different U.S. and Soviet interpretations of the veto. Vandenberg called the idea "impossible," saying "it would not only leave the vital Charter question in doubt" but "give Stalin the very 'veto' for which he is contending." It would be "a 'climax in humiliation'" for the

United States." Vandenberg was worried that a U.S. retreat would set a dangerous precedent, send a damaging signal to nations that were deciding whether to align with Washington or Moscow, and encourage further Soviet aggressiveness that eventually would force a more serious U.S.-Soviet confrontation. Stettinius reassured Vandenberg that he had reached the same conclusion and showed him the message he had sent to Hopkins. "I was amazed," Vandenberg recalled. "It was *magnificent* in its unqualified assertion of our position. It would not have been stronger if I had written it myself."[11]

As it turned out, Stettinius was right about Stalin. Hopkins raised the big-power veto with him on June 6 in between their discussions about U.S.-Soviet relations in general and Poland in particular. Stalin "had not understood the issues," Hopkins cabled to Truman. "After considerable discussion in which Molotov took an active part, Stalin overruled Molotov and agreed that the American position was acceptable to him." The U.S. victory left Truman delighted and Vandenberg euphoric.

"This," Truman wrote later, "meant the end of a deadlock that had threatened to disrupt the whole conference."[12] Stettinius received the official word from Gromyko and relayed it to Vandenberg, who wrote with great enthusiasm in his diary,

> *America Wins!* . . . It is a complete and total surrender. No attempt at any weasel-worded compromise . . . I think everyone is convinced that the blunt, unconditional message which Stettinius sent to Moscow turned the trick. I *hope* some of our people have learned a lesson. Many of them were beginning to weaken under the "war of nerves." If Stalin had held out, I am afraid we would have been under heavy pressure from some of our own people to yield. I am equally sure that Stettinius would not have yielded short of instructions from the President. At any rate, we have discovered (I hope) that we can get along with Russia *if and when* we can convince Russia that *we mean what we say.*[13]

America's victory now left the Big Five to resolve a related issue about the reach of the Security Council. If any of the five permanent members could veto UN military action, could nations protect themselves militarily by forming regional defense pacts? Truman and Vandenberg thought the answer must be "yes."

. . .

"The grave problem," Vandenberg reflected in early May, "is to find a formula which will reasonably protect legitimate regional arrangements without destroying the overall responsibility of united action through the Peace League and without inviting the formation of a lot of dangerous new 'regional spheres of influence' etc."[14]

Truman and Vandenberg's collaboration on this issue would prove propitious when, four years later, Washington reacted to further Soviet aggression in Europe by teaming with eleven European nations to establish the North Atlantic Treaty and, with it, NATO. At the moment in San Francisco, however, America's hopes for "regional arrangements" were focused not on Europe but on the Western Hemisphere.

For more than a century, U.S. policy in its own hemisphere had been driven by the "Monroe Doctrine," under which President James Monroe told Europe's great powers in 1823 that "we should consider any attempt on their part to extend their system to any portion of this hemisphere as dangerous to our peace and safety." Despite that well-established policy, Stettinius discovered in early 1945 that Latin American nations feared that the Dumbarton Oaks draft—with its proposed Security Council—could leave them unprotected particularly from Soviet aggression. If the Security Council was supposed to keep the peace, and if the Soviets could veto Security Council action, where did that leave Latin America?

To reassure America's neighbors to the south, Stettinius had worked with nineteen Latin American nations in Mexico City in late February and early March to craft the "Act of Chapultepec," stating that an attack against any of the signatories "shall . . . be considered as an act of aggression against" the others and urging them to establish a defense treaty.[15] The Latin nations welcomed the act but, heading into San Francisco, the question was whether the United States, as a party to both, would stick by Chapultepec or the Dumbarton Oaks draft. Several Latin nations expressed their concerns to State Department official Leo Pasvolsky. But, while Pasvolsky followed proper protocol by relaying those concerns to Stettinius, he himself did not lend the Latin officials a sympathetic ear. He feared that regional pacts would mean regional "spheres of influence," and, he believed, spheres of influence would undermine the United Nations. More support came from the new assistant secretary of state for American republic affairs, a thirty-six-year-old man by the name of Nelson Rockefeller, who had played a key role at Chapultepec and signed the act on behalf of the United States. When Rockefeller heard about the Latin Americans' meeting with Pasvolsky, he requested a quick follow-up meeting with Stettinius. When Stettinius rebuffed him, Rockefeller reached out to Vandenberg.

By then, the San Francisco conference already had carved out an exception to the rule of Security Council primacy. It had adopted an amendment to the charter that allowed for "regional arrangements" to protect countries from "enemy states"—i.e., Germany, which had not yet surrendered. The amendment constituted a limited European exception, allowing it to act alone in the face of revived German aggression after World War II. Fine, Vandenberg thought. But if the United Nations would allow for a European exception, why not a Latin American one? For Vandenberg the issue was less about whether Latin American nations felt secure than about whether the United States could act on its own. If the Soviets attacked a nation in America's backyard, would Washington have to await action by the Security Council (which Moscow would veto) or could it defend its neighbor?

Truman left the question largely to his team in San Francisco to resolve. For Stettinius and Vandenberg, it would quickly prove complicated.

. . .

On Saturday, May 5, Vandenberg dined with Rockefeller and suggested language for the charter that would create an exception related to Chapultepec. Rockefeller expressed support and, that night, he consulted with Cuban and Colombian officials, who were equally enthused. Vandenberg sent the proposal to Stettinius the next morning. Pasvolsky's earlier chat with Latin officials portended trouble, however, because he was influential with the delegation. Unlike the veto controversy, during which Truman and the delegates remained united, the regional issue split the delegation wide open.

When the delegates met on the morning of Monday, May 7, and discussed Vandenberg's proposal, it received support from Sol Bloom and Charles Eaton, the Democratic chairman and senior Republican on the House Foreign Affairs Committee, respectively. But it was opposed by Harold Stassen, who shared Pasvolsky's deep concern that it would undermine the whole idea of a global organization. Pasvolsky outlined the issue in dramatic terms: "If we open up the Dumbarton Oaks proposals to allow for regional enforcement action on a collective basis, the world organization is finished . . . We will convert the world into armed camps and end up with a world war unlike any we have yet seen." Dulles opined that the existing charter language did not prohibit U.S.-led self-defense for Latin America anyway, whether driven by Chapultepec or the Monroe Doctrine.

Stettinius found himself pulled in multiple directions. His delegates were split and, were they to back Vandenberg's amendment, the secretary would have to convince Moscow to go along. Meanwhile, he wanted to prevent the Latin nations from bolting from San Francisco in disgust, which might convince the Senate to reject the charter. After he received Vandenberg's proposal but before the delegation discussed it, a frustrated Stettinius accused Rockefeller of masterminding Vandenberg's action (which was largely true) and said that it threatened the conference itself. So, too, did Dulles, who lashed out at Rockefeller harshly, saying he had "hoodwinked the Senator" and adding, "You've taken a man I was sent out here to keep from doing some goddamn fool thing, and you've gotten us into a real pickle." Nevertheless, Rockefeller continued working closely with Latin officials on the issue.[16]

With no consensus in sight, Vandenberg pulled his Senate card, reminding everyone that he could cause trouble in Washington if his desires went unmet. "I served notice on the Delegation, as a matter of good faith," he relayed, that if this question is not specifically cleared up in the Charter, I shall expect to see a Reservation [i.e., a dissent] on the subject in the Senate and that I shall support it. I do not see how we could tolerate a possible situation in which (under the Charter) we could not deal with a bad Pan-Am [Pan American] situation at all because (1) we are not permitted to act under Chapultepec and (2) the Security Council is stopped by a Russian or a British or a Chinese or a French veto. Neither do I see how we can desert the demands of our united Pan-Am neighbors in this matter.[17]

Vandenberg's proposal, however, was threatening to open a Pandora's box of regionalism. Australia sent word that it wanted the power to spearhead regional action, while Arab nations were coming together as a regional group as well. The senator hoped to thread a very thin needle, writing on May 9, "Our great problem is to find a rule which protects legitimate existing regional groups (like Pan-Am) without opening up the opportunity for regional balance-of-power groups."[18] That day, the *New York Times* brought the delicate behind-the-scenes maneuvering over regionalism into the open.

With the U.S. delegation still split, Vandenberg mused that Truman would have to resolve the issue.

. . .

It was not, in fact, Truman who brought victory. Nor was it Vandenberg. It was, instead, Stettinius and Stassen.

Stassen, who had reached out to Rockefeller at Stettinius's request, suggested a substitute to Vandenberg's amendment that focused less on the hot-button issue of regionalism than on self-defense. In the coming days, Stettinius gathered the delegation behind the new language, won Truman's support over the phone, and negotiated further changes between British officials who wanted it broadened to give them flexibility in Europe and the Mediterranean and Latin officials who wanted a specific mention of Chapultepec.

Vandenberg proved helpful. He backed the amendment, which did not mention Chapultepec, to help Stettinius. But he also assured Latin officials that he'd steer a resolution through the Senate to make clear that,

"Victory against War"

as far as the United States was concerned, it referred to Chapultepec. When Latin officials persisted in their quest for specific language, Stettinius countered by offering Assistant Secretary of State Jimmy Dunn's idea that the United States hold a conference that fall to turn Chapultepec into a formal regional pact. After securing Truman's approval and cutting a final deal with Latin officials, Stettinius went public, announcing agreement over the amendment as well as the fall conference. The secretary was risking public embarrassment because the Soviets had not yet agreed to the final language, but they did so quietly a few days later.

Vandenberg praised Stettinius afterward while taking credit for his performance:

> I had a private chat with Stettinius (I called it "fatherly") in which I urged him to take hold of this problem with a firm hand and *to be the Secretary of State* in fact as well as name. I told him this Regional problem involves a decision as to what the *Administration's foreign policy* is in respect to Inter-American relations; that this can't be settled by us Republicans at Frisco; that the *Administration* has got to say what it intends to do to justify the work of the Mexico City Conference (Chapultepec) which *it* sponsored only two months ago. I told him that if he settled *this*, we would have little further trouble with our Latin friends.

Nevertheless, Vandenberg wrote that Stettinius is "entitled to immense credit for having made a job of it and for having driven it through. It shows what he can do. I hope he continues to *be* Secretary of State."[19]

6

"A Solid Structure upon Which We Can Build"

"IT HAS BEEN THE crowning privilege of my life to have been an author of the San Francisco Charter," Vandenberg wrote on June 23.

By then, the major powers had resolved all of their differences but, because the Soviets wanted three days to review the charter, the various delegations could not yet sign it, and Truman, who was in Olympia, Washington, on his way to San Francisco, could not yet close the conference. It was, however, a mere speed bump on the road to victory. The United States had successfully spearheaded history's largest gathering of nations, maintaining unity among its allies and overcoming Soviet obstructionism. Truman and Vandenberg worked in concert, albeit largely through Stettinius. The secretary dutifully fulfilled the president's dictate to keep Vandenberg happy, and Vandenberg helped Stettinius at key moments, supporting his efforts and encouraging his leadership.

Truman arrived in San Francisco on June 25, motorcading from the airport at Hamilton Field to the Fairmont Hotel and passing huge crowds that lined Market Street to see him. Also that day, Vandenberg announced that he would support the charter and seek its Senate ratification. That was big news—the *New York Herald Tribune's* headline of June 26 blared, "Truman in San Francisco to Close Parley Today; Vandenberg for Charter." Though Vandenberg had worked feverishly to secure an acceptable charter, he had not announced his final verdict on it. And his approval virtually guaranteed that the Senate would follow.

"Our intelligent American self-interest indispensably requires our loyal co-operation in this great adventure to stop World War Three before it starts," Vandenberg said in a prepared statement.[1]

Truman, alas, would not suffer Wilson's fate.

. . .

"The Charter of the United Nations which you have just signed is a solid structure upon which we can build a better world," Truman told the conference on June 26. "History will honor you for it. Between the victory in Europe and the final victory in Japan, in this most destructive of all wars, you have won a victory against war itself."

Vandenberg returned to Washington on June 27 aboard a flight that included foreign delegates and other dignitaries. The Senate Foreign Relations Committee met him at the airport along with a band, and he and Connally were feted enthusiastically upon their arrival in the full Senate. Connally spoke to the chamber the next day, Vandenberg the day after. Reflecting its significance for the events that would follow, the *Washington Post* printed Vandenberg's long address in its entirety.

The charter, Vandenberg told a hushed Senate, "represents a great, forward step toward the international understanding, the cooperation and fellowship which are indispensable to peace, progress and security. If the spirit of its authors can become the spirit of its evolution I believe it will bless the earth. I believe it serves the intelligent self-interest of the United States which knows, by bitter experience in the valley of the shadow of two wars in a quarter century, that we cannot live entirely unto ourselves alone. I believe it is our only chance to keep faith with those who have borne the heat of battle . . .

"None of its authors will certify to its perfection," he concluded. "But all of its authors will certify to its preponderant advantages. It is the only plan available for international cooperation in the pursuit of peace and justice. It is laden with promise and with hope. It deserves a faithful trial. America has everything to gain and nothing to lose by giving it support; everything to lose and nothing to gain by declining this continued fraternity with the United Nations in behalf of the dearest dream of humankind."

. . .

On July 2 the president took the unusual step of traveling to Capitol Hill and presenting the charter in person to the Senate, telling its members that "it is good of you to let me come back among you."

In an oblique reference to 1919, Truman said, "the Charter . . . has been written in the name of 'We the people of the United Nations.' Those people—stretching all over the face of the earth—will watch our action here with great concern and high hope. For they look to this body of elected representatives of the people of the United States to take the lead in approving the Charter and the Statute [of the International Court of Justice] and pointing the way for the rest of the world."

By then, neither Truman nor Vandenberg needed to do much to bring the Senate along because, beyond Washington, the country was increasingly rallying around the United Nations. *The New York Times, New York Herald Tribune, Washington Post, Christian Science Monitor, Baltimore Sun, Philadelphia Inquirer, Miami Herald, Atlanta Constitution, Nashville Tennessean, Milwaukee Journal, New Orleans Times-Picayune, Des Moines Register, Detroit Free Press, St. Louis Post-Dispatch, San Francisco Chronicle*, and scores of other newspapers across the nation had expressed support for it, as had such influential magazines as *Life, Harper's,* and *The Nation.*

The Senate Foreign Relations Committee held five days of hearings in early July before sending the charter to the full Senate on a 21–1 vote, with the lone dissent coming from California's flamboyant Republican isolationist, Hiram Johnson. On July 28 the Senate ratified it on an 89–2 vote, with the dissents this time from Republican isolationists William Langer of North Dakota and Henrik Shipstead of Minnesota (though Johnson would have made it three were he not hospitalized at the time).

During the hearings Vandenberg spoke only occasionally and, for the most part, only to clarify a point about Security Council powers or regional defense pacts or U.S. obligations to participate in collective military action. On the Senate floor, he was equally sparse in his comments, though he felt compelled to reiterate his support for the charter at some length on July 23 for two reasons. First, he didn't want his "temporary silence interpreted as reflecting any sort of default in my continuing deep and abiding conviction that this is man's best hope for a safer and happier world." Second, sensitive to public criticism, he wanted to respond to a "two-column editorial in certain important metropolitan newspapers" that attacked the charter as well as "Vandenberg and his cohorts." He was no doubt pleased when, upon concluding his remarks, his colleagues applauded.

Proud when the Senate ratified the treaty, Vandenberg couldn't resist a final blast of ego. "Everybody now seems to agree," he wrote to his wife, "that I could have beaten the Charter if I had taken the opposition tack."[2]

. . .

By turning Tennyson's utopianism, FDR's vision, and the Dumbarton Oaks draft into reality, and by securing an overwhelming Senate vote for the charter, Truman and Vandenberg sent the world an unmistakable message: 1945 was not 1919. The United States was now on the world stage to stay.

Not surprisingly, global affairs progressed after 1945 in ways that didn't meet the highest hopes of Truman, Vandenberg, and the UN's other architects. The world avoided World War III, but far less because global leaders created the United Nations than because rationality prevailed in Washington and Moscow at moments of great tension. Rather than work together to provide "collective security" through the Security Council, the United States and Soviet Union battled through proxy wars in Asia, Africa, and Latin America. Rather than "promoting and encouraging respect for human rights and fundamental freedoms for all," as its charter promises, the United Nations has ignored egregious human rights abuses in many countries while decrying far less serious ones in just a few.

Moreover, the UN's record in imposing sanctions to change governmental behavior and deploying peacekeepers to maintain order has

"Victory against War"

been mixed. Sanctions proved effective in Libya, Liberia, and the former Yugoslavia, but they failed in Somalia and Rwanda and prompted a multibillion-dollar scandal with Iraq's oil-for-food program. Peacekeeping proved useful in the Suez, Namibia, El Salvador, Cambodia, Mozambique, and Haiti, but failed dramatically in Somalia and the Balkans.

Nevertheless, the United Nations has proved useful in other ways. To Churchill's point that "jaw-jaw" is better than "war-war," the body has hosted high-profile debates that helped to defuse such conflicts as the 1962 Cuban Missile Crisis and the 1973 Arab-Israeli War. Meanwhile, the United Nations has crafted global treaties to promote certain causes and prevent certain actions, and it has created institutions to spur economic and social advancement.[3]

Perhaps most important for our purposes, the United Nations has played a major role in keeping America on the international stage since its founding. Through its role at the Security Council and its influence through various UN bodies, the United States couldn't fully retreat from the world even if it wanted to.

. . .

"Everything, in the final analysis, depends on Russia (and whether we have *guts* enough to make her behave)," Vandenberg wrote to his wife after the Senate ratified the UN Charter.[4]

In the preceding months, Truman and Vandenberg had learned much about their adversary in Moscow. They had witnessed Soviet intransigence in San Francisco and were increasingly shaken by Stalin's ruthlessness in Europe. They had each tangled with Molotov, and, as the Senate debated the charter, Truman was again facing off with Stalin, this time at the Potsdam Conference near Berlin.

Truman and Vandenberg understood that, for all the good that a United Nations might do, it could not prevent the continuing emergence of a U.S.-Soviet global rivalry. With World War II drawing to a close, the world was now dominated by two superpowers with dramatically different ideologies, political structures, economic systems, and global interests. As U.S.-Soviet relations worsened and their clashes grew more frequent, the United States desperately needed a framework, a doctrine, a set of operating principles by which to view the world and confront the challenge.

It would emerge in the midst of crisis more than a year later—with Britain abandoning its longtime obligation to protect Greece and Turkey, the Soviet Union poised to fill the vacuum left by Britain's retreat, and the United States forced to decide how big of a role it would play on the world stage.

PART 2

"To Support Free Peoples"

AT 10:00 A.M. ON February 27, 1947, Harry Truman was meeting with Arthur Vandenberg and six other congressional leaders at the White House. George C. Marshall, who had replaced Jimmy Byrnes as secretary of state a month earlier, was explaining why Congress should give $400 million in economic and military aid to Greece and Turkey to enable them to fend off Soviet-backed threats to their independence. Just days earlier, Great Britain had officially informed the United States that—bankrupt and exhausted by World War II and lacking enough food and fuel for its own people during an unusually cold winter—it could no longer fulfill its commitments to defend those two nations. Truman and his team recognized the earthshaking implications: the United States would have to step up and replace Britain as the world's leading defender of freedom, or it would leave a vacuum on the world stage for an increasingly hostile and aggressive Soviet Union to fill.

Marshall, then sixty-six, with white hair that he parted neatly on the left, was an iconic figure, highly accomplished and widely respected in both parties. Franklin Roosevelt appointed him the army's chief of staff on the eve of World War II, *Time* named him "Man of the Year" in 1943, and Winston Churchill dubbed him the "organizer of victory" after the war. In later years, he would serve as secretary of defense and win the Nobel Peace Prize. But, though normally commanding, Marshall this time was neither sharp nor convincing. The lawmakers did not grasp the stakes, and they began picking apart Marshall's presentation with questions about what the effort would cost and whether America would be merely "pulling British chestnuts out of the fire."

A worried Dean Acheson, the undersecretary of state who was sitting beside Marshall, leaned over and asked softly, "Is this a private fight or can anyone get into it?" After Marshall asked Truman to let Acheson speak, Acheson took over, outlining the stakes in dramatic terms and making clear that both the future of freedom around the world as well as U.S. national security were at risk. The issue, he explained, was much bigger than Greece and Turkey. After locking up Eastern Europe soon after World War II, the Soviet Union was working feverishly to expand its empire far beyond. Over the prior eighteen months, Soviet advances had put the world's democracies on their heels. Now, with victories in Greece and Turkey—which seemed likely if the two countries did not get outside help—the Soviets could lay claim to the Mediterranean region and threaten the Middle East. With the growing influence of Soviet-directed Communists in France, Italy, and elsewhere, they also could destabilize the U.S.-led democracies of Western Europe. Not since the days of Athens and Sparta, of Rome and Carthage, Acheson said, was the world divided between two great powers as it was now between the United States and the Soviet Union. The question was whether the United States would aid Greece and Turkey and, more broadly, make it clear to its allies, to the Soviets, and to Third World nations that would soon choose sides that America would defend free and democratic governments around the world in the face of mounting Soviet aggression.[1]

Acheson hit his mark. His dramatic ten- to fifteen-minute oration was followed by perhaps ten seconds of stunned silence. Breaking it was Vandenberg, who was now chairman of the Senate Foreign Relations Committee because Republicans had won control of both houses of Congress the previous November. "Mr. President," Vandenberg pledged, leaning forward on a sofa, "if you will say that to the Congress and the country, I will support you and I believe most of its members will do the same."[2]

. . .

Truman did just that in a major address to Congress on March 12, 1947; Vandenberg worked with him to nourish the needed support for his aid package on Capitol Hill; and the result was the second major element of America's revolutionary new foreign policy. Washington provided the requested $400 million, enabling Greece and Turkey to overcome the Soviet-led challenges. More importantly, the aid came wrapped in what was soon dubbed the "Truman Doctrine"—the president's declaration that the United States would "support free peoples who are resisting attempted subjugation by armed minorities or by outside pressures," would "assist free peoples to work out their own destinies in their own way," and would do so "primarily through economic and financial aid which is essential to economic stability and orderly political processes."

If America's work to create the United Nations in early 1945 marked its decision to replace isolationism with global engagement, the Truman Doctrine represented its determination to seize the reins of global leadership by defending freedom and confronting Soviet expansionism. The doctrine marked the culmination of two years of hardening U.S. attitudes toward Moscow, driven by growing concerns over Soviet activities in Eastern Europe and Soviet threats to expand far beyond. As Truman and Vandenberg grew more alarmed about Soviet behavior, they drew closer to one another in their desire that the United States stop appeasing the Soviets and start confronting them.

Truman and Vandenberg worked closely on the strategy for selling this dramatic new approach to U.S. foreign policy, and on the particulars of its first manifestation in the form of Greek-Turkish aid. They explained to lawmakers and the public why America must step up and why the United Nations at that point was ill equipped to step in. While, two years earlier on the United Nations, they had worked largely through Edward Stettinius, the key go-between in this case was the suave, savvy, and sophisticated Acheson.

The roots of this dramatic change date back to 1945, when euphoria over America's victory in war began to give way to disillusionment in Washington over the breakdown of U.S.-Soviet cooperation.

7

"What Is Russia Up To Now?"

"I'm tired of babying the Soviets," Truman told Secretary of State Jimmy Byrnes in early January of 1946.

By then, a growing number of other U.S. officials had grown tired of it as well. Watching global developments, analyzing Soviet motives, they increasingly abandoned hopes of U.S.-Soviet cooperation and advised Washington to prepare for relentless confrontation with Moscow. Truman and several of his key advisers had harbored hopes of cooperation in his initial months in office, with the president even noting that he "liked" Stalin and admired his taste in culture. Vandenberg never harbored such hopes; he was an unsentimental Soviet critic from well before Truman's presidency.

As 1945 gave way to '46, the Soviets continued to implant their puppet regimes in Eastern Europe and, more ominously, Stalin signaled that he wanted to extend the Soviet sphere all the way to Iran. At a meeting of the Council of Foreign Ministers—the ministers or their equivalents of the United States, Soviet Union, Britain, France, and China—in London in September of 1945, U.S., Soviet, and British officials had agreed to withdraw all of their respective troops from Iran (which they had protected from possible German attack during the war) by March 1946. In November 1945, however, Washington received reports that Moscow was adding to Soviet forces in that country, casting doubt on its withdrawal commitment. In December Soviet officials rejected a U.S. proposal that Washington, London, and Moscow withdraw their troops more quickly, and they refused to discuss the matter when Byrnes attended the Council of Foreign Ministers meeting that month in Moscow.

For Truman and Vandenberg the Moscow meeting, from December 16 to 26, proved particularly consequential. They agreed that it portended more Soviet intransigence—and that Byrnes had not represented the United States well there. They both thought Byrnes was too eager to cut deals with the Soviets and declare victory. That Byrnes would face criticism for excessive deal making was hardly surprising, for he had made his name on Capitol Hill, where deal making was the coin of the realm. He served in the House from 1911 to 1925 and the Senate from 1931 to 1941, and, in the latter body, he was a close confidante of FDR, helping to shepherd much of his New Deal into law. FDR rewarded him with a Supreme Court seat in 1941 but called him back to the administration just a year later to run his Office of Economic Stabilization.

To both Truman and Vandenberg's later dismay, Byrnes also was a man of no small ego. He boldly exerted so much power at the Office of Economic Stabilization and then as head of FDR's Office of War Mobilization that many lawmakers and journalists called him the "Assistant President."

Byrnes's behavior in Moscow even forced Truman and Vandenberg to scramble to avoid an open breach with one another.

. . .

On the evening of December 27, 1945, Truman and Vandenberg both read a State Department communiqué that Byrnes had issued that night, outlining what he, the Soviet Union's Vyacheslav Molotov, and Britain's Ernest Bevin had decided in Moscow. Neither of them was happy with it.

By then, Truman had been seething for months that Byrnes was trying to make U.S. foreign policy on his own rather than implement the president's decisions. Now, he was angry that Byrnes didn't show him the communiqué before releasing it. Beyond that, Truman was angry that it didn't address his concerns about Soviet behavior in Eastern Europe and Iran. Byrnes had no idea that Truman's anger had been building, and, earlier that day, he pressed for greater public glory—asking White

"Support Free Peoples"

House aides to arrange for him to address the nation by radio about the conference before he had even briefed Truman about it. Truman's aides wisely ignored the request. The next day, Truman instructed his press secretary, Charlie Ross, to tell Byrnes to "come down here posthaste" and "make your report" to the president, who was then sailing on the *Williamsburg*, the presidential yacht. A fatigued Byrnes was reluctant to comply, agreeing only grudgingly. On the yacht and then at a January 5 White House meeting between them, Truman dressed down Byrnes for making U.S. policy without first clearing it with him. It was at the January 5 meeting, at the end of his lecture to Byrnes, when Truman said he was "tired of babying the Soviets."[1]

Meanwhile, Vandenberg objected strongly to a section of the communiqué suggesting that U.S., Soviet, and British officials would discuss the possibility of transferring control of atomic energy to an international body without first ensuring that proper safeguards were in place to protect U.S. interests. This was no new issue for Vandenberg. Soon after Hiroshima and Nagasaki in August of 1945, Vandenberg urged the United States not to share atomic secrets with any nation until there was an "absolute free and untrammeled right of intimate inspection all around the globe." The next month he met with Truman to discuss his idea of a new House-Senate committee to oversee atomic energy (which eventually came to life in the form of a new Senate committee). Through the fall Vandenberg promoted "a system of complete worldwide inspection which shall guarantee to civilization that no nation (including ourselves) shall use atomic energy for the construction of weapons of war." When, on December 10, Byrnes told Vandenberg and other senators that, in the upcoming Moscow meeting, he would offer to share atomic information with the Soviets, Vandenberg led a group of outraged senators to the White House the next day to meet with Truman. Truman told the senators he agreed that unfettered inspections were a prerequisite for any atomic information-sharing, and he later directed Acheson to cable Byrnes, who was on his way to Moscow, not to disclose any information in Moscow or pledge to do so without an agreement over an ironclad inspection system.[2]

Meanwhile, Truman notified Vandenberg by letter on December 21 that he was appointing him to the U.S. delegation for January's UN General Assembly meeting in London. When, six days later, Byrnes issued his communiqué about the Moscow meeting, Vandenberg wrote that he "very nearly resigned [from the delegation] . . . because I could not possibly subscribe to what it said about the atomic bomb. I am unwilling to endorse any atomic disclosures to Russia unless and until we have adequate and dependable methods of international inspection and control which will guarantee the world that atomic weapons are never made again anywhere. The Moscow Communique sounds like one more typical American 'give away' on the subject."

Vandenberg phoned Truman on the evening of December 27 to complain and met with him the next day at the White House. Acheson attended the Truman-Vandenberg meeting, and he later drafted a public statement for Truman to make clear that Washington would not take any steps toward international information-sharing on atomic energy until the necessary safeguards were in place. Vandenberg then issued his own statement, saying that Truman's statement "helpfully clarifies the situation." Next, Vandenberg met with Byrnes, who then announced that U.S., Soviet, and British officials had agreed to focus on security safeguards at *all* stages of discussion about international control and that any agreement among them would go to Congress for approval. With his concerns now addressed, the senator turned to the UN General Assembly meeting that was set for January 10, climbed aboard the *Queen Elizabeth* with his wife, and set sail for London.[3]

For Truman and Vandenberg, the Moscow meeting was but the tip of an emerging iceberg of growing U.S.-Soviet conflict that would increasingly absorb their time. In the coming months, positions hardened in Washington and Moscow, laying the groundwork for Truman's dramatic speech of a year later.

. . .

"This is a privilege for me," Harry Truman told the heads of federal agencies and personnel directors in the White House's Motion Pic-

"Support Free Peoples"

ture Room on February 9, 1946. Truman had "called [them] together" to focus their attention on his recent executive order that returned the civil service to a "peacetime basis." The pivot to "peacetime" was all too ironic because on that very day, half a world way, Joseph Stalin was suggesting that war between the United States and Soviet Union was inevitable. The only question was when.

Stalin's February 9 speech at the Bolshoi Theater ignited a series of events over the ensuing weeks—in which Truman and Vandenberg participated heavily—that gave the Cold War a new momentum. U.S. concern over Stalin's remarks was understandable, for they carried a frightening tone. Announcing a new five-year economic program at a rally before "elections" to the Supreme Soviet, Stalin said World War II was the "inevitable result of the development of world economic and political forces on the basis of present-day monopolistic capitalism" and that "catastrophic wars" are inevitable "under the present capitalist conditions of world economic development." Supreme Court Justice William Douglas called the speech "the declaration of World War III" while *Time* termed it "the most warlike pronouncement uttered by any top-rank statesman" since the war.[4]

In the weeks before Stalin spoke, Truman and his top advisers had been struggling to understand Soviet motives. Why was Moscow so aggressive on the world stage? Did it want a sphere of influence to protect itself against future invasion, or did it seek world domination? Truman later reflected on his dismay that winter. "I had hoped," he wrote, "that the Russians would return favor for favor, but almost from the time I became President I found them acting without regard for their neighboring nations and in direct violation of the obligations they had assumed at Yalta."[5] At the State Department, officials expected Stalin's Bolshoi speech to trigger a thoughtful analysis from its Moscow embassy. After all, the second-ranking U.S. official in Moscow often sent cables to explain the latest Soviet activities, and a high-profile speech from Stalin begged for perspective.

But George F. Kennan, who would turn forty-two a week after Stalin's speech, wasn't inspired to send anything to Washington because he didn't think it was particularly necessary. Tall, lanky, blue-eyed, and balding, Kennan was an intellectual giant among his Foreign Service peers, but he was also a sensitive, brooding, often lonely figure who frequently took to bed for long periods for diseases that were both real and imagined. He had felt particularly ignored in recent months as he sent cable after cable, urging U.S. officials to discard their rose-colored glasses about the Soviets, recognize that Moscow didn't share Washington's interests, and proceed accordingly. In fact, he thought U.S. policy toward Moscow should have hardened after the Polish uprising of late 1944 when the Soviets stopped advancing into Poland and let the Nazis slaughter Polish resistance fighters. "For eighteen long months I had done little else but pluck people's sleeves, trying to make them understand," he recalled. "So far as official Washington was concerned, it had been to all intents and purposes like talking to a stone."[6] Moreover, Kennan didn't see anything new in Stalin's speech, for it reflected the Soviet outlook about which he had already written so much.

But after receiving nothing from Kennan for several days, State Department officials gave him a nudge, suggesting by cable that they hungered for his insights. It was the Friday night of a holiday weekend, and the embassy was quiet. Nevertheless, Kennan had an audience in Washington that was surprisingly eager to hear his thoughts, and he wasn't about to waste the opportunity. So Kennan, who was in bed with a cold, sinus infection, and other maladies, summoned his "long suffering" secretary to type up the draft he would dictate while lying flat on his back. "They asked for it—," he told a staffer who would send it to Washington by cable that night, "now they're going to get it!"

The Soviet Union, Kennan wrote in his "Long Telegram" of more than 5,000 words—the longest in State Department history—believes it "still lives in antagonistic 'capitalist encirclement' with which in the long run there can be no permanent peaceful coexistence." Capitalism's "internal conflicts" generate wars, either between capitalist states or against the "socialist world." The Soviets believed they must do whatever they could to "advance relative strength" around the world and reduce that of the "capitalist powers." "At bottom of Kremlin's neurotic view

"Support Free Peoples"

of world affairs," he wrote, "is traditional and instinctive Russian sense of insecurity . . . they have learned to seek security only in patient but deadly struggle for total destruction of rival power, never in compacts and compromises with it." To advance its goals, Kennan warned, Moscow would work through Communist parties, labor unions, youth leagues, women's organizations, racial societies, and media organs far beyond its borders, as well as the Russian Orthodox Church, other governments, and governing groups. The Soviets would try to undermine Western countries at home and reduce their influence in the Third World, and, when necessary, they would remove governments that stood in their way.

Whether Truman ever saw Kennan's cable remains unclear. Nevertheless, it proved enormously influential with his top aides, for it arrived when they were finally ready to absorb its message. It provided a philosophical foundation for America's unfolding global efforts. Such influential officials as Acheson, Bohlen, Harriman, and James Forrestal, the navy secretary, read it closely and circulated it widely. "It hit Washington at just the right moment," Harriman recalled. "It was very fortunate."[7]

. . .

Arthur Vandenberg, by contrast, didn't hunger for the kind of theory that Kennan was propagating; he was more practical. He didn't think deeply about Soviet neuroses; he tracked Soviet behavior.

Just days after Kennan's telegram reached Washington, Vandenberg returned to the capital after thirty-seven days at the UN meeting in London. He found the meeting frustrating and Soviet behavior ominous. The General Assembly had voted to create a UN Commission on Atomic Energy and to continue relief efforts in war-torn areas. But the Soviets caused trouble when the General Assembly forwarded two items to the Security Council—the continuing presence of British and French troops in Lebanon and Syria, and of Soviet troops in northern Iran. While the British and French pledged to withdraw their troops, the Soviets offered nothing. So, with Truman's team still mulling the implications of Kennan's telegram, Vandenberg considered what he had witnessed in London and decided to relay his thoughts in a high-profile speech that would draw attention, shape public opinion, and feed his ego. With a cigar dangling from his lips, he pounded out one draft after another on his manual typewriter and tested out his words on his wife and friendly newsmen until he was ready to deliver them. The moment came on February 27 when, with the galleries packed and most senators on hand, he rose on the Senate floor.

"What is Russia up to now?" Vandenberg asked, gripping the lectern at his desk with both hands and shaking his head on occasion for effect. "It is, of course, the supreme conundrum of our time. We ask it in Manchuria. We ask it in Eastern Europe and the Dardanelles. We ask it in Italy where Russia, speaking for Yugoslavia, has already initiated attention to the Polish Legions. We ask it in Iran. We ask it in Tripolitania. We ask it in the Baltic and the Balkans. We ask it in Poland. We ask it in the capital of Canada. We ask it in Japan. We ask it sometimes even in connection with events in our own United States. What is Russia up to now?" Vandenberg urged U.S. officials to speak candidly about U.S. interests so that Washington and Moscow could reach at least a cold understanding. Washington, he said, should make clear what America stood for, what it would and wouldn't tolerate, and where it would draw its line. "The United States," he said, "has no ulterior designs against any of its neighbors anywhere on earth. We can speak with the extraordinary power inherent in this unselfishness. We need but one rule. What is right? Where is justice? There let America take her stand." Vandenberg finished and senators stood, applauding and shaking his hand.

While Kennan's "Long Telegram" educated officials atop Washington's policymaking circle—and has since acquired a legendary status— Vandenberg's oration received far greater public attention at the time. It reached Americans across the country through broad newspaper coverage, including much laudatory commentary. The *Washington Post* called it "magisterial." "There have been few occasions," wrote James A. Wechsler of New York's *PM* newspaper, "on which a single Senator has so dramatically and so decisively dominated Senate opinion on world-wide issues." "It left you," the *Detroit Free Press'* James M. Haswell wrote, "with a sense of history going on right here now." "This," the *Omaha World-Herald*

"Support Free Peoples"

declared, "is the voice of responsibility, the voice of statesmanship, the voice that America has been longing to hear." It was, the *Houston Post* wrote, "the most important speech since the declaration of war."

Time, the *New York Times*, and other leading organs, however, focused on the political atmospherics. They noted that Byrnes planned to speak the next night in New York to the Overseas Press Club of America, and they portrayed Vandenberg's speech as a preemptive attack on Byrnes and, more generally, on Truman's foreign policy. If so, Byrnes got the message. Echoing Vandenberg's hard line, and clearly referring to Moscow, he said that "we cannot allow aggression to be accomplished by coercion or pressure or by subterfuges such as political infiltration." "Great powers as well as small powers," he went on, "have agreed under the United Nations Charter not to use force or the threat of force except in defense of law and the purposes and principles of the charter. We will not and we cannot stand aloof if force or the threat of force is used contrary to the purposes and principles of the charter." Byrnes had signaled to U.S. and global audiences that Truman was toughening his posture toward the Soviets, and a delighted Vandenberg later praised him repeatedly.[8]

After Kennan's telegram, Vandenberg's speech, and Byrnes's rejoinder, two things were clear: First, Truman and Vandenberg were closer than ever in their views on the Soviet Union. Second, Vandenberg's stature continued to grow, for political wags dubbed Byrnes's speech the "Second Vandenberg Concerto."

. . .

Byrnes's speech proved a turning point in his relationship with Vandenberg. It eliminated Vandenberg's doubts about Byrnes's willingness to confront the Soviets. Now that Vandenberg fully trusted Truman's secretary of state, he could more easily work with the president both through Byrnes and more directly.

Vandenberg's change of heart toward Byrnes was long in coming. He had harbored ill feelings about him ever since Truman announced in mid-1945 that Byrnes would replace Stettinius as secretary of state. For starters, Vandenberg was disgusted by what he viewed as Truman's shabby treatment of Stettinius, whom he had come grudgingly to respect for his work at that year's UN conference in San Francisco. Truman's political aide, George Allen, visited Stettinius in San Francisco as the conference was ending, hinted that Truman might want to name another secretary, and suggested that Stettinius take Truman's offer to make him the U.S. representative to the new United Nations. Only after Stettinius asked about Byrnes did Allen admit that, yes, Truman already had promised him the job. Stettinius "deserved better treatment after his rare performance at Frisco," Vandenberg wrote at the time. "It just shows how cruel and ruthless 'politics' can be."

Vandenberg, however, also didn't think Byrnes was right for the job. "Jimmy Byrnes is a grand guy (for any *other* job down here)," Vandenberg wrote to his wife. "But his whole life has been a career of compromise." With a disparaging reference to FDR, Byrnes's close ties to him, and the Yalta conference of early 1945, Vandenberg went on, "Just as we have, at long last, got Russia to understand (through Stettinius) that we occasionally mean what we say, Stettinius gets the axe and Jimmy (who helped surrender at Yalta) comes back in! . . . The peace of the world *really* depends on whether Russia and America can live together in this new world. I believe we can if Russia is made to understand that we can't be pushed around. That was our greatest victory at Frisco. Stettinius was its symbol. Now we lose him—and get back Byrnes and Yalta. Oh, well—."[9]

Nor was December's Moscow meeting the only time Vandenberg thought that Byrnes had performed poorly in the job. When, in the early weeks of 1946, Poland's Soviet-backed government was murdering opposition leaders, Britain's foreign minister, Ernest Bevin, strongly denounced it in the House of Commons and called for free elections. From London, the U.S. delegation to the UN meeting urged Byrnes, who had returned to Washington, to reinforce Bevin's denunciation. When, instead, Byrnes directed the U.S. embassy in Warsaw to tell Poland's government that "we are relying" on it to "take the necessary steps to assure the freedom and security" necessary for free elections, Vandenberg was left disgusted.[10]

After the "Concerto," however, Vandenberg saw Byrnes in an entirely new light, praising his "courageous candor."[11]

"Support Free Peoples"

8

"The Russians Are Trying to Chisel Away a Little Here, a Little There"

TRUMAN AND VANDENBERG PROCEEDED apace through 1946, each pursuing America's tougher anti-Soviet line. They worked less directly with one another than on parallel tracks. Truman addressed a host of Soviet-related crises from home, while Byrnes and Vandenberg collaborated overseas while they represented the United States at meetings of the Council of Foreign Ministers and other gatherings.

In early March, Truman introduced Winston Churchill to an audience at Fulton, Missouri's Westminster College, symbolically embracing the dramatic words that would follow: "From Stettin in the Baltic to Trieste in the Adriatic," Churchill declared, "an iron curtain has descended across the Continent. Behind that line lie all the capitals of the ancient states of Central and Eastern Europe. Warsaw, Berlin, Prague, Vienna, Budapest, Belgrade, Bucharest and Sofia, all these famous cities and the populations around them lie in what I must call the Soviet sphere, and all are subject in one form or another, not only to Soviet influence but to a very high and, in many cases, increasing measure of control from Moscow." Churchill proposed an Anglo-American alliance to counter Moscow's aggression. Truman had urged Churchill to accept the Westminster invitation, volunteered to introduce him, learned from Churchill what he planned to say, read his speech while the two traveled by train from Washington to Fulton, and applauded repeatedly while Churchill delivered it. Truman never sought to soften his words, no doubt because they reflected the president's views. But when Americans reacted coolly to Churchill's call to arms, Truman disingenuously denied prior knowledge of it and sidestepped a chance to endorse it. He even offered Stalin a comparable speaking venue and pledged to introduce him, too, but Stalin never pursued the offer.

Around that time, Truman also made clear to Stalin that the United States would not ignore specific Soviet provocations around the world. The March 1946 deadline for Soviet troop withdrawals from Iran came and went with Moscow announcing that, rather than comply, it would leave some troops there. Meanwhile, the Soviets were stoking a Communist-led separatist movement in Azerbaijan, a northern Iranian province. That Moscow was operating so far from home didn't escape notice in U.S. circles. "The USSR aims not only at acquiring a privileged position in northern Iran," George Kennan cabled from Moscow, "but at virtual subjugation, penetration and domination of the entire country, and Bahrein and Kuwait as well." Its goal, he wrote, was "ultimate political domination of the entire Asiatic mainland."[1] Truman worried about Moscow's disregard for its commitments, its implicit threat to Turkey and other neighbors, and a potential Soviet seizure of Iran's oil reserves—the last of which carried frightening implications for the U.S. and Western economies. The president was concerned enough about war with the Soviets if Moscow threatened U.S. interests further that he appointed Harriman, the former U.S. ambassador to Moscow, as ambassador to Great Britain because he needed a trusted aide in that crucial capital in case war erupted.

At Truman's request, U.S. officials in March confronted the Soviets over Iran at the United Nations. Meanwhile, Byrnes followed his "Second Vandenberg Concerto" of February 28 with a March 16 address in which he called for extending the draft and said that "our military strength will be used to support the purposes and principles of the [UN] Charter."[2] In April Truman sent the U.S. battleship *Missouri* to the eastern Mediterranean in a bold display of U.S. power and its commitment to the region. Apparently moved by U.S. resolve, the Soviets withdrew their troops from Iran in May.

. . .

"Support Free Peoples"

That spring and summer, Washington and Moscow clashed again over the Mediterranean region, prompting Truman to stare down Stalin again—and setting the stage for the Truman-Vandenberg collaboration on Greek-Turkish aid a year later.

Everyone understood the region's strategic and symbolic importance. Greece was located on the Mediterranean Sea, at the southern tip of Europe and near the Middle East and Northern Africa. It was, thus, a potentially important naval base for either the United States or the Soviet Union, depending on its status. It also was symbolically important as the cradle of Western civilization and birthplace of democracy. Just to the east, Turkey was the gateway from the Mediterranean to the Black Sea through the Turkish Straits, an international waterway that was under Turkish control.

By early 1946 Truman suspected, correctly, that the Soviets were eyeing the Mediterranean for expansion. Unbeknownst to him, Stalin told his aides that spring that he was pleased with where World War II and its aftermath had left Soviet borders to the north, west, and east. The south, however, was different. "Here," Stalin said, pointing on a map toward Turkey, "I don't like our border." Stalin wanted to reclaim Turkish land that the Soviets had lost years earlier and to create a Soviet role for the Turkish Straits. "Historically," Stalin said of the south, "this is where the threat [to Soviet national security] has always originated."[3] That summer, Moscow pressured Turkey to put the Turkish Straits under joint Soviet-Turkish control. A year earlier at the Potsdam Conference, Stalin had sought a Soviet role over the straits but Truman firmly rejected the idea and Stalin backed off.

Truman was determined to prevent any Soviet inroads. For Greece, the United States helped oversee its national elections in March. Truman also told America's ambassador in Athens that the United States would guarantee that country's independence. For Turkey, as Moscow confronted Ankara over the Turkish Straits, Truman directed Turkish officials to hold firm, sent the supercarrier *Franklin D. Roosevelt* to join the *Missouri* in the Mediterranean, and directed Acheson to inform Moscow that the United States was prepared to enforce Turkey's sovereignty and its sole responsibility for the straits. In August Truman signed a policy memorandum declaring Turkish independence a vital U.S. interest, and he told Acheson that he'd stand by it "to the end." Late that summer Truman approved a decision to station a U.S. naval task force in the region permanently.[4]

"We might as well find out," Truman told top U.S. foreign and military officials on August 15 as they gathered around his desk in the White House, "whether the Russians are bent on world conquest." General Dwight Eisenhower, who was then the army's chief of staff, whispered his concern to Acheson that officials had not fully explained to Truman that his approach could mean war with the Soviets. Truman, who noticed Eisenhower whispering, told him to speak up. When Eisenhower expressed his concern aloud, the president reached into his desk, took out a map of the region, and began to talk. Dipping into the rich history he had learned while reading voraciously as a child, Truman lectured his aides on the region's strategic importance and the need to keep it free of Soviet control. Acheson later pronounced himself "awed" by Truman's knowledge.[5]

Once more, the Soviets backed off. But no one thought Stalin was done pressing for greater Soviet influence in the region.

. . .

While Truman confronted Stalin from Washington, Vandenberg battled the Soviets from Paris.

Vandenberg had joined Byrnes in Paris for Council of Foreign Ministers meetings, which ran on and off from late April through mid-July and focused on drafting postwar peace treaties for Italy, Hungary, Rumania, Bulgaria, and Finland. Byrnes and Vandenberg returned to the French capital for the Paris Peace Conference, which ran from late July to mid-October and was held to consider the five peace treaties more formally.

With U.S., Soviet, British, and French officials at the table, Byrnes and Vandenberg battled mostly with Molotov, the Soviet foreign minister, but also with his deputy, Andrei Vishinsky. At the Council of Foreign Ministers meetings, they clashed, for instance, over reparations from

Italy for World War II; the fate of Italy's colonies; Italy's final borders with France, Austria, and Yugoslavia; the final status of Trieste; the fate of some Greek islands; and, in abbreviated form, the mega-issue of a final settlement over Germany. While supporting Byrnes as he parried Soviet delaying tactics and roadblocks to progress, Vandenberg also provided important behind-the-scenes assistance. In mid-May he drafted a statement for Byrnes to release upon calling for the council to recess until June 15, since Washington and Moscow were deadlocked over key issues.

In between meetings, Byrnes and Vandenberg shared more leisurely pursuits, bonding further in the process. In late April Byrnes shared his idea for a four-party treaty for Germany, with the former Nazi state fully disarmed, prompting Vandenberg to recall that he had urged Germany's disarmament in his "speech heard 'round the world" of January 10, 1945. Then, while the two watched the horses at Longchamp Racecourse, Byrnes shared his concerns about the Soviet-sympathizing Commerce Secretary Henry Wallace and Senator Claude Pepper, a Florida Democrat, who were both criticizing Byrnes for his hard-line anti-Soviet views. Vandenberg grew ever more comfortable with Byrnes as the latter came around to Vandenberg's way of thinking about the Soviets.

"Byrnes gives every evidence of '*no more appeasement*' in his attitudes," Vandenberg wrote,

> and I am *certain* this is the way, if there *is* one to reach common ground with the Soviets. I want to be scrupulously fair and reasonable with them: but I want to be relentlessly firm in our insistence upon these American positions. No more Munichs! If it is impossible for us to get along with the Soviets on such a basis, the quicker we find out the better. America must behave like the *Number One World Power* which she is. Ours must be the world's moral leadership—or the world won't have any.[6]

With the council meetings recessed that spring, Vandenberg praised Byrnes for his "magnificently courageous and constructive job."[7] When Vandenberg then asked Byrnes whether he could beg off when the council resumed in June, saying he needed to address his Senate duties at home, Byrnes insisted that he attend. Returning to Paris in June, Byrnes and

Vandenberg dug in even more with the Soviets, negotiating in blunter language. By mid-July the council had completed its work, finishing drafts of the five treaties and establishing the Paris Peace Conference to consider them formally.

Vandenberg returned home in July and took to the Senate floor, reviewing the accomplishments of Paris—and issuing a warning to Soviet leaders. "You should understand with complete conviction," he said, "that we deeply respect the great Russian people . . . we are just as determined as you are that military aggression—from any source and no matter what its guise—shall never curse the earth again; and we are enlisted in the cause for keeps . . . You should also understand with equally complete conviction," he went on, "that we cannot be driven, coerced, or pressured into positions which we decline voluntarily to assume; and that we will not bargain in human rights and fundamental liberties anywhere on earth."[8]

. . .

At the other end of Pennsylvania Avenue, the president was feeling much the same way. "The Russians are trying to chisel away a little here, a little there," a frustrated Truman told his staff in July.

As he prepared that summer for a speech to promote his anti-Soviet hard line, Truman asked White House Counsel Clark Clifford to compile a list of international agreements that the Soviets had violated. With that list in hand, Truman would be ready to slam the Soviets if the Paris Peace Conference fell apart over Soviet intransigence. Clifford reached out to his aide, George Elsey, who suggested that they broaden the topic of their work to Soviet behavior in general on the world stage. When Truman agreed, Clifford and Elsey solicited input from such officials as Byrnes; Admiral William D. Leahy, who spoke for the Joint Chiefs of Staff; Secretary of War Robert Patterson; Secretary of the Navy James Forrestal; Attorney General Tom Clark; and Director of Central Intelligence Sidney Souers. They also consulted with Kennan and Bohlen.

The 26,000-word product—officially "American Relations with the

Soviet Union," though far better known as the Clifford-Elsey report—was important both because it reflected the administration's thinking at the time about the Soviets and because it presaged major U.S. initiatives that were soon to come. It echoed Churchill's assertion in his "iron curtain speech" that the Soviets understood power more than anything else, recommended that the United States always maintain sufficient military strength to deter them, urged that America even "be prepared to wage atomic and biological warfare," proposed political and economic aid for Soviet bloc countries in Eastern Europe, and suggested that the United States support democracies that faced Soviet threats.

Indeed, the report's passage on the last of these points bears a striking resemblance to the Truman Doctrine that Truman would enunciate months down the road: "The United States should support and assist all democratic countries which are in any way menaced or endangered by the USSR. Providing military support in case of attack is a last resort; a more effective barrier to communism is strong economic support. . . . The United States can do much more to ensure that economic opportunities, personal freedom and social equality are made possible in countries outside the Soviet sphere by generous financial assistance."

Truman received the report from Clifford on September 24 and read it that evening. He immediately grew alarmed that it would leak and "blow the roof" off the White House and Kremlin. He called Clifford the next morning and ordered him to bring every other one of the twenty copies to him immediately for safekeeping. It wasn't until twenty years later, after an interview in which Truman revealed its existence, that the *New York Times'* Arthur Krock brought the report to light in his memoirs.[9]

. . .

As 1946 came to a close, Truman and Vandenberg had grown more closely aligned over foreign policy than ever. But all around them, threats to their bipartisan collaboration were mounting. It was a congressional election year, the country was roiling in economic and social turmoil, Truman was weakened by political attacks from within and outside Democratic ranks, and the Republicans smelled blood. Democrats fought to maintain control of Congress while Republicans, who had not enjoyed it since the early 1930s, sought it desperately.

Truman and Vandenberg would have to work hard to ensure that their partnership could survive the brutal campaign and its inevitable fallout.

"Support Free Peoples"

9

"Halfbright"

IN 1946 VANDENBERG WAS seeking a fourth six-year term as a senator, and he was worried that his time away from Michigan and his focus on issues far from the everyday concerns of his constituents threatened his victory.

The senator had spent 213 days overseas in 1946, with his trip to London in January followed by three trips to Paris and then one to New York. The Congress of Industrial Organizations (CIO), which represented industrial unions before its merger with the AFL in 1955, targeted Vandenberg for defeat over his labor record. Meanwhile, the uncompromisingly isolationist *Chicago Tribune*, which enjoyed a wide circulation in Michigan, criticized him fiercely over his foreign policy.

Nearly a year before Election Day, Vandenberg expressed concern to John W. Blodgett, a philanthropist and prominent Michigan Republican, that his absences would prove a "very serious liability." "There is an entirely new generation of voters in Michigan since I first ran for the Senate," he wrote. "I must be more or less of a legendary character to many of them. Similar circumstances have been fatal to better men than I. It is an excellent reason why I should have sense enough to 'call it a day' and voluntarily retire."[1] Vandenberg's wife, Hazel, hoped he would, enabling the two to spend more time together.

Vandenberg never seriously considered retirement, however, for he needed the Senate like a fish needed water. He didn't *work* as a senator; he *was* a senator—from the tips of his toes to the top of his balding pate. He refused to shortchange his foreign policy responsibilities for the time-consuming tasks of campaigning, writing to his campaign office from Paris in late 1946, "Politics are important; but *peace is indispensable.*" Nevertheless, he wouldn't roll the dice completely on his reelection. Instead, he made a virtue out of his duties, tapping the pride of his constituents by positioning himself as the senator with an influential voice on the world stage. His campaign erected billboards that advertised his award that year from *Collier's* as the Senate's most valuable member and carried the tagline: "The world listens to this man from Michigan." The campaign distributed flyers across the state that included reprints of his speeches and positive newspaper commentary.

Also for political purposes, Vandenberg exploited the attacks on him from Soviet officials and the Communist press for his firm stand against Moscow, telling Michiganders, "I am flattered to find myself at the top of the Communist 'purge' list all around the world . . . If the people understand that they are 'dropping a letter to Stalin in the mailbox' when they drop their votes into the ballot box, I have no doubt of the outcome." The state's pliable media played along in strikingly supportive ways. Radio stations broadcast a program that put Vandenberg's career and speeches to dramatic music, while leading newspapers urged his reelection as an endorsement of bipartisan foreign policy.

As it turned out, Vandenberg faced no Republican primary opponent, and the Democratic candidate didn't mount much of a challenge. In November, he won in a landslide, capturing 67 percent of the 1.6 million votes cast. The victory ratified his strong desire to maintain his bipartisan approach to foreign affairs. "The outcome means much more to me than a personal victory," he wrote in an election night statement. "This is secondary. It means unmistakable endorsement of the united, bipartisan foreign policy through which we are striving for national security and world peace with justice on the basis of sound American ideals. I take it the national returns present a similar mandate. They mean that this policy will continue. Those who may have been led to doubt our

"Support Free Peoples"

unity in this regard now have their eloquent answer from the people of the United States."[2]

. . .

Meanwhile, with Democrats and Republicans campaigning ferociously for months all over the country, Truman and Vandenberg did little on the campaign trail to threaten their working relationship.

Truman wasn't out much anyway because worried Democrats didn't want any unnecessary public association with an increasingly unpopular president. Nor did Truman let the sweeping GOP victories that fall, which gave Republicans control of the House and Senate simultaneously for the first time since the early 1930s, embitter him for the long term. After first sulking about the election results, which marked a strong public rebuke to his leadership, Truman gathered his strength and opted to discard caution in the interest of boldness. "I think the proper thing to do," he decided, "is to do what I think is right and let them all go to hell."[3]

Vandenberg, who could have proved helpful to Republican candidates beyond Michigan, chose not to campaign nationally. "I certainly shall not make a broadcast under the auspices of the Republican National Committee," he wrote to his campaign office in late September. "I think it would be sheer political suicide on a national scale for the Republicans, after two years' forbearance, to be the ones who should wreck the non-partisan character of our official attitudes toward America's foreign policy."[4]

. . .

Soon after Election Day, a Senate Democrat from Arkansas offered a novel idea that spoke both to Truman's extraordinary political weakness and Vandenberg's unusually elevated stature.

J. William Fulbright was concerned that, with Republicans running Congress, the nation faced two years of divided government and, thus, gridlock at a time of mounting challenges. He suggested that Truman appoint Vandenberg as secretary of state, putting him first in line for the presidency because there was no vice president at the time. Truman then would resign, Fulbright went on, elevating Vandenberg to president.

That prompted Truman, who naturally ignored the idea, to thereafter call the senator "Halfbright."

. . .

As Harry Truman pondered the implications of Britain's withdrawal from Greece and Turkey in early 1947, he worried that a Republican-controlled Congress would not support his proposed response.

"The vital decision that I was about to make," Truman wrote later, "was complicated by the fact that Congress was no longer controlled by the Democratic party. While expecting the help of such fine supporters of the idea of bipartisanship in foreign affairs as Senator Vandenberg and Congressman [Charles] Eaton of New Jersey [chairman of the House Foreign Affairs Committee], I realized the situation was more precarious than it would have been with a preponderantly Democratic Congress."[5]

At first blush, Truman had reason to worry. House Republican leaders wanted to cut taxes by 20 percent and cut spending enough to cover the cost—and, as isolationist sentiments reemerged within GOP ranks, defense and foreign aid were natural candidates for the chopping block. Fears mounted in the White House and State Department that the Republican majority would try to steer the country back to its isolationism of the 1920s and '30s. That would undercut Truman's efforts to reinforce America's new leadership position on the world stage, boosting the chances for global mayhem.

On foreign affairs, however, the 1946 elections would prove a blessing in disguise for the besieged president. With the British retreat, Greek and Turkish vulnerability, and Soviet aggressiveness on the world stage, Truman would soon contemplate the kind of dramatic response that begged for bipartisan consensus in Congress. Change of that magnitude would prove controversial under the best of circumstances, raising serious questions in Congress and across the country. The only way for such change to sustain broad public support, and to remain in place through Democratic and Republican presidencies to come, was for it to emerge from bipartisan consensus.

And, in the new Republican-controlled Eightieth Congress, no one was more interested in bipartisan consensus than the new chairman of the Senate Foreign Relations Committee, one Arthur H. Vandenberg.

10

"Vandenberg Expressed His Complete Agreement with Me"

VANDENBERG HAD MIXED EMOTIONS about Truman's outreach to him as the Greek-Turkish crisis unfolded in early 1947.

As he often did, Vandenberg felt that Truman was seeking his help without fully consulting him beforehand. Vandenberg first learned about the crisis during the February 27 meeting at which Acheson spoke in dramatic fashion. "The trouble," he reflected later, "is that these 'crises' never reach Congress until they have developed to a point where Congressional discretion is pathetically restricted. When things finally reach a point where a President asks us to 'declare war' there usually is nothing left except to 'declare war.'"[1]

Vandenberg was torn, however, for he recognized the larger stakes at hand. Over the previous year, he had often sounded the public siren about Soviet adventurism, and he shared Truman's view that Washington must take a stand. So he was generous about Truman's late notice, convincing himself that the crisis had come upon the president unexpectedly, leaving him without the time for a more leisurely consultation. "It must be remembered," he wrote, "that the whole thing was precipitated upon our government so suddenly that there really was very little opportunity for preliminary consultation and studies."[2]

In reality, the crisis had not arrived "so suddenly" for Truman or Vandenberg. Through the early weeks of 1947, each could see that Britain was nose-diving economically, retreating militarily, and reducing its footprint in the Mediterranean. Increasingly, its financial resources were drained, its factories were idle, and its people were jobless, freezing, and starving. "We have not enough resources to do all that we want to do," British officials wrote in a white paper they sent to the State Department in early January. "We have barely enough to do all that we *must* do. Whether we reckon in man power, coal, electricity, steel or national production as a whole, the conclusion is unavoidable."[3]

Moreover, Britain's government had sold at least half of its assets and assumed huge debt during the war, and it was now accumulating more debt and quickly draining $5 billion in U.S. and Canadian loans of the previous year—$3.75 billion of it from the United States, due largely to the efforts of Truman and Vandenberg. Britain's production and exports were too low, driven by inadequate manpower and productivity. Industry was using coal far faster than the country was mining it, the government cut coal allotments to industry in half in January, railroads lacked the cars to transport coal quickly enough to where it was needed, and some localities shut off their electricity temporarily because they lacked the coal to power it.

Britain's record cold of that winter made matters far worse, as Truman and Vandenberg could read in the newspapers. The worst blizzards since 1881 hit the country on January 25, dropping nearly a foot of snow in some places. Within days, Britain was paralyzed. "Roads and railways were blocked, rivers were frozen solid, ships were held in port, hundreds of communities were isolated, coal pits were closed, and winter wheat was killed," a State Department official wrote later. "Utility companies began to cut down immediately on electricity and gas supplies, and factories began closing in droves: they had been living hand to mouth as far as fuel was concerned, and now the hand was frozen."[4] February brought more calamitous, almost unfathomable news. By February 7, more than half of Britain's industry was idle. The government announced that, for several days, it would cut all electricity for industrial users in London and other major parts of the country and it would cut electricity to homes between 9:00 a.m. and noon and between 2:00 and 4:00 p.m. In London, offices, businesses, and restaurants resorted to candles and hurricane lamps. Across the country and beyond, observers called it an "Economic Dunkirk."

. . .

As Truman and Vandenberg watched from Washington, an exhausted, bankrupt, and desperate Britain reacted to its economic troubles by drastically curtailing its global presence. In the early days of 1947, Britain's government decided to reduce its armed forces from more than 1.4 million men to less than 1.1 million. On February 3, its embassy in Athens announced that Britain would cut its troops stationed in Greece in half. Eleven days later, Britain referred the future of Palestine, over which it had long exercised a mandate, to the United Nations. Four days after that, it announced that it would end its control over India.

In late February, London officially notified Washington that it would end its aid to Greece and Turkey in six weeks, prompting Truman's February 27 meeting with congressional leaders. Britain's notification came in complicated maneuvers between Friday, February 21, and Monday, February 24. By official protocol, Britain's ambassador, Lord Inverchapel, had to deliver the notification to Secretary of State George C. Marshall. When the ambassador sought Marshall that Friday, however, he had already left for a speaking engagement at Princeton University. So, Britain's embassy transmitted a copy of the official message to the State Department on Friday, giving officials a head start to consider the implications and begin sketching out U.S. responses. Lord Inverchapel delivered the official one to Marshall on Monday.

As Truman and Vandenberg soon realized, the United States would be replacing Britain on the world stage at a particularly perilous time in the Mediterranean region. Greece was split between ultra-right government sympathizers and Communist insurgents. Meanwhile, Moscow's puppet governments in Albania, Bulgaria, and Yugoslavia were arming and training the Communists in camps along the Greek border, hoping to topple the government and bring that nation into the Communist sphere. From Moscow, U.S. ambassador Walter Bedell Smith wrote that "only the presence of British troops had so far saved Greece from being swallowed into the Soviet orbit."[5] Turkey faced imminent danger as well but, as we have seen, less from Communist insurrection from within than Soviet designs from without. Though Moscow had backed down months earlier, U.S. officials recognized in early 1947 that a British retreat left the door open for a quick Soviet move against Turkey and the waterways it controlled.

Of Britain's collapse and growing Communist threats to democratic government not only in Greece and Turkey but across Europe, the *New York Times*' Anne O'Hare McCormick previewed on February 17 what Truman, Marshall, and Acheson would describe to congressional leaders ten days later. The crises "reveal how battered and shaken are the old strongholds of democracy in Europe, and how few these strongholds are. Most of all they throw the ball to us, giving notice that if freedom as we know it is to survive it's up to the United States to save it."[6]

. . .

As Truman and Vandenberg focused on the Greek-Turkish crisis, Acheson replaced Byrnes as the key go-between for the two—and he played the role masterfully.

Born on April 11, 1893, in Middletown, Connecticut, Dean Gooderham Acheson was the quintessential aristocratic blue blood; he both looked and acted the part. He was tall, mustachioed, and dapper. A graduate of Groton and Yale—where he was a member of Phi Beta Kappa and the Scroll and Key Society—he finished fifth in his class at Harvard Law School and clerked for Supreme Court Justice Louis Brandeis. He could be more than a little arrogant, especially when stirred by the mindless questions of publicity-seeking lawmakers at public hearings. He had a devilish sense of humor, which he often deployed to puncture the air at what he considered overly solemn events. When, in late 1944, Secretary of State Edward Stettinius presided over the swearing in of his new aides and asked Acheson, who was already serving as an assistant secretary, to say a few words, he began his remarks this way, "These little pigs went to market, but this little pig stayed home."[7]

"Support Free Peoples"

Truman and Acheson were very different. If the former was straightforward in language, the latter was often indirect and flowery, his writings filled with colorful adjectives. Here, in typical fashion, is how Acheson described Britain's foreign minister, Ernest Bevin: "His gait was the rolling one of a fat man; his clothes gave the impression of being enormous. His best feature was his eyes which, even behind heavy, horn-rimmed spectacles, lit up a face made undistinguished by an unusually broad and flat nose above full lips."[8] But, whatever his stylistic differences with Truman, Acheson was "unfailingly polite, patient, and deferential"[9] to him. Never, unlike Byrnes, did he confuse his role with Truman's. The president, in turn, appreciated Acheson's worldly wisdom and sober judgment. Nor did Truman ever forget that, when he returned to Washington by train after the dismal 1946 congressional elections, Acheson was the sole cabinet official who came to greet him at Union Station.

As for Vandenberg, Acheson's attitude toward him was a mix of deep respect for his statesmanship and lighthearted bemusement over his pomposity. Acheson understood the vital role that Vandenberg was playing in rallying Republican support for Truman's foreign policy. But he mocked Vandenberg's ego, his bursts of outrage at White House efforts to advance its policy without first paying due deference to the esteemed senator from Michigan. "Without warning a hurricane struck," Acheson later wrote of an incident with Vandenberg in 1943. "Its center was filled with a large mass of cumulonimbus cloud, often called Arthur Vandenberg, producing heavy word fall. Senator Vandenberg, for whom I came to have great respect and considerable admiration, had the rare capacity for instant indignation, often before he understood an issue, or even that there was one."

Of aid to Greece and Turkey, Acheson wrote, "Arthur Vandenberg's part in the enactment of this proposal into law was invaluable. He was born to lead a reluctant opposition into support of governmental proposals that he came to believe were in the national interest." Of the senator's vainglorious style, Acheson continued, "One of Vandenberg's stratagems was to enact publicly his conversion to a proposal, his change of attitude, a kind of political transubstantiation. The method was to go through a period of public doubt and skepticism; then find a comparatively minor flaw in the proposal, pounce upon it, and make much of it; in due course propose a change, always the Vandenberg amendment. Then, and only then, could it be given to his followers as true doctrine worthy of all men to be received . . . He was not engaged in strategy; rather he was a prophet pointing out to more earthbound rulers the errors and spiritual failings of their ways."[10]

Beyond Truman and Vandenberg, however, this was Acheson's moment, and he seized it with an unusual zealotry. America, he believed, faced "a task in some ways more formidable than the one described in the first chapter of Genesis."[11] That's why Acheson was so effective at Truman's February 27 meeting with congressional leaders after Marshall had failed to deliver; he believed in the cause enough to describe it in jaw-dropping fashion. That's also why his zeal could get the better of him on occasion. At a dinner party in April, he had an ugly confrontation with influential columnist Walter Lippmann, who was raising questions about the Truman Doctrine as Congress continued to debate it. After accusing Lippmann that night of "sabotaging" U.S. foreign policy, he called him the next morning to apologize.[12]

Acheson helped Truman by driving administration efforts, and he helped Vandenberg to convince skeptical lawmakers that these efforts were vital to U.S. national security.

. . .

Truman took a call from Acheson about Britain's retreat on the afternoon of February 21, 1947, and he quickly approved Acheson's plan of action.

It was Acheson who had suggested to Inverchapel, a close friend, that the British Embassy provide a copy of his message to Marshall on Friday, February 21, so that Truman's team could begin work that weekend. With the copy in hand, Acheson called Truman and Marshall. With their separate assents, he directed State Department officials to outline the implications and options for the United States. They produced a flurry of papers, to which Acheson and his staff gave a final review on

Sunday, February 23, at his Georgetown home before putting them on Marshall's desk for his review on Monday. "At that," Acheson recalled, "we drank a martini or two toward the confusion of our enemies."[13]

Truman met on February 26 with Marshall, Acheson, Eisenhower, and other officials, all of whom agreed that the United States would have to fill the void left by the British. "Greece and Turkey were still free countries being challenged by Communist threats both from within and without," Truman recalled.

> These free peoples were now engaged in a valiant struggle to preserve their liberties and their independence. America could not, and should not, let these free countries stand unaided. To do so would carry the clearest implications in the Middle East and in Italy, Germany, and France. The ideals and the traditions of our nation demanded that we come to the aid of Greece and Turkey and that we put the world on notice that it would be our policy to support the cause of freedom wherever it was threatened. The risks which such a course might entail were risks which a great nation had to take if it cherished freedom at all. The studies which Marshall and Acheson brought to me and which we examined together made it plain that serious risks would be involved. But the alternative would be disastrous to our security and to the security of free nations everywhere.[14]

The next morning, Vandenberg walked into Truman's office for the February 27 briefing on the Greek-Turkish crisis along with other key lawmakers—Senator Tom Connally, the Senate Foreign Relations Committee's top Democrat; Senate Democratic Leader Alben Barkley; Senator Henry Styles Bridges, the Republican chairman of the Joint Committee on Foreign Economic Cooperation; House Speaker Joseph W. Martin; House Democratic Leader Sam Rayburn; Republican Charles Eaton, chairman of the House Foreign Affairs Committee; and Rep. Sol Bloom, the House Foreign Affairs Committee's top Democrat. Truman, Marshall, and Acheson spoke; Vandenberg offered his support if Truman took his message "to the Congress and the country"; and administration officials began to draft a presidential address.

It wasn't long before the news leaked, the debate unfolded, and the challenges for Truman and Vandenberg grew larger.

. . .

Truman had asked all attendees on February 27 to stay mum about the meeting but—Washington being Washington—it was a forlorn hope. The ties between officials and journalists were too close and plentiful. The next day, the *New York Times'* James Reston described the meeting in considerable detail in a front-page story headlined, "Truman Asks Aid to Greece; British Unable to Bear Cost."

Vandenberg may have been the leaker. He was close to Reston, who sometimes served as a confidante to him. Most striking in Reston's write-up was his recognition, echoed in the coming days by leading lawmakers and other influential journalists, that the world was potentially witnessing a historic passing of the torch from Great Britain to the United States. "In choosing to put [its] economic stability first and in turning to the United States for assistance," Reston wrote, "the British have in effect asked whether the United States was prepared to assume a great part of the responsibility for world peace and stability assumed by Britain in the nineteenth century. That is what is at issue rather than the appropriation of a loan to a small Mediterranean country."[15]

Truman left Washington on March 2 to visit his mother in Grandview, Missouri, on his way to Mexico for a long-planned official trip, leaving his aides to fashion the speech that Vandenberg had suggested before returning on March 6. Vandenberg didn't know precisely what Truman would say when he spoke to Congress and the country, but he clearly understood the stakes. In a March 5 letter to House Republican and fellow Michigander John B. Bennett, Vandenberg pledged to avoid public comment until he had "all of the facts," but he nevertheless added, "I sense enough of the facts to realize that the problem in Greece cannot be isolated by itself. On the contrary, it is probably symbolic of the world-wise ideological clash between Eastern Communism and Western Democracy; and it may easily be the thing which requires us to make some very fateful and far-reaching decisions."[16]

"Support Free Peoples"

With Truman gone and Vandenberg mulling matters, a sense of crisis, foreboding, and transformation pervaded Washington. On March 2 the influential journalist Joseph Alsop, who wrote the thrice-weekly column "Matter of Fact" for the *New York Herald Tribune* with his brother Stewart, opined, "In the last week the optimistic foundation of American world policy has quite literally been shattered by a series of hammer blows."[17] On March 7 Truman cancelled a Caribbean cruise for which he was to leave the next day and scheduled a March 10 meeting on the Greek-Turkish crisis with a larger group of congressional leaders than that of February 27. On March 11 Walter Lippmann wrote, "Every one recognizes that what is called the Greek crisis is only a first installment of a very much greater challenge, arising from the fact that the British Empire is no longer able to do what it has done for more than a century—that is to block the expansion of the Russian empire into the Mediterranean, the Middle East, and into the Persian Gulf and the Indian Ocean. The United States is compelled to act because the collapse of Greece, Turkey and Iran would precipitate unmanageable turmoil and disorder, conflict and violence in Europe and in Asia."[18]

Vandenberg returned to Truman's office on March 10 as part of the larger group. Accounts differ as to what ensued. "Vandenberg expressed his complete agreement with me,"[19] Truman recalled later, and no one voiced opposition. Truman's account, however, seems rose-colored. A day before, some lawmakers had predicted a "showdown" with Truman over the details of what he was proposing, and Acheson acknowledged later that this congressional delegation was decidedly cooler to Truman's message than that of February 27. Vandenberg reiterated his call for Truman to speak publicly, and, Acheson said, no one committed himself to publicly support the president's request. News soon leaked that Truman would ask Congress for $250 million for Greece and $150 million for Turkey.

On Capitol Hill, opposition was growing to anything that would overtly support Greece's autocratic government, rescue Britain's empire, or establish a permanent U.S. beachhead in the Balkans. Concerned about that opposition, Vandenberg called Republican lawmakers together on the evening of March 10 to preview what Truman would announce two days later. Vandenberg said that he'd withhold his ultimate judgment until he saw the details, but he made a pitch for bipartisan cooperation. "This is a matter which transcends politics," he said. "There is nothing partisan about it. It is national policy at the highest degree."[20]

. . .

Complicating matters for Truman and Vandenberg were the foreign and domestic environments in which they were operating.

Truman sought congressional support not only because he believed that his Greek-Turkish package was necessary but also because, at that moment, Marshall was attending a Council of Foreign Ministers meeting in Moscow. A congressional rebuff of Truman's efforts to confront the Soviets would not just weaken the president politically at home, but it also would undercut Marshall's desire to speak in Moscow on behalf of a united America.

Also at that moment, Vandenberg was fighting a rearguard action to limit Republican efforts to cut federal spending so dramatically that it would leave no room for the Greek-Turkish funding. By late February the House had voted to limit total annual spending to $31.5 billion, cutting Truman's budget request by $6 billion (or more than 15 percent). Vandenberg, facing strong support among Senate Republicans for the House-passed funding ceiling, was forced to work with Democrats on compromise Senate legislation to raise it to $33 billion. Republicans were caught between hard-line conservatives who sought to fulfill their party's 1946 campaign promise to cut taxes across the board by 20 percent, and Vandenberg and like-minded colleagues who sought to secure funds for America's emerging global needs. "The real problem now facing the White House," wrote Joseph Alsop, who sympathized with Truman's efforts, "is how to deal with an economy-minded Congress, which has for months been living in a kind of dream world."[21]

Another obstacle that stood before Truman and Vandenberg—mostly in Republicans circles in Washington but also among the public—was renewed isolationism. At the late February speaking engagement at

Princeton that delayed his receipt of Britain's official notification about Greece and Turkey, Marshall expressed deep concern about the "natural tendency" of postwar Americans to turn inward, become "indifferent to what I might term the long-term dangers to the nation's security," and adopt the posture of a "spectator" who is "interested, yes, [in global affairs] but whose serious thinking is directed to local immediate matters . . . We should think now in long terms of years rather than in terms of months and their immediate political issues," Marshall said in words that he directed to Princeton's students. "You should fully understand the special position that the United States now occupies in the world, geographically, financially, militarily, and scientifically, and the implications involved. The development of a sense of responsibility for world order and security, and the development of a sense of overwhelming importance of this country's acts, and failures to act, in relation to world order and security—these in my opinion are great musts for your generation."

Truman shared Marshall's concerns about revived isolationism. "This was the time to align the United States of America clearly on the side, and the head, of the free world," he wrote later, describing his thoughts at the time. "I knew that George Washington's spirit would be invoked against me, and Henry Clay's, and all the other patron saints of the isolationists. But I was convinced that the policy I was about to proclaim was indeed as much required by the conditions of my day as was Washington's by the situation in his era."[22]

. . .

As Truman prepared to make his case, a team of writers was struggling to craft the words he would deliver.

Joseph Marion Jones, a State Department speechwriter, spent Sunday, March 2, crafting a five-page, triple-space draft, while, separately that day, State Department officials Loy Henderson and Gordon Merriam wrote a full-length draft. After Henderson sent both documents to Acheson, the latter called Jones on Monday night and assigned the drafting to him. Acheson held review sessions in his office with Jones and others on March 4, 5, and 6, with Jones taking notes at each session and then refining his draft. On March 6 Jones convinced Acheson to recommend that Truman not deliver a fireside chat by radio, which was then under consideration, arguing that the speech would be more forceful and, thus, more effective if Truman delivered it in person to Congress. On March 7 Acheson widened the circle of reviewers, sending the working draft both to Marshall, who was in Paris on his way to Moscow, and to White House Counsel Clark Clifford, Truman's trusted wordsmith. Marshall requested some deletions while Clifford suggested structural changes.

Also on March 7 Truman met at the White House with Acheson, Clifford, and other top White House aides and decided to seek congressional support for his Greek-Turkish proposals as soon as possible. He then met with the cabinet, told them what he planned to seek, and solicited advice about tactics. The consensus was that, as Acheson and Clifford had sought, the president should deliver an address to Congress. A day later, Clifford expressed his concern to Truman that the State Department draft lacked focus, and Truman directed him to involve himself more deeply in the drafting. Clifford worked closely with Acheson, Jones, and other State Department officials on March 9 and 10 on multiple drafts, some produced by Jones, others by Clifford and his aide, George Elsey.

In steering the final drafting by White House and State Department aides, Truman opted for salesmanship over nuance. Thus, he sided with Acheson and Clifford over Marshall, Bohlen, and Kennan, all of whom wanted him to tone down the rhetoric. On the morning of Sunday, March 9, as they were about to edit Jones's latest draft, Clifford told Elsey that the speech represented "the opening gun in a campaign to bring people to the realization that the war isn't over by any means." Thus, he pushed for crisper, sharper, tougher verbiage—for the kind of language that can rally a nation.

So, too, did Truman. He read the speech for the first time in the White House Cabinet Room on March 10, working with Clifford and other White House aides. He made some wording changes and sug-

"Support Free Peoples"

gested that the speech still needed what Clifford called "more punch." Meanwhile, Elsey circulated the draft to other key White House officials who, in turn, submitted their own suggestions for changes. Clifford then met with Acheson to negotiate the final additions and deletions.[23]

Marshall had cabled from Paris to suggest that Truman ease off a bit. "It seemed to General Marshall and me," recalled Bohlen, who was traveling with Marshall, "that there was a little too much flamboyant anti-Communism in that speech." Kennan, who was then teaching at the War College, agreed wholeheartedly with Marshall and Bohlen after State Department officials shared a draft with him. "The Russians might even declare war!" he warned. Acheson, however, agreed with Truman and Clifford that to sell the policy to Congress and the public, Truman needed to outline it in dramatic fashion.[24]

"I wanted no hedging in this speech," Truman wrote later. "This was America's answer to the surge of expansion of Communist tyranny. It had to be clear and free of hesitation or double talk."[25]

11

"The President's Message Faces Facts"

IN THE EIGHTIETH CONGRESS, which convened in January of 1947, Arthur Vandenberg was not just chairman of the Senate Foreign Relations Committee. His colleagues had chosen him to serve as the Senate's president pro tempore, its highest position. So after House Speaker Joseph W. Martin called the House to order on March 12 at about 12:45 p.m., Vandenberg walked down the middle aisle, flanked by the Senate secretary and House sergeant at arms, before ascending the dais that was just above and behind the podium. About fifty other senators then found good seats in the front of the House chamber.

Minutes later, Harry Truman walked down the aisle, escorted by senior lawmakers and carrying a black folder. Passing the rows of lawmakers, Truman noticed the seven-year-old daughter of House Democrat Thomas G. Abernathy of Mississippi sitting on his lap, pen and pad in hand in case she grew bored and wanted to draw. "Hello, little girl," the president said, beaming, before continuing his walk to the podium, where he would deliver one of the most consequential foreign policy addresses of any president.

"Mr. President, Mr. Speaker, Members of the Congress of the United States," Truman began. "The gravity of the situation which confronts the world today necessitates my appearance before a joint session of the Congress. The foreign policy and the national security of this country are involved." He reviewed the dire situations in Greece and Turkey, the urgent challenges they confronted, their desperate need for assistance, and the strategic stakes for the United States and the free world.

Greece, he said, "is today threatened by the terrorist activities of several thousand armed men, led by Communists, who defy the government's authority at a number of points, particularly along the northern boundaries." They were exploiting the "human want and misery" caused by retreating Nazis in early 1945 who had destroyed "virtually all" of the railways, roads, port facilities, communications, and the merchant marine and had burned more than a thousand villages. Now, some 85 percent of children were "tubercular," livestock and poultry had almost disappeared, and soaring inflation had wiped out almost all savings. Turkey, Truman said, was spared such wartime cruelty, but it nevertheless needed U.S. help just as badly to fend off threats to its "national integrity." Truman noted that, with Britain abandoning its commitments, no other nation but the United States had the wherewithal to replace it. Nor, he said, was the United Nations ready to do the job.

Truman made clear what a U.S. move to help Greece and Turkey would mean. "To ensure the peaceful development of nations, free from coercion, the United States has taken a leading part in establishing the United Nations. The United Nations is designed to make possible lasting freedom and independence for all its members. We shall not realize our objectives, however, unless we are willing to help free peoples to maintain their free institutions and their national integrity against aggressive movements that seek to impose upon them totalitarian regimes. This is no more than a frank recognition that totalitarian regimes imposed on free peoples, by direct or indirect aggression, undermine the foundations of international peace and hence the security of the United States."

Truman highlighted the increasingly bipolar world of U.S.-Soviet competition about which Acheson had spoken so forcefully on February 27. "At the present moment in world history," he explained, "nearly every nation must choose between alternative ways of life. The choice is too often not a free one. One way of life is based upon the will of the majority, and is distinguished by free institutions, representative government, free elections, guarantees of individual liberty, freedom of speech and religion, and freedom from political oppression. The second way of life is based upon the will of a minority forcibly imposed upon the majority. It relies upon terror and oppression, a controlled press and radio, fixed elections, and the suppression of personal freedoms."

Truman trotted out what became known years later as the "domino theory"—that the fall of one nation to Communism would prompt the fall of its neighbor, akin to a contagious disease. Greece's fall would endanger Turkey, cause "confusion and disorder" that "might well spread throughout the entire Middle East," and have a "profound effect" on Europe, where people were struggling to maintain freedom while rebuilding their societies from the devastation of war. "The seeds of totalitarian regimes," Truman explained, "are nurtured by misery and want. They spread and grow in the evil soil of poverty and strife. They reach their full growth when the hope of a people for a better life has died. We must keep that hope alive . . . If we falter in our leadership, we may endanger the peace of the world—and we shall surely endanger the welfare of our own nation."

With all that in mind, Truman enunciated the three sentences that, before long, would become the Truman Doctrine:

I believe that it must be the policy of the United States to support free peoples who are resisting attempted subjugation by armed minorities or by outside pressures.

I believe that we must assist free peoples to work out their own destinies in their own way.

I believe that our help should be primarily through economic and financial aid which is essential to economic stability and orderly political processes.

Its first installment would be $250 million for Greece and $150 million for Turkey. Reaction came swiftly.

. . .

The vision that Truman outlined, and that Vandenberg supported from the start, sent shock waves at home and abroad.

Truman's speech, the *Washington Post* wrote, was "one of the most momentous ever made by an American Chief Executive." It "raised a question," the Scripps-Howard newspaper chain stated, "as grave as any that has ever confronted the American people, and the answer to it may, for better or worse, decide our own ultimate destiny as a free people." "This is a time of decision—" the *Christian Science Monitor* declared, "one of the most momentous decisions in American history." "What the President was saying," the *New York Herald Tribune* concluded, "was that if the American system is to survive, it must prove its value— just as the totalitarian system has been trying to prove its own value."[1]

Truman's words delighted Western Europe. "Not since the United States entered World War II and assured the Allied victory have Europeans been so stirred by an American diplomatic act as they were by the President's message," the *New York Times'* Harold Callender wrote from Paris. "Some of those in closest touch with foreign affairs thought that, by checking Russian expansion, these new United States commitments would prevent the clash between Russia and the West that long has been regarded by many Europeans as inevitable." Echoes of Europe's recent pain resonated in its reactions to Truman's pledges. "They were viewed as the kind of commitments that, if given in 1936 or even in 1938, would have stopped Nazi Germany's expansion and prevented World War II."

Vandenberg expressed his support, further reassuring the allies. "The President's message faces facts and so must Congress," Vandenberg told reporters in words that he had worked out beforehand with Acheson. "The independence of Greece and Turkey must be preserved, not only for their own sakes but also in defense of peace and security for all of us. In such a critical moment the president's hands must be upheld. Any other course would be dangerously misunderstood." From the perspective of a relieved Europe, Vandenberg's words "indicated that the Republicans would back Mr. Truman" not only on the loans but, more importantly, the underlying policy.[2]

But if Truman's vision was big, bold, and revolutionary, what did it actually mean? No one was sure. "Congress stepped into its new task somewhat bewildered," the *New York Times* wrote the next day. "Mem-

"Support Free Peoples"

bers, as they listened to the Chief Executive, saw their country's foreign policy undergo radical change in the space of twenty-one minutes." Critics feared that Truman's words amounted to a "declaration of war" against Moscow, a proposal for limitless Lend-Lease–type aid for besieged governments, and a pronouncement that "intervention" was now the new U.S. foreign policy.[3]

At the broadest level, Truman was taking the Monroe Doctrine of 1823, through which President James Monroe warned European powers to stay out of the Western Hemisphere, applying it to the Soviet Union, and expanding its reach to the world writ large. If, Truman was telling the Soviets, they challenged "free peoples" who sought to "work out their own destinies in their own way," America would respond. Monroe had told Europe's powers that America's hemispheric backyard was vital to its national security; Truman was now telling Moscow that, in an age in which oceans no longer protected nations from the modern technology of warfare, the world was America's backyard—and the United States planned to protect it from Soviet encroachment.

· · ·

With Marshall in Moscow through late April, Acheson was Truman's key salesman on Capitol Hill for the Truman Doctrine and Greek-Turkish aid. He and Vandenberg worked together, often in tightly orchestrated ways, to ensure that the proposal advanced through the various stages of congressional review.

Their work began immediately after Truman's speech as lawmakers questioned the proposal's scope and criticized the details; it encompassed Senate Foreign Relations Committee hearings in late March; and it stretched through the Senate floor debate of early April. "I have never seen such willingness to cooperate with the legislature," Vandenberg said of Acheson that spring. "I think if I called him at ten in the morning and asked him to deliver the Washington Monument to my office by noon, he would somehow manage to treat this as a proper request and deliver it."[4]

Truman, of course, needed majority votes in both the Senate and

House. So Acheson and other top officials like Will Clayton, the undersecretary of state for economic affairs, also spent lots of time on the House side. But Vandenberg remained the main target of the administration's congressional outreach. He was undoubtedly the most influential Republican lawmaker on foreign policy. If Vandenberg could steer the Greek-Turkish aid through the Senate, the House surely would follow.

In addressing concerns and nourishing support, Acheson and Vandenberg were forced to walk a fine line. To secure the requisite votes, they needed to make two contradictory points—first, that the situation in the Mediterranean region was dire enough that the United States had to act boldly; and second, that the proposal did not presage a policy of unlimited U.S. action in which America would be everywhere, do everything, and bankrupt itself in the process. It would prove a delicate walk indeed.

Vandenberg invited the broadest possible Senate debate, one that extended beyond what his committee normally conducted. In the days after Truman's speech, he invited *all* senators—not just the thirteen on his committee—to submit questions that he would compile and send to the State Department for answers. That would make it likelier that, when the time came for the Senate to vote, non-committee senators would support the proposal. Senators sent 400 questions to Vandenberg, who consolidated them into 125 that he passed along to the State Department on Thursday, March 20, hoping to receive answers by the start of his committee's hearings the following Monday (although the State Department missed that deadline). The House Foreign Affairs Committee started its own hearings on March 20, with Acheson in the hot seat as its first witness. Vandenberg's committee—which reviewed Truman's proposal in a private meeting with Acheson and other top officials on March 13—opened its hearings on schedule on March 24, also with Acheson as the lead witness. Vandenberg invited non-committee senators to join the hearings and question the witnesses.

With Acheson's assistance, Vandenberg tried to leave no stone unturned in his quest for a Senate majority.

. . .

"Support Free Peoples"

Vandenberg was keenly aware of broad congressional concern over the implications of Truman's proposal, both for America's expanding global posture and for the funds needed to underwrite it. Just how broad should this new U.S. commitment be? Vandenberg made clear that he recognized his colleagues' worries.

"Congress must carefully determine," he said in his remarks to reporters after Truman's speech, "the methods and explore the details in so momentous a departure from our previous policies. The immediate problem may be treated by itself. But it is vitally important also to frankly weigh it for the future. We are at odds with communism on many fronts. We must primarily consult American welfare."[5]

Vandenberg had worked intensely in San Francisco to bring the United Nations to fruition, and he didn't want a new U.S. foreign policy to undermine it. This policy, he said, "must keep faith with the pledges to the Charter of the United Nations which we all have taken. We should proceed as far as possible within the United Nations." But Vandenberg also recognized that "that is not practical at the moment because the United Nations has no relief funds; and it has not yet concluded agreements with member nations for military support. We should immediately insist in the Security Council that these latter plans be consummated. We should also seek an immediate report from the United Nations Commission investigating alleged external invasion of Greek sovereignty."

Nevertheless, Vandenberg noted, the issue was less a global than a bilateral one. "The plain truth is that Soviet-American relationships are at the core of this whole problem. Every effort should be made to terminate these controversies. This effort must occur in plain understanding of basic principles which we shall not surrender. I repeat my own belief that it ought to be possible for Moscow and Washington to 'live and let live' since neither wants anything like war. Yet we find ourselves in constant disagreement respecting our mutually pledged objectives. There should be frank consultations between us—with all the cards face up on the table—in final search for mutual understanding."[6]

Truman's speech and Vandenberg's response set the terms of battle that would ensue on Capitol Hill through May.

12

"The Administration Made a Colossal Blunder in Ignoring the UN"

AS TRUMAN AND VANDENBERG steered the proposal to enactment, they benefited from a significant foundation of support on and off Capitol Hill.

"The President's address to Congress on March 12 has been the subject of almost unprecedented nation-wide discussion, and has been regarded as proposing a 'new' foreign policy of the greatest import," the State Department wrote in an undated memo as the debate unfolded. The department tracked public opinion, media coverage, and congressional support to help the administration and its allies (like Vandenberg) shape their messages, reinforce popular notions, and alleviate concerns.

The public favored economic aid to Greece and Turkey "by a wide margin," the State Department reported, but was divided over sending military supplies and opposed to deploying military advisers. Public support was rooted in agreement about "halt[ing] Soviet or Communist expansion," though Americans accepted that role "with reluctance and misgivings." The strongest opposition came from "'liberals' of the Henry Wallace school" and "consistent opponents of foreign policy measures which project the United States actively in world affairs." Specific concerns involved the "failure" to consider the UN route, the "efficacy and ultimate cost of 'trying to fight Communism with dollars,'" and the possibility that Greek and Turkish aid would lead to war.

Most of the press and public commentators expressed support, including a broad swath of newspapers of the left, right, and middle.

"This broad support," the State Department concluded, "was based largely on the conviction that American national interests require resistance to the threat of Soviet expansionism, and that the program laid down by the President offered such resistance." Leading newspapers that backed Truman's proposal included the *New York Times*, *New York Herald Tribune*, *Washington Post*, *Washington Star*, *Baltimore Sun*, *Chicago Times*, *Atlanta Constitution*, and *Denver Post*. *Time* and *Barron's* were among the supportive periodicals, and key public figures who backed the proposal included former GOP presidential nominees Thomas Dewey and Alf Landon and labor leader David Dubinsky. Congressional support crossed party lines, and, at the time of this memo, the twenty-six senators (including Vandenberg) and thirty-five House members who expressed support or "qualified" support outnumbered the fourteen senators and twenty-nine House members who expressed opposition.

Nevertheless, partisan politics reared its ugly head early on, embarrassing Truman, angering Vandenberg, and complicating their task.

. . .

Vandenberg was eager to help Truman convince Congress to support Greek-Turkish aid because he believed the stakes were too high to do otherwise. But Vandenberg always portrayed himself as a loyal Republican and stressed his independence from the administration. He knew he would lose influence with Republicans if they began to believe he had evolved from bipartisan collaborator to administration lackey. "Many people seem to think that I act as sort of a Co-secretary of State in connection with foreign policy decisions," he reflected that spring. "This of course is totally erroneous. Indeed, it would be a physical impossibility."[1]

That explains why Vandenberg reacted so strongly to a March 17 effort by the Democratic National Committee to convince its Republican counterpart to embrace the Truman Doctrine officially. Gael Sullivan, the Democratic National Committee's executive director, had invited Carroll Reece, the Republican National Committee's chair-

"Support Free Peoples"

man, to cosign a public statement "reaffirming both parties' support of America's foreign policy as outlined by President Truman with the concurrence of Arthur H. Vandenberg." Sullivan called Vandenberg the "authorized spokesman for the Republican party in matters of foreign policy" and said that because he had expressed support for the president's policies, the two parties should do so as well, thus sending a unified message to the world.[2]

Vandenberg was furious. "When bipartisan foreign policy gets into the rival hands of partisan national committees," he declared in a Senate floor speech, "it is in grave danger of losing its precious character. No matter how worthy the announced intentions, it can put foreign policy squarely into politics which, under such circumstances, are no longer calculated to stop at the water's edge . . . Bipartisan foreign policy is not the result of political coercion but of nonpolitical conviction. I never have even pretended to speak for my party in my foreign policy activities . . . What I decline to do myself I cannot permit the executive director of the Democratic National Committee to do in my name."[3] Tom Connally, the Senate Foreign Relations Committee's top Democrat, agreed. So did Truman, who later told reporters that he didn't know of Sullivan's letter until he read about it in the newspaper.

When the furor eased, Sullivan suggested that he wouldn't propose any more bold ideas without checking first with a higher-up.

. . .

"The Administration made a colossal blunder in ignoring the UN," Vandenberg wrote in an undated note to himself sometime after Truman's speech. It was the most controversial aspect of Truman's proposal, the issue with the biggest potential to derail congressional approval, and, thus, the problem Vandenberg tried to address even before his committee's hearings began.

On Capitol Hill a revolt erupted in both chambers. In the Senate on March 25, Democrats Claude Pepper of Florida (nicknamed "Red Pepper" for his frequent defense of Moscow) and Glenn H. Taylor of Idaho proposed legislation to provide $100 million in U.S. economic aid to

Greece and let the United Nations administer it. "There is no reason why," Pepper declared, "to help the Greek people, we have to destroy the United Nations." In the House, Minnesota Rep. John A. Blatnik, a Democrat-Farmer Laborite, proposed the same measure. Such other notables as New York's former mayor, Fiorello H. La Guardia, also proposed a UN approach. They had public sentiment on their side, with Americans favoring a UN solution by more than two to one.[4]

Acheson blamed himself for the ruckus, conceding he should have recommended that Truman first seek a UN effort to protect Greece and Turkey and, after it died at the hands of an inevitable Soviet veto, propose unilateral U.S. action. Vandenberg and Acheson understood that UN supporters needed the "political cover" that would enable them to support a U.S. effort. Rather than accept Acheson's offer to solve the problem, however, Vandenberg seized the chance to put his name on a solution.

The senator pursued a two-step approach that amounted to literary window dressing. First, he drafted a preamble to Truman's proposal that recognized the UN's stature but acknowledged that it was "not now in a position to furnish Greece and Turkey the financial and economic assistance which is immediately required." Second, he teamed with Connally to add a provision that enabled the Security Council or the General Assembly to end the U.S. aid program if the United Nations had taken its own action.

Vandenberg's efforts, Acheson wrote later, "must have seemed either silly or cynical or both in London, Paris, and Moscow." The preamble amounted to soothing words, while the provision on UN action was equally meaningless because neither the Security Council nor the General Assembly would find the agreement or the resources to create a program. "Nevertheless," Acheson added, "it was a cheap price for Vandenberg's patronage and warmly welcomed by Warren Austin, our representative at the United Nations."[5]

It would prove to be enough.

. . .

"Support Free Peoples"

Vandenberg opened his committee's hearings at 10:00 a.m. on March 24, with his colleagues seated on the dais in Room 318 of the Senate Office Building and Acheson situated across from them at the witness table.

Acheson, who was serving as acting secretary with Marshall in Moscow, read a long statement that built on Truman's speech of March 12, bringing the president's points to life in richer, more graphic, and more dramatic terms. He also sought to answer some of the questions that senators had submitted as part of the 125 queries that Vandenberg had sent to the State Department. On the United Nations, Acheson said that Greece had, in fact, received "substantial relief assistance" from the United Nations Relief and Rehabilitation Administration (UNRRA), which was created in 1943 and folded into the United Nations, but that UNRRA was going out of business that spring and couldn't help more. The United Nations, he explained, had no other funds or experts to assist Greece and Turkey. On concerns about a huge U.S. commitment to Greece and Turkey, Acheson said the administration had no plans to send troops and didn't see the need to do so anyway. On suspicions that Greek-Turkish aid would underwrite continuing British policy in the region, Acheson said that Washington alone would design the aid program and implement it through agreements with Greece and Turkey. On worries that Greek-Turkish aid would trigger an unending series of aid packages for countries across the globe, Acheson said the administration would weigh any other aid request on its own and not necessarily model future action on Greek-Turkish aid. On fears that Greek-Turkish aid would lead to war with the Soviets, Acheson said, "These are not acts which lead to war. They lead in the other direction. They help to maintain the integrity and independence—what the United Nations Charter calls the 'sovereign equality'—of states."

When Acheson finished, Vandenberg relinquished his right as chairman to begin questioning him, letting other committee members go first. At times during the questioning, however, he piped up to throw a question or two at Acheson in ways that would help alleviate the concerns that senators were airing. Rather than grill Acheson, Vandenberg tried to help him make his case.

At one point, Vandenberg's questioning highlighted the reality that transferring the problem to the United Nations would delay aid to Greece and Turkey—and the United States would end up providing the bulk of it anyway.

VANDENBERG: If it were transferred, the first necessity would be— would it not?—to call a special meeting of the General Assembly, which requires action either by the Security Council or by a majority of the member nations. Is that correct?

ACHESON: Yes, sir. That is correct.

VANDENBERG: That would involve, I suppose, on a most hopeful basis, thirty days?

ACHESON: I should think at least thirty days, senator.

VANDENBERG: Then when you got into the General Assembly, the only thing it would do, in order to get relief funds, would be to make a special assessment upon the member nations, inasmuch as it has no such funds and is not organized for the purpose of administering such funds. It would have to make a special assessment, would it not? And in that special assessment, under the allocation of assessments, we immediately would confront the major burden of the assessment. Is that correct?

ACHESON: That is right.

At another point, Vandenberg sought to allay continuing fears that the Truman Doctrine portended an unending series of U.S. responses to aggression overseas that would mirror the Greek-Turkish proposal.

VANDENBERG: In other words, I think what you are saying is that wherever we find free peoples having difficulty in the maintenance of free institutions, and difficulty in defending against aggressive movements that seek to impose upon them totalitarian regimes, we do not necessarily react in the same way each time, but we propose to react.

ACHESON: That, I think, is correct.

With its major concerns alleviated, Vandenberg's committee voted unanimously on April 3 to send Truman's proposal to the full Senate.

. . .

"Let us be totally plain about it," Vandenberg told the Senate on April 8 as it opened debate on Truman's proposal.

"It is a plan to forestall aggression which, once rolling, could snowball into global danger of vast design. It is a plan for peace. It is a plan to sterilize the seeds of war. We do not escape war by running away from it. No one ran away from war at Munich. We avoid war by facing facts. This plan faces facts."

Vandenberg painted a picture of unrelenting Soviet aggression and dire threats to U.S. national security if the United States rejected the urgent pleas of Greece and Turkey. "The plain fact seems to be," he told his colleagues,

> that if the Greeks, in their extremity, are not successfully helped to help themselves to maintain their own healthy right to self-determination, another Communist dictatorship will rise at this key point in world geography. Then Turkey, long mobilized against a Communist war of nerves, faces neighboring jeopardy. The two situations are inseparable. Turkey confronts no such internal extremity as does Greece; but it requires assistance to bulwark its national security. The president says that the maintenance of its national integrity is essential to the preservation of order in the Middle East. If the Middle East falls within the orbit of aggressive Communist expansion, the repercussions will echo from the Dardenelles to the China Sea and westward to the rims of the Atlantic. Indeed, the Middle East, in this foreshortened world, is not far enough away for safety from our own New York or Detroit or Chicago or San Francisco.

Most noteworthy—as in his remarks after Truman's speech— Vandenberg highlighted the signal that the Senate, with its decision, would send to U.S. allies and adversaries alike. "To repudiate the president of the United States at such an hour," he declared, "could display a divisive weakness which might involve far greater jeopardy than a sturdy display of united strength. We are not free to ignore the price of noncompliance." That price, he explained,

> would be the forfeiture of all hope to effectively influence the attitude of other nations in our peaceful pursuit of international righteousness from now on. It would stunt our moral authority and mute our voice. It would encourage dangerous contempts. It would invite provocative misunderstandings of the tenacity with which we are prepared to defend our fundamental ideals . . . What would you think if you were a citizen of Athens? . . . What would you think if you were a citizen of Ankara? What would you think if you were a citizen of any other of the weary, war-torn nations who are wondering this afternoon whether the torch still burns in the upraised hand of liberty; whether it is hopeless to struggle on toward democratic freedom? And what would you think . . . if you were the Politburo in Moscow's Kremlin?

Through the Senate debate, which ran on and off until April 22, Vandenberg replied to senators' wide-ranging questions, clarified details, and explained strategic goals. He strongly opposed efforts to scale back Truman's proposal by, for instance, assisting Greece but not Turkey or by providing the economic but not military aid. Though acknowledging that neither he nor anyone else could confidently predict the future, he argued strenuously that the risks of U.S. inaction far outweighed those of action.

So inspired, the Senate voted 67–23 for the measure on April 22; the House followed suit on a 287–107 vote on May 6.

. . .

Compared to Vandenberg's stirring words, which earned him the applause of his colleagues, Truman's language was muted when he signed the measure on May 22.

"The Act," he said, "is an important step in the building of the peace. Its passage by overwhelming majorities in both Houses of the Congress is proof that the United States earnestly desires peace and is willing to make a vigorous effort to help create conditions of peace. The conditions

"Support Free Peoples"

of peace include, among other things, the ability of nations to maintain order and independence, and to support themselves economically."

Despite Truman's modest description, the doctrine that he had enunciated and that he and Vandenberg brought to life in the form of Greek-Turkish aid not only marked a dramatic break with America's isolationist past. It also would help shape the foreign policies of presidents to come for well over a half century. Truman's policy "to support free peoples who are resisting attempted subjugation by armed minorities or by outside pressures" and to "assist free peoples to work out their own destinies in their own way" came to life again in Truman's defense of South Korea after the North's invasion in 1950; in John Kennedy's stirring words at the Berlin Wall in 1963; in America's calamitous war in Vietnam; in Jimmy Carter's naive promise to make human rights the unchallenged driver of his foreign policy; in Ronald Reagan's covert assistance to democratic forces in Eastern Europe that helped end the Cold War; in Bill Clinton's successful effort to halt Serbian atrocities in the Balkans in the 1990s; in George W. Bush's Freedom Agenda that helped inspire the so-called Color Revolutions in Georgia, Ukraine, and Kyrgyzstan in the early twenty-first century; and in the military protection that Barack Obama provided to enable rebels to topple Muammar Gaddafi in Libya.

What was revolutionary in 1947 became routine in the decades to come. America assumed the mantle of global leadership not just to protect itself, not just to offset the aggressive designs of its superpower rival, but to provide tangible assistance to advance freedom far from home. Over the years, Americans came to see this role as intrinsic to U.S. foreign policy and reacted adversely when presidents refused to play it. In response to the short shrift that Richard Nixon and Gerald Ford gave to human rights in the mid-1970s, Congress wrote laws that elevated human rights in the operations of the State Department as well as in the disbursal of foreign aid. George H. W. Bush was widely criticized for doing nothing as slaughter ensued in the Balkans, while Obama came under similar attack as horror unfolded in Syria.

. . .

By early 1947, however, Truman and Vandenberg recognized that the challenge to U.S. national security was not just military, not just rooted in the designs of a hungry rival in Moscow. The challenge was rooted as well in a European economy that had collapsed, leaving millions of people across a devastated continent without food, housing, or hope. The United States had allocated more than $15 billion in relief for a host of European countries since 1945, but the patchwork measures could not keep pace with demand. As desperation grew, so, too, did opportunities for Soviet-backed Communists in France, Italy, and elsewhere to win elections or mount insurrections by sowing social discord.

Even before Truman signed the Greek-Turkish aid bill, he and his top advisers were coalescing around a landmark approach to the economic collapse across the Atlantic, a way to confront the problem comprehensively. It would bear the name of Truman's iconic secretary of state, George C. Marshall. And it would require a close collaboration with Vandenberg to bring it to fruition.

PART 3

"The World Situation Is Very Serious"

ON THURSDAY, JUNE 5, 1947, Harry Truman was tending to his duties in Washington. He held his 108th press conference; worked the phones; and conducted separate meetings with his cabinet, Commerce Secretary Averell Harriman, Republican foreign policy adviser John Foster Dulles, and a delegation of House members.

At the morning press conference, Truman announced his appointments of Nebraska's former governor, Dwight Griswold, as chief of the United States mission to Greece and former top Red Cross official Richard F. Allen as field administrator for relief in Europe. He also responded forcefully to Senator Robert Taft's charge that, in providing $400 million in Greek-Turkish aid, he was abandoning efforts to control inflation. "The Administration did not advocate the Greek-Turkish aid program for the purpose of bringing prices down," Truman explained, reading a long statement that he also distributed to reporters. "It advocated that program for two important reasons—first, to extend aid to starving millions and to help restore their economies so that the world may regain its prosperity in the long run; and second, to help those nations which want to preserve their freedoms and to set up a bulwark against totalitarian aggression."

That afternoon, Arthur Vandenberg was at his seat in the Senate, where he and his colleagues were ratifying peace treaties between the "Allied and Associated Powers" (including the United States) and the defeated nations of Italy, Rumania, and Hungary. While working months earlier in Europe with Jimmy Byrnes, the then-secretary of state, Vandenberg had helped bring those treaties to fruition. On the Senate floor that day, however, he was quiet. No one mounted a serious challenge to any of the treaties, so Vandenberg merely provided his votes for them.

For Truman and Vandenberg, their focus would shift later that day to a far more dramatic initiative. In the quaint town of Cambridge, Massachusetts, Secretary of State George C. Marshall would, as he had promised Harvard president James B. Conant a week earlier, "make a few remarks . . . and perhaps a little more"[1] at a luncheon to follow Harvard's commencement (where he would receive an honorary degree). Truman didn't know precisely what Marshall would say at the luncheon in Harvard Yard for alumni, parents, and others because Marshall continued refining his remarks on his way to Cambridge. Truman wasn't worried, however. He knew that, broadly speaking, Marshall would invite Europe's teetering nations to come together, assess their financial needs, craft a comprehensive strategy to rebuild their economies, and ask the United States for the funds to implement it. Besides, he trusted Marshall to the point of hero worship.

For two years, Truman had proposed multiple rounds of short-term relief for particular nations, and Vandenberg had spearheaded the successful efforts to secure their congressional approval. As recently as February of 1947, Truman had proposed $350 million for Austria, Hungary, Poland, Italy, Trieste, China, and Greece "to assist in completing the great task of bringing relief from the ravages of war to the people of the liberated countries." "On humanitarian grounds, and in the light of our own self-interest as well," he said, "we must not leave the task unfinished. We cannot abandon the peoples still in need. To do so would be to replace hope with despair in the hearts of these peoples and thus to undermine the spiritual and economic stability upon which our own hopes for a better world must rest." Vandenberg agreed, cautioning the Senate that, without the aid, "famine, disease, and disaster will stalk a desperate Europe."[2] By May, Vandenberg had convinced the Senate Foreign Relations Committee to approve it unanimously, steered it through the Senate, and persuaded the House to rethink its initial decision to cut the request to $200 million.

That spring, however, Truman and Vandenberg both came to realize what other officials had already suspected—that by providing only short-term relief for individual countries, they were like skippers on a leaky boat, plugging holes to ensure that it didn't sink but leaving it ill equipped to make its way to shore through increasingly turbulent waters. Europe's economy still hadn't recovered from the destruction of war, and, across the continent, its member nations needed a comprehensive strategy to restore the smooth operations of business and labor, factory and farm, currency and trade. Without it, U.S. officials feared that desperate populations across Europe would vote for Soviet-sympathizing Communist parties or Communists would mount successful violent insurrections.

"It is already evident," Marshall stated over lunch at Harvard in a dry, business-like manner that belied the earthshaking ramifications of his remarks,

> that, before the United States government can proceed much further in its efforts to alleviate the situation and help start the European world on its way to recovery, there must be some agreement among the countries of Europe as to the requirements of the situation and the part those countries themselves will take in order to give proper effect to whatever action might be undertaken by this government. It would be neither fitting nor efficacious for this government to undertake to draw up unilaterally a program designed to place Europe on its feet economically. This is the business of the Europeans. The initiative, I think, must come from Europe. The role of this country should consist of friendly aid in the drafting of a European program and of later support of such a program so far as it may be practical for us to do so. The program should be a joint one, agreed to by a number, if not all European nations.

...

The Marshall Plan—the third major element of America's revolutionary new foreign policy—spurred a year-long collaboration between Truman and Vandenberg, in which they crafted the details and plotted the strategy to bring it to fruition.

Through the summer and fall, as Western Europe catalogued its needs, Truman and Vandenberg met at the White House with top administration officials to sketch out the details of how the Marshall Plan would work. Capping off months of study, Truman asked Congress in December of 1947 for a then-stunning $17 billion over four years to fund it. To put the figure in perspective, *total* federal spending for all foreign and domestic activities in 1947 was $34.5 billion. With spendthrift and isolationist Republican opponents in the Senate and House plotting to kill the plan, Vandenberg convinced Truman to accept a series of changes over the next few months to address legitimate concerns and clear the political hurdles to passage. Most importantly, the administration deleted the four-year, $17 billion figure and agreed to seek funds on an annual basis, reduced the first installment from $6.8 billion for fifteen months to $5.3 billion for twelve months, and moved the program out from the State Department so that its administrator would report to the president. As Vandenberg calibrated each move carefully to dilute the opposition, support for the plan grew.

At Vandenberg's direction, the Senate Foreign Relations Committee held hearings from January 8 through February 5 of 1948, taking testimony from more than ninety witnesses and receiving written statements from scores of others. The witnesses included cabinet members and ambassadors; business, labor, and agricultural leaders; college professors and editors; and officials from church, women's, civic, veterans, trade, and other groups. The committee approved the first installment unanimously on February 13; Vandenberg opened the Senate debate on March 1 with a 9,000-word address that his colleagues applauded heartily; and the Senate approved the plan on a 69–17 vote on March 14. The House approved it in somewhat different form, a House-Senate conference committee drafted a compromise that both chambers then passed, and the president signed it into law on April 3, 1948.

. . .

Truman knew that Marshall's words at Harvard—quickly labeled the "Marshall Plan"—would carry huge geopolitical implications.

After all, the United States was taking dead aim at Soviet efforts to exploit the chaos and expand its reach across Europe. Washington was proposing to spend enormous sums to ensure that Western European governments remained free and democratic. By offering those governments an economic lifeline, the Marshall Plan was designed to provide hope to the millions of aimless, jobless, starving, and freezing people of Western Europe, restoring their faith in the West and convincing them to eschew the tempting promises of Communism.

Vandenberg recognized the implications as well. He later called Marshall's speech a "shot heard 'round the world."

13

"Desperate Men Are Liable to Destroy the Structure of Their Society"

AS TRUMAN AND VANDENBERG gazed across the Atlantic in the spring of 1947, they feared the same nightmare.

A full two years after the Nazis had surrendered, Europe remained ravaged, its economy in disarray. Millions were starving, freezing, or sick, and many roads, rails, and ports were still damaged and unusable. The harsh winter of 1946–47 had killed millions of animals and destroyed millions of acres of cropland, causing severe springtime shortages of milk, eggs, butter, meat, fish, oils, fats, wheat, bread, flour, cereal, beans, potatoes, and other vegetables and driving food prices sky high. Even with millions of tons of U.S. food aid, Europeans survived on daily rations that fell far short of recommended minimums. Tuberculosis returned as Europe's number one killer, while typhus raged across the Balkans. Meanwhile, as the *Washington Post* reported in April, "doctors still are few, hospitals scarce, housing inadequate and fuel almost nonexistent."[1] Across Europe, frustration boiled over. In Germany's British-controlled zone, hundreds of thousands of people across several cities protested food shortages in the largest mass demonstrations since Hitler's rule, smashing windows and overturning vehicles. In Vienna, protestors squared off with police in front of the Federal Chancellory.

"It took almost two years for Europeans and Americans to realize," journalist Theodore White wrote from the continent, "that Europe was not only incapable of resistance to the Russians, but that she was engaged in a desperate ordeal of survival that had nothing to do with the Soviet

Union. The tides of trade in which Europe lived had vanished. Like a whale left gasping on the sand, Europe lay rotting in the sun."[2]

Aid alone could not rescue Europe because its economy was not functioning. Businesses weren't operating, workers weren't working, factories weren't producing, farmers weren't harvesting, and nations weren't trading. A continent that was still struggling to survive would have to rebuild the architecture of a working economy if it hoped to address the needs of its people. The more Europe struggled, the angrier its people grew—and the more endangered its governments became.

"But what is Europe now?" Winston Churchill asked in a speech at London's Royal Albert Hall in May of 1947. "It is a rubble-heap, a charnel-house, a breeding-ground of pestilence and hate. Ancient nationalistic feuds and modern ideological factions distract and infuriate the unhappy, hungry populations. Evil teachers urge the paying-off of old scores with mathematical precision, and false guides point to unsparing retribution as the path to prosperity. Is there then to be no respite?"[3]

It was, as Truman and Vandenberg recognized, a situation ripe for exploitation, with Soviet-led Communists plotting to overthrow Western democracies through the niceties of electoral ballots or the violence of bloody coups.

. . .

Truman understood the challenge and focused intensely on Europe's suffering almost from the moment he assumed the presidency, describing the situation in graphic terms and pushing relentlessly for America to respond.

"Europe today is hungry," Truman told the nation by radio after returning from the Potsdam Conference with Soviet and British leaders in August of 1945. "I am not talking about Germans," he said, recognizing that Americans had little empathy for them.

> I am talking about the people of the countries which were overrun and devastated by the Germans, and particularly about the people of Western Europe. Many of them lack clothes and fuel and tools and shelter and raw materials. They lack the means to restore their cities and their factories. As the win-

ter comes on, the distress will increase. Unless we do what we can to help, we may lose next winter what we won at such terrible cost last spring. Desperate men are liable to destroy the structure of their society to find in the wreckage some substitute for hope. If we let Europe go cold and hungry, we may lose some of the foundations of order on which the hope for worldwide peace must rest.

At that point, Vandenberg was less certain than Truman that the United States should come to Europe's rescue. When, after months of discussion between top U.S. and British officials in late 1945, Truman proposed a $3.75 billion loan to Britain, Vandenberg expressed his uncertainty in a December 19 letter to Dulles. "The British loan is a tough conundrum for me and for my Republican colleagues," he wrote. Vandenberg worried that a U.S. loan to Britain would invite a request from Moscow—and, if Washington rejected the latter due to its growing unhappiness over Moscow's global aggressiveness, that that, in turn, would end all cooperation among Washington, London, and Moscow. Further, he took offense at British complaints that Washington was offering only $3.75 billion. "We are notified in advance that we are going to get no good will out of this largesse," Vandenberg observed, asking Dulles, "If we are not going to get good will what are we going to get?"

Vandenberg eventually came around, however, lending his support to the legislation that reached Truman's desk in July of 1946. He was swayed by Europe's growing struggles and Moscow's brash efforts to exploit them. On the Senate floor, Vandenberg told his colleagues that the United States must seize "the economic as well as the moral leadership in a wandering world which must be stabilized just as necessarily for us as for others."[4]

With isolationist sentiment running high in the isolationist Midwest, Vandenberg received lots of mail from unhappy constituents.

. . .

Truman was particularly concerned about Europe's food crisis, and his efforts to alleviate hunger on the continent were frequent, creative, and increasingly urgent. While deploying governmental resources, he also tapped the private sector. In May of 1945, he ordered the heads of his war-related agencies, such as the War Production Board, to make European relief a priority. In June, he urged Americans to conserve food "in every possible way" so the United States could send surpluses to Europe.

Truman intensified his efforts in 1946. In February, he ordered emergency measures to conserve food and ship it overseas—including a "vigorous campaign" to convince Americans to conserve bread and other food; the discontinued use of wheat to produce alcohol and beer; inventory controls for wheat and flour; and preferences to move wheat, corn, meat, and other foods by rail for shipment to Europe.

"We in this country," he told the nation that month in a statement, "have been consuming about 3,300 calories per person per day. In contrast, more than 125 million people in Europe will have to subsist on less than 2,000 calories a day; 28 million will get less than 1,500 calories a day and in some parts of Europe, large groups will receive as little as 1,000 calories. Under these circumstances it is apparent that only through superhuman efforts can mass starvation be prevented. In recognition of this situation Great Britain only yesterday announced cuts in rations of fats and a return to the dark wartime loaf of bread." In April Truman told the nation by radio, "America is faced with a solemn obligation. Long ago we promised to do our full part. Now we cannot ignore the cry of hungry children. Surely we will not turn our backs on the millions of human beings begging for just a crust of bread. The warm heart of America will respond to the greatest threat of mass starvation in the history of mankind."

In the ensuing months Truman created a committee of leading citizens to craft a public campaign of voluntary food conservation; appealed to Americans by radio to cut their food consumption two days each week to what the average person in "hungry lands" eats; urged individuals and groups to send food packages through the private Cooperative for American Remittances to Europe (which later became CARE); threatened to seize control of the railroads if striking workers didn't return to work not only because the strike was hurting America's economy, but because it was jeopardizing bread supplies for forty-five million people in Europe; and appointed former top federal official Granville Conway to serve as coordinator of emergency export programs and ensure that Washington met its goals for food exports.

By the middle of 1947, the United States had provided more than $15 billion in postwar relief, mostly for Europe. Congressional critics suggested the figure was even higher.[5] The enormous sums raised questions: Why did Europe's needs remain so great? Was the money doing any good? Was Europe wasting it? Should Washington provide more?

. . .

In the spring of 1947, Truman and Vandenberg recognized that the United States needed to try a new approach.

At Truman's direction that spring, the administration was a flurry of activity in pursuit of a new goal—systemic change. Rather than continue distributing aid to address this particular need or that, administration officials came to see that the United States needed to help rebuild the foundation of Europe's economy. It was a monumental challenge, one that Truman telegraphed publicly and on which many of his top aides contributed significantly.

"Everywhere on earth, nations are under economic pressure," Truman said at Baylor University in March. "Countries that were devastated by the war are seeking to reconstruct their industries. Their need to import, in the months that lie ahead, will exceed their capacity to export. And so they feel that imports must be rigidly controlled. Countries that have lagged in their development are seeking to industrialize. In order that new industries may be established, they, too, feel that competing imports must be rigidly controlled.

"Nor is this all," the president continued. "The products of some countries are in great demand. But buyers outside their borders do not hold the money of these countries in quantities large enough to enable them to pay for the goods they want. And they find these moneys difficult to earn. Importing countries, when they make their purchases, therefore seek to discriminate against countries whose currencies they do not possess. Here, again, they feel that imports must be rigidly controlled."

Truman's views were reinforced a month later by Marshall, who had returned from Moscow after attending a Council of Foreign Ministers meeting. There, Marshall and his aide, Charles Bohlen, had met privately with Stalin. As the Soviet dictator brushed off concerns about mounting U.S.-Soviet disagreements while unnervingly doodling wolves' heads in red pen, Marshall concluded that Stalin wanted more European chaos that he could exploit, helping Communists to seize power across Western Europe. On his flight home from Moscow, Marshall spoke to his aides about a systemic approach to Western Europe's troubles. Addressing the nation by radio after his return, he said of Europe, "the patient is sinking while the doctors deliberate." Marshall summoned George Kennan, the new head of his new Policy Planning Staff, and ordered him to craft a plan to address Europe's economic crisis within two weeks. When Kennan asked Marshall whether he had any further guidance, the general replied, "Avoid trivia."[6]

Around that time, Truman also heard from Will Clayton, a top State Department official whom the president had sent to Europe to study the problems up close. Clayton, who drafted Truman's Baylor speech, had developed a deep understanding of economics through a lifetime of private sector success. Born on February 7, 1880, in Tupelo, Mississippi, Clayton was a multimillionaire cotton trader before he was forty. He believed in free trade and stable money, aligning himself with FDR in the 1930s when Republicans tilted toward protectionism and delivering speeches across the country to promote his free-market views. Reflecting his prominence, *Time* dubbed him "King Cotton" on its cover. After working for the War Industries Board's Cotton Distribution Committee during World War I, Clayton returned to government in 1940 as a "dollar-a-year" man with the Reconstruction Finance Corporation. He then moved to the Export-Import Bank before Roosevelt brought him to the State Department in 1944 as its first assistant secretary for economic affairs; Truman later promoted him to undersecretary. Clayton was tall and powerfully built, with white hair and dark eyebrows that sloped toward his nose. He wore pin-striped suits over a matching vest, a handkerchief in his breast pocket, and a stern expression on his face.

A man of great discipline, he walked several miles to work every morning for exercise and didn't drink until he was fifty-eight, doing so then only because his doctor said that sweet sherry would be good for his health. He was beloved at the State Department for his mild manner and long hours; no one there worked harder. As much as anyone, Clayton was the intellectual force behind the Marshall Plan.[7]

"It is now obvious that we grossly underestimated the destruction to the European economy by the war," Clayton wrote in a May 27 memo to Marshall.

> We understood the physical destruction, but we failed to take fully into account the effects of economic dislocation on production—nationalization of industries, drastic land reform, severance of long-standing commercial ties, disappearance of private commercial firms through death or loss of capital, etc., etc. . . . Europe is steadily deteriorating. The political position reflects the economic. One political crisis after another merely denotes the existence of grave economic distress. Millions of people in the cities are slowly starving. More consumer goods and restored confidence in the local currency are absolutely essential if the peasant is again to supply food in normal quantities to the cities . . . Without further prompt and substantial aid from the United States, economic, social, and political disintegration will overwhelm Europe.[8]

Around the same time, Vandenberg, too, was sensitized to the threat of a European collapse. The State Department had sent Dulles on a clandestine mission to Paris to assess chances of a Communist takeover or civil war. Alarmed by the mounting strikes and threats of violence, Dulles briefed Vandenberg by phone.

. . .

On May 8, 1947, Truman was supposed to be in Cleveland, Mississippi. He had accepted an invitation to speak at Delta State Teachers College, fulfilling a promise to friends from the area. But as the date neared, Truman wanted to avoid entanglement in a local political fight. So he stepped aside and announced that Dean Acheson, the undersecretary of state, would speak in his place.

Rural Mississippi was hardly the ideal place for a top Washington official to make news, particularly about U.S. foreign policy. But, the timing was propitious. Acheson recognized an opportunity to deliver a call to "reveille" that would awaken the American people "to the duties of that day of decision" and to float some ideas that were surfacing at the White House and State Department. "I am going to throw up a ball," Acheson told Truman before heading south on an air force DC-3, "and it's going to have to come down somewhere." Thus, the northeastern aristocrat who was most comfortable in Washington's halls of power and New York's corporate boardrooms traveled enthusiastically to a remote town in the Deep South.[9]

"The devastation of war has brought us back to elementals," Acheson said after removing his jacket and rolling up his sleeves in the hot, crowded gymnasium, "to the point where we see clearly how short is the distance from food and fuel either to peace or to anarchy." He reviewed some "basic facts of life with which we are primarily concerned today in the conduct of foreign affairs"—Europe and Asia's "physical destruction or economic dislocation, or both"; Germany and Japan's inability to rebuild in the absence of final peace settlements; and severe winter storms and summer droughts of the prior two years that had devastated European crops and fuel production. The United States would have to provide more assistance to Europe, but concentrate it "where it will be most effective in building world political and economic stability, in promoting human freedom and democratic institutions, in fostering liberal trading policies, and in strengthening the authority of the United Nations." In other words, the United States must turn from episodic relief to systemic rebirth.

The implications of Acheson's remarks skipped past many in the crowd, but they didn't escape the notice of top international and national media. Acheson had teed up the speech in off-the-record discussions with leading British reporters, and they gave it a big splash when Acheson delivered it. The White House announced beforehand that it would be "an important foreign policy speech," and the State Department briefed the top wire services and influential syndicated columnists. Asked later by

the *New York Times'* Reston whether the speech represented administration policy, Acheson directed him to the White House where Truman confirmed that it did.

Nor did the implications escape the notice of one Arthur Vandenberg. Sitting at his desk in Washington, he grew livid as he read about
the speech. Once again, the administration was telegraphing a costly new
initiative that would demand Vandenberg's collaboration and legislative
skills to steer through Congress—and once again the president and his
team hadn't brought him into the planning process. After demanding
a meeting with Truman, and with Marshall and Acheson in the room
for it, Vandenberg unloaded, waiving the speech around in his hand.

"I want you to understand from now on," the senator told the president, repeating one of his favorite expressions, "that I'm not going to
help you with crash landings unless I'm in on the takeoff."[10]

. . .

Vandenberg's anger was rooted in both personal pique and political reality. Just two days before Acheson spoke, the House approved the first
installment of the Truman Doctrine—the $400 million aid package for
Greece and Turkey. It had been no easy sell in the Republican-controlled
Eightieth Congress, for which tax cutting at home and isolationism
abroad were strong themes. A robust plan of the kind that Acheson
sketched out in Mississippi would invite far bigger legislative battles.

Months earlier, Truman had anticipated the coming clash between
America's growing global role, which would demand more federal
resources, and countervailing Republican sentiments. In his "Budget
Message to the Congress" in January, the president declared, "There is
no justification now for tax reduction." He urged lawmakers to retain the
higher wartime excise tax rates that were due to expire on July 1. Although
his Budget Message of January predated the Truman Doctrine and Marshall Plan of March and June, respectively, Truman clearly envisioned
by then that the costs of America's overseas obligations would rise. "We
have to carry our proper share of the expense of building world organization," he said. "We must make effective provision for national defense."

When, in June, Congress sent Truman a bill to cut tax rates, he vetoed it, saying that it was both economically unnecessary and fiscally irresponsible in light of government's needs for foreign-related resources. "We are still meeting heavy obligations growing out of the war," the president explained. "We continue to be confronted with great responsibilities for international relief and rehabilitation that have an important bearing on our efforts to secure lasting peace. We are still in a transition period in which many uncertainties continue. In the face of these facts, common prudence demands a realistic and conservative management of the fiscal affairs of the Government." That legislation would have cut tax rates on July 1. After the veto, Congress sent Truman an identical bill except that it would have cut tax rates six months later. He vetoed that one as well.

A loyal Republican on domestic issues, Vandenberg voted for the tax cuts and supported GOP efforts to override Truman's veto. But his heart wasn't in it. He knew that tax cutting could threaten the resources needed to fund America's global role. He didn't speak on behalf of either bill when it came to the Senate floor. Thus, he could express fealty to Republican principles on the domestic side while knowing full well that Truman would stop the effort in its tracks.

Republican tax cutting reflected the party's deep-seated predisposition for smaller government, and it showcased one of the biggest hurdles that Vandenberg would have to overcome when the Marshall Plan came before Congress.

14

"I Have No Illusions about
This So-Called 'Marshall Plan'"

TRUMAN'S APPOINTMENT OF MARSHALL as secretary of state in January of 1947 irritated Vandenberg because he had grown quite fond of Byrnes, with whom he spent so many days at global conferences in 1946.

Truman didn't tell Vandenberg beforehand that he was replacing Byrnes, and, not surprisingly, the senator took umbrage at the snub. In a Senate speech days later, he questioned Truman's "sudden and unusual interruption of the State Department's personnel." Vandenberg's anger quickly subsided, however, and he vowed to work with Marshall as he had worked with Byrnes and, before him, Edward Stettinius. He steered Marshall's confirmation through his committee and the Senate by unanimous votes on the same day.

That neither Vandenberg nor any other senator opposed Marshall was hardly surprising, for he was a man of unusual stature. Born on December 31, 1880, in Lewiston, Pennsylvania, he graduated the Virginia Military Institute in 1901 and quickly moved up the army's ranks, serving as a top aide to General John J. Pershing during World War I. From there, it was one key position after the next—army chief of staff during World War II, secretary of state, and, later, presidential envoy to China, and secretary of defense. On different occasions, Truman called him "the great one of the age" and "one of the most astute and profound men I have ever known," and the well-read president considered Marshall a greater military leader than Hannibal, Khan, or Napoleon.[1]

He was "George" to his wife, "General Marshall" to everyone else, and he exuded a discipline and purposefulness, a seriousness and self-confidence, a calm and sober-mindedness that even his most accomplished colleagues envied. In a *New York Times* profile in early 1947, Reston wrote, "He listens to the facts; he questions carefully; he grants wide authority to his aides, rewards clarity and industry, punishes inefficiency; he listens patiently to men who have a clear idea of what they are talking about and impatiently to 'ramblers'; then, having heard them out, he makes his estimate of the immediate situation just as he did on the various military campaigns."[2] Marshall spoke in a low, staccato voice that, while awkward before large crowds, commanded respect in smaller settings. "Don't fight the problem, gentlemen," he would say as debates raged among his staff. "Solve it."

Unlike Byrnes (the former senator), Marshall (the former military man) did not immediately understand the need to stroke Vandenberg or other lawmakers in order to nourish congressional support for administration policy. He assumed that Congress would support the Marshall Plan or any other initiative if the administration made a convincing case for it. Encouraged by his politically seasoned aides, however, he began to seek out Vandenberg on a consistent basis. Five days after his Harvard speech, he wrote to Vandenberg to suggest that the latter craft a Senate resolution that would endorse the concept behind the Marshall Plan. In July Vandenberg announced that Marshall had agreed to meet regularly with his committee in private on a range of issues. In August, the two traveled together to Rio de Janeiro as part of the U.S. delegation to an inter-American defense conference.

Marshall shared with Vandenberg the administration's thinking about how to convert the Marshall Plan speech into a legislative proposal, soliciting his views. The two met twice a week at Blair House, the president's guesthouse across Pennsylvania Avenue from the White House, through the fall and winter.

"We could not have gotten much closer," Marshall said later, "unless I sat in Vandenberg's lap or he sat in mine."[3]

. . .

Truman wanted Marshall's name associated with the big, bold plan to save Europe out of both high-mindedness and political reality.

To be sure, he respected Marshall greatly and was happy to let him bask in the limelight. At a practical level, though, Truman also knew that a Republican Congress was far likelier to approve a sweeping initiative of mind-boggling cost if it were associated with an iconic figure rather than a controversial president.

In May, as top administration officials studied Europe's condition, White House Counsel Clark Clifford suggested to Truman that he announce the coming plan and put it in his own name. That Clifford would do so was hardly noteworthy; presidents normally assume brand-name ownership of their major initiatives. In addition, Clifford, a top White House political adviser, was eyeing Truman's 1948 campaign for reelection and viewed the plan as a fortuitous opportunity for presidential glory.

Truman was hesitant, however. He knew that Republicans, too, were eying the presidential race and he feared that, with no desire to help Truman politically, a Republican Congress would not treat a "Truman Plan" well. Flashing a knowing smile to Clifford, the president said, "We have a Republican majority in both Houses. Anything going up there bearing my name will quiver a couple of times, turn belly up, and die." Mulling matters further for another day or so, Truman then told Clifford definitively, "I've decided to give the whole thing to General Marshall. The worst Republican on the Hill can vote for it if we name it after the General."[4]

· · ·

"I need not tell you gentlemen that the world situation is very serious," Marshall stated at Harvard while Truman and Vandenberg toiled away in Washington. "That must be apparent to all intelligent people."

Marshall reviewed "the physical loss of life" and "visible destruction of cities, factories, mines and railroads," but he focused on the more serious "dislocation of the entire fabric of European economy." He explained that "the feverish preparation for war and the more feverish maintenance of the war effort engulfed all aspects of national economies," leaving machinery in "disrepair" or "entirely obsolete." "Longstanding commercial ties, private institutions, banks, insurance companies and shipping companies disappeared, through loss of capital, absorption through nationalization or by simple destruction," Marshall explained. "In many countries, confidence in the local currency has been severely shaken. The breakdown of the business structure of Europe during the war was complete," and "the rehabilitation of the economic structure of Europe quite evidently will require a much longer time and greater effort than had been foreseen . . .

"The truth of the matter," he continued, "is that Europe's requirements for the next three or four years of foreign food and other essential products—principally from America—are so much greater than her present ability to pay that she must have substantial additional help, or face economic, social and political deterioration of a very grave character. The remedy lies in breaking the vicious circle and restoring the confidence of the European people in the economic future of their own countries and of Europe as a whole. The manufacturer and the farmer throughout wide areas must be able and willing to exchange their products for currencies the continuing value of which is not open to question."

Marshall outlined America's self-interest in underwriting Europe's systemic rebirth, invited all European nations to participate, but warned that only nations that contributed positively would receive U.S. help. "It is logical," he stated,

> that the United States should do whatever it is able to do to assist in the return of normal economic health in the world, without which there can be no political stability and no assured peace. Our policy is directed not against any country or doctrine but against hunger, poverty, desperation and chaos. Its purpose should be the revival of a working economy in the world so as to permit the emergence of political and social conditions in which free institutions can exist. Such assistance, I am convinced, must not be on a piecemeal basis as various crises develop. Any assistance that this government may render in the future should provide a cure rather than a mere palliative.

Any government that is willing to assist in the task of recovery will find full cooperation, I am sure, on the part of the United States government. Any government which maneuvers to block the recovery of other countries cannot expect help from us. Furthermore, governments, political parties, or groups which seek to perpetuate human misery in order to profit therefrom politically or otherwise will encounter the opposition of the United States.

The funds would come from America, but the systemic vision would have to emerge from a unified Europe.

. . .

At that point, the Marshall Plan was not really a "plan." It was a concept. To convert it to a plan, Truman would propose a legislative package, with a request for federal dollars and details of the program's architecture.

Presumably, Vandenberg would lead the effort on Capitol Hill, pushing the legislation through Congress in a form Truman could accept. With Truman needing his help, it was now time for Vandenberg to reveal what he wanted in return.

"Current discussion, in and out of public life," Vandenberg said in a statement to reporters on June 13, "is directed toward new foreign programs of large-scale post-war American rehabilitation—as distinguished from direct relief—to prevent social and economic collapse in many parts of the world. It is a good thing that these discussions are under way in the open," he went on. "But they should not be misunderstood at home or abroad. At home, they should not invite anxieties that we shall rush into imprudent and inadequately seasoned plans. Abroad, they should not be taken as evidence that our foreign friends can depend upon us as a substitute for depending on themselves."

Though he endorsed Marshall's idea, Vandenberg recognized the tight-fistedness of Republican lawmakers and their skepticism toward bold U.S. global action. Seeking to assure his GOP colleagues that he would address their concerns, he declared that he would closely scrutinize the administration's detailed proposal for any signs of excess. "I endorse the importance of facing this problem on an over-all basis instead of dealing with anticipated crises, one by one . . . ," he stated, "but equally I recognize that intelligent American self-interest immediately requires a sound, over-all inventory of our own resources to determine the latitudes within which we may consider these foreign needs. This comes first because if America ever sags, the world's hopes sag with her."

Specifically, Vandenberg proposed that Truman appoint a bipartisan committee of "our ablest and most experienced citizenship" to assess America's capacity to help Europe, and he made clear that he wouldn't assist Truman until he did so.[5]

With little choice to do otherwise, Truman agreed.

. . .

On Truman's behalf, the State Department's Will Clayton officially endorsed Vandenberg's idea of a bipartisan committee on June 18, and the president announced its creation four days later.

Commerce Secretary Harriman would chair it, and its nineteen members would include business leaders like Procter & Gamble's R. R. Deupree and Studebaker's Paul G. Hoffman (who, at Vandenberg's behest, Truman later chose to run the Marshall Plan); labor leaders like the AFL's George Meany and the CIO's James B. Carey; academic leaders like Harvard's Edward S. Mason and Cornell's William I. Myers; and public officials like Chester C. Davis, president of the Federal Reserve Bank of Saint Louis, and Robert M. La Follette Jr., the former senator from Wisconsin.

Truman said the Harriman Committee "will be requested to determine the facts with respect to the character and quantities of United States resources available for economic assistance to foreign countries, and to advise me, in the light of these facts, on the limits within which the United States may safely and wisely plan to extend such assistance and on the relation between this assistance and our domestic economy." At the same time, the president ordered up two additional reports: his Council of Economic Advisers would study how foreign aid of the size envisioned would affect America's economy, and government experts headed by Interior Secretary Julius Albert Krug would assess whether large-scale U.S. foreign aid would imperil America's national resources.

By early November the three committees had delivered their reports.

Krug's panel concluded that America had the resources to protect national security, retain U.S. living standards, and assist Europe to the extent envisioned by the Marshall Plan. The Council of Economic Advisers concluded that America had the financial capacity to do so. The Harriman Committee concluded that America had vital economic, political, and humanitarian interests in Europe's recovery; that while requiring U.S. sacrifice, Europe's recovery was achievable; and that it would cost $12 billion to $17 billion.

The Harriman Committee's report proved the most influential by far, largely because Vandenberg promoted its findings widely. When Harriman's panel unveiled it in November, the senator reacted with glee even before digging in, as if declaring victory for forcing the administration to fulfill his demands. "It is a magnificent piece of work," he wrote to his wife, while acknowledging that he hadn't yet read it. "But it is three inches thick! I brought it home with me tonight. That'll keep me busy over the weekend (although I will divert long enough to tend to the crossword puzzles)."[6]

After reading a bit of it, Vandenberg congratulated Harriman by cable, writing, "Only a Hollywood press agent could do justice to it."[7]

. . .

Truman and Vandenberg recognized that, beyond the rich data of committee reports and the views of top officials, the public would play a large role in determining the Marshall Plan's ultimate fate. Vandenberg raised concerns about public willingness to support the plan and the administration's ability to make the case for it effectively.

"I have no illusions about this so-called 'Marshall Plan,'" Vandenberg wrote in late June of 1947 to Clark M. Eichelberger, director of the American Association for the United Nations. "I certainly do not take it for granted that American public opinion is ready for any such burdens as would be involved unless and until it is far more effectively demonstrated to the American people that this (1) is within the latitudes of their own available resources and (2) serves their own intelligent self-interest."[8]

Vandenberg recognized that without strong public support for it, Republican isolationists and Democratic pacifists could oppose the Marshall Plan without fear of political retribution. He highlighted the issue with the influential columnists with whom he was close. "The problem is here," he told Joseph and Stewart Alsop in early August, by which he meant (according to the Alsops) "the indifference still widely prevailing in this country" to "the dark, gigantic background of the world drama."[9] Vandenberg repeated his concerns to columnist Marquis Childs, who wrote a week later, "Above all, as Vandenberg is acutely aware, the supreme task is to get the American people to see how our obligation fits in with the desperate need for recovery and rehabilitation in non-Communist Europe."[10]

Truman shared Vandenberg's concern, and, in the fall of 1947, he sought to convince Americans that the Marshall Plan was essential. In prepared speeches and off-the-cuff remarks, he outlined the rationale behind it.

"The sick and the hungry," Truman told an inter-American defense conference outside of Rio de Janeiro on September 2, "cannot build a peaceful world. They must have the support of the strong and the free. We cannot depend upon those who are weaker than we to achieve a peace for us to enjoy. The benefits of peace, like the crops in the field, come to those who have sown the seeds of peace. It is for us, the young and the strong, to erect the bulwarks which will protect mankind from the horrors of war forever."

The president returned to Europe's desperation and America's responsibility in remarks to newspaper editors on September 30, in a discussion with editorial writers on October 17, and in a radio address to the nation on October 24.

. . .

For Truman and Vandenberg, deteriorating U.S.-Soviet relations proved an influential backdrop to the Marshall Plan, shaping their decisions and prompting them to view the plan in increasingly urgent terms.

Marshall's invitation for *all* European countries to participate had come after an administration debate over what to do about the Soviets and their satellites. Invite them in, and Washington would position Moscow to undermine the program from within. Shut them out, and Washington would subject itself to charges that it was the United States, not the Soviet Union, that was dividing Europe in two.

Truman left the decision to Marshall, who turned to Kennan, his well-regarded Soviet expert. "Play it straight," Kennan advised. That is, invite the Soviets to participate. Moscow would never do so, he said, because it would have to open its books to Western scrutiny and reveal the details of its economic weakness. Marshall took the advice—thus, at Harvard he spoke of "Europe" rather than "Western Europe"—but neither he nor such top-ranking officials as Bohlen, Harriman, and Robert Lovett were very confident about what the Soviets would do. To raise the odds that Moscow would reject the offer, U.S. officials shared their thoughts with their British counterparts, making clear that they weren't enthused about Soviet participation and soliciting London's help to derail it.

While the United States fretted about the coming Soviet decision, the Soviets played into Washington's hands by opting for obstruction over cooperation. Britain's foreign minister, Ernest Bevin, and France's foreign minister, Georges Bidault, invited their Soviet counterpart, Vyacheslav Molotov, to meet with them in late June in Paris. As the three discussed a response to Marshall's invitation, Molotov sought to convince the others that, despite what Marshall had proposed, individual European nations should submit individual requests for aid to Washington. When Bevin and Bidault rejected the idea, Molotov walked out—and Moscow's state-run radio attacked the Marshall Plan in ever more strident tones.

"It seems," Acheson wrote later, based on Bevin's recollection, "that Molotov has a bump on his forehead which swells when he is under emotional strain. The matter was being debated and Molotov had raised relatively minor questions or objections at various points, when a telegram was handed to him. He turned pale and the bump on his forehead swelled. After that, his attitude changed and he became much more harsh."[11] Apparently, Stalin had hardened his approach to the Marshall Plan and instructed Molotov accordingly.

When, in early July, Bevin and Bidault invited twenty-two other European nations to craft a response, Czechoslovakia first accepted and Poland expressed interest. The Soviets, however, forced the former to withdraw and the latter to stay out, positioning the United States exactly where Truman wanted it. The president had "played it straight" by offering the Marshall Plan to the Soviets and their satellites, and they had rejected the offer, putting the blame squarely on Moscow for further dividing Europe.

. . .

At the home of Thomas Jefferson on July 4, Truman mocked the Soviet decision. "Certain nations today are withholding their support of reconstruction plans on the ground that this would mean interference by some nations in the internal affairs of others. This is as fallacious as the refusal of a man to enter a profitable business partnership on the ground that it would involve interference in his private affairs."

Europe's division into U.S.- and Soviet-led blocs deepened that summer and fall, with the Marshall Plan playing a major role in the split. In Western Europe, sixteen nations—Britain, France, Austria, Greece, Norway, Switzerland, Belgium, Iceland, Portugal, Turkey, Denmark, Ireland, Sweden, Italy, Luxemburg, and the Netherlands—convened in Paris on July 12 to craft a detailed response to Marshall's invitation ("bravely," Vandenberg told the Senate months later, "because it was in virtual defiance of the Russian bear, which promptly showed its teeth"). In Eastern Europe in response, Moscow would ink trade and other agreements with several of its satellites in the coming weeks.

Meanwhile, attitudes about the Soviets further stiffened in Washington. In July the journal *Foreign Affairs* published "The Sources of Soviet Conduct," in which Kennan (writing anonymously as "X") advised that "any United States policy toward the Soviet Union must be that of a long-term, patient but firm and vigilant containment of Russian expansive tendencies."[12] In August Bohlen told a meeting of top State Depart-

"Very Serious"

ment and Defense Department officials, "There is virtually no chance of any of the problems" between the U.S.- and Soviet-led worlds "being settled" until a crisis between them "comes to a head . . . It is not a matter of several years in the future. It is more likely a question of months."[13]

In September the sixteen Marshall Plan nations agreed to six sets of economic reforms that were recommended by Clayton, who was monitoring their efforts in Paris, including financial and monetary changes and lower trade barriers. In late September they presented Washington with their official response to the Marshall Plan, requesting a combined $19 billion for Europe's systemic rebirth. In October the Soviet newspaper *Pravda* announced that the Communist parties of the Soviet Union and eight Soviet-bloc nations had created the "Cominform" to oppose the Marshall Plan and, more broadly, U.S. imperialism.

The world was now more divided than ever.

15

"The Perils of Hunger and Cold in Europe"

IN THE SUMMER OF 1947, Truman anticipated that he would propose the detailed legislation to implement the Marshall Plan much later that year, that Congress would consider it carefully in early 1948, and that, until then, Europe would live off the billions in U.S. aid that it had received to that point.

Asked on July 10 whether Congress should proceed with its plan to adjourn later that month and return in January, Truman told reporters that he foresaw nothing in its way. Of the possible "necessity" for Congress to approve the Marshall Plan more quickly, he said, "I don't see any necessity in the immediate future now." When Truman met with Vandenberg and other congressional leaders on July 14, he said that he didn't envision the need to call Congress into "special session" that fall to speed action. He would have the Marshall Plan ready for Congress when it returned after New Year's Day.

Europe's sinking fortunes, however, threatened Truman's leisurely timetable. "Europe is bleeding to death," Ernest Bevin, Britain's foreign minister, told columnists Joseph and Stewart Alsop in late July, adding that Europe could well die if America did not step in expeditiously.[1] By August reports were increasingly reaching Washington that, without additional aid very soon, the governments of France and Italy could fall to Communist challenge. Later that month, the Alsops reported that the odds of a special session of Congress that fall to address the issue were rapidly growing.

Truman was facing pressure not only from Europe but, increasingly, from his staff. Marshall returned from the Rio conference on inter-American defense in early September and received an alarming briefing on Europe's descent from Lovett, who had replaced Acheson as undersecretary of state two months earlier. That same day, Lovett also outlined the situation publicly, telling reporters that Europe was suffering from Britain's quick drain of dollars as well as from unexpected crop failures that forced European nations to spend their remaining dollars on food and fuel.

As a result, Truman began to shift his position on a special session, signaling that he'd be more amenable to one. In September he sailed leisurely to Washington on the battleship *Missouri* from Rio, where he also had attended the defense conference, with a scheduled arrival on September 19. But he sent White House Counsel Clark Clifford to fly ahead to Washington and consult with Marshall. The stage was set for Marshall and Clifford to recommend a special session and for Truman to call one.

Vandenberg, meanwhile, refused to pressure Truman one way or the other about a special session because he refused to share ownership of Europe's troubles with him. Truman and his team, he said, had the most up-to-date information about Europe, and they were best placed to suggest America's next steps. While Congress had "no disposition to dodge any emergency which the President may identify," Vandenberg said, "the information is not up here. It's down there [i.e., at the White House]."[2]

. . .

The issue, however, wasn't just whether Truman should call a special session that fall. It also was what, exactly, Vandenberg and his fellow lawmakers would do in one.

The Marshall Plan was big, bold, and complicated, and, not surprisingly, administration officials needed time to flesh it out. Moreover, they could not fully control the timetable. As Marshall had made clear at Harvard, his plan was predicated on a request from Europe—once Europe had come together to inventory its needs. The United States and

Europe were operating on parallel tracks, and those tracks would affect one another. Privately, Truman's top aides pushed Western European officials to adopt bold economic reforms and scale back their funding request so that it wouldn't prove unpalatable to lawmakers or the American public. Only after receiving Europe's official request could U.S. officials complete the detailed proposal for Congress. Thus, depending on what the sixteen Marshall Plan nations decided, the administration might not finish crafting its proposal until well into the winter—that is, beyond the time of any special session that fall.

Besides, even if Truman sent the proposal to Capitol Hill in the fall, a Republican-controlled Congress wasn't going to rubber-stamp it quickly into law. Vandenberg would hold hearings at his Senate Foreign Relations Committee, and Chairman Charles Eaton would do the same at the House Foreign Affairs Committee. The measure would then go to the Senate and House floors for full debates. For a proposal of that magnitude, the process would surely take many weeks, if not many months.

Could Europe hold out until early 1948, if not later? Among Truman's top aides, doubts mounted. In August of 1947 Clayton began to call for another round of short-term aid that would tide Europe over until the Marshall Plan was enacted, preventing a European collapse. That Clayton was witnessing Europe's troubles firsthand at the time made his call particularly noteworthy in Washington. In September Lovett began to echo that call publicly. By late September Clayton and Lovett had convinced Marshall.

Within days Truman was convinced by Marshall, Lovett, and Clayton that Europe couldn't wait for the Marshall Plan; it needed short-term aid. He called Vandenberg and other congressional leaders to the White House on September 29 and proposed $580 million in additional aid, with the bulk focused on France and Italy—the two nations that were most quickly running out of food and fuel and, thus, most vulnerable to Communist takeover. "The situation in western Europe has, in the last few months, become critical," Truman wrote the next day in a letter to Vandenberg, Eaton, and the chairmen of the Senate and House appropriations committees, which also had to approve the funding request. "This is especially true in the cases of France and Italy, where slow recovery of productivity, particularly of goods for export, combined with the increasing drain on their dollar resources, has produced acute distress . . . Political groups that hope to profit by unrest and distress are now attempting to capitalize on the grave fears of the French and Italian people that they will not have enough food and fuel to survive the coming winter."

Truman wrote that he would soon send the Marshall Plan to Congress. He stated, however, that it could not succeed if Europe first collapsed. "Prompt and effective aid to meet the urgent needs of the present is essential," he wrote, "lest the strains become too great and result in an expanding economic depression which would engulf western Europe and, eventually, spread over much of the rest of the world." He asked the chairmen to call their committees together at the earliest possible time to consider his request. With many lawmakers in Europe at the time to examine the crisis in person, the committees would have to await their return. Consequently, Vandenberg and Eaton announced that their panels would come together for a joint meeting on November 10.

Although he respected Truman's request that his committee consider short-term aid at its earliest convenience, Vandenberg was rankled by the president's approach. Once again, he felt squeezed. Rather than approach Vandenberg when his aides first began to worry about Europe's collapse, Truman dropped the issue on Vandenberg's doorstep when the crisis had reached an acute stage. After Lovett outlined the problem at the September 29 White House meeting, Truman asked congressional leaders for their views.

"You gentlemen have had five weeks to think this over," a resentful Vandenberg blurted, "and now you give me five minutes."[3]

. . .

"I have met this afternoon with a group of congressional leaders," Truman told reporters on October 23, announcing that he would call a special session of Congress for the following month.

"I presented to them detailed information concerning the alarming and continuing increase in prices in this country and the situation regarding the need for emergency foreign aid. I informed them that I had concluded it was necessary to convene the Congress on Monday, November 17th."

On the foreign front, the pace of activity quickened. France would need help by year-end, Italy even sooner. After briefing the lawmakers on October 23, Truman addressed the nation the next evening by radio. "A period of crisis is now at hand," he declared. "The perils of hunger and cold in Europe make this winter a decisive time in history. All the progress of reconstruction and all the promise of future plans are endangered. If European nations are to continue their recovery, they must get through this winter without being crippled by economic paralysis and resulting chaos."

Specifically, he said, crop failures in France and Italy were forcing those countries to import half the grain they needed for food for the coming months. Their fuel also was running low, and they couldn't replenish their fuel stocks because their miners were ill nourished and their railroads remained damaged from the war. Short of money, France and Italy soon wouldn't be able to buy food or fuel at all. Washington also needed to allocate more funds for the occupied areas of Germany, Japan, and Korea.

Vandenberg and Eaton held their joint committee meeting as scheduled on November 10. The two committees then held several days of separate hearings at which administration officials testified. On the Senate side, Vandenberg sought to address congressional concerns about the mounting costs of U.S. aid to Europe, asking Marshall for a "total balance sheet" of anticipated costs through the fiscal year, which would end on June 30. He also helped the administration make its case, engineering an exchange with Lewis Douglas, the U.S. ambassador to Great Britain, on the stakes at hand.

"It is almost certain," Douglas told the Senate Foreign Relations Committee on November 11, "that if we do nothing, the chaos and disorder that would result would fill men's minds with queer, quaint and fantastic ideas hostile to our own interests." Helpfully, Vandenberg then asked a leading question.

VANDENBERG: Well, what would really happen if the United States did nothing?

DOUGLAS: If Congress refuses this interim aid, it is likely that by spring it will be too late to enact a long-range program for the recovery of Europe. The next four or five months will be the critical months.

. . .

Truman tied short-term aid closely to the Marshall Plan when he addressed the opening of Congress's special session.

"Emergency assistance by itself will not solve the European problems," Truman told the senators and House members who had gathered in the House chamber on the afternoon of November 17, with Vandenberg and House Speaker Joseph W. Martin on the dais behind him. "Emergency aid is no substitute for a long-range recovery program, but it is a vital prerequisite to such a program. If the Western European nations should collapse this winter, as a result of our failure to bridge the gap between their resources and their needs, there would be no chance for them—or for us—to look forward to their economic recovery. The providing of interim aid will give us time to plan our part in an economic recovery program and it will give the peoples of Europe the strength to hold out until such a program begins."

Seeking to help Truman gather the votes for short-term aid, however, Vandenberg took a different approach than Truman due to the political realities on Capitol Hill. Rather than tie such aid closely to the Marshall Plan, Vandenberg drew a clear distinction between them. A growing number of lawmakers were making clear that their vote for short-term aid did not necessarily presage their vote for the Marshall Plan, or they were already expressing opposition to the Marshall Plan; among the latter was Robert Taft, the influential Republican senator. Vandenberg didn't want senators to withhold their support for short-term aid out of fear that, by supporting it, they'd be signaling their support for the Marshall Plan.

"I want to make it plain that the Senate is not confronting in this pending vote any sort of an obligation to other and subsequent relief

"Very Serious"

programs of greater magnitude," he told his colleagues as the Senate debated short-term aid on November 24. "The only question here, and there are no other implications, is interim, emergency aid for France, Italy and Austria for the period ending March 31, 1948."

Vandenberg's fears were overblown, however. By the time Truman spoke on November 17, short-term aid had become inevitable. Through the summer and early fall, hundreds of House and Senate members had traveled to Europe to assess the crisis up close. They had returned by November, a large majority of them convinced that Washington would have to step in quickly to prevent a catastrophic collapse.

Two days after Truman spoke, Vandenberg's committee voted unanimously to approve the president's request for $597 million for France, Italy, and Austria. On December 1, after a week of Senate debate, Vandenberg steered the measure through the full chamber on an 83–6 vote. After the House approved a different measure later in December, the chambers ironed out a compromise measure that passed both chambers and received Truman's signature on December 23.

. . .

On this latest short-term crisis, Vandenberg's collaboration with Truman proved striking. For the president, Vandenberg was not just the most helpful Republican lawmaker on foreign policy; he was the most helpful lawmaker of either party. The *New York Times'* Reston described it this way in late November:

> The Democrats in the Senate have developed a new way of demonstrating their respect for Senator Arthur H. Vandenberg's aid on foreign policy issues. They all gather politely in the upper chamber, as they did this morning, to hear him launch the debate. They nod their assent and applaud warmly at the right places. But when he finishes, and the real debate starts, they vanish immediately, leaving him alone to deal with the dissenters of both parties . . .

"The surprising thing about this," Reston continued, "is that there has been such a revolution in our foreign policy affairs in the Senate that everyone now takes this extraordinary situation for granted."[4]

16

"The Commies Will Be Completely Back in the Saddle"

"I AM HOME AFTER a hectic day at the White House and the State Department," Vandenberg wrote to his wife in the fall of 1947.

As Truman and his top team developed the Marshall Plan legislation, they brought Vandenberg into their deliberations. "About 20 of us met in the [White House] Cabinet Room this morning," Vandenberg continued in that same letter. "The President is trying to discriminate between 'stop-gap aid' for France and Italy to keep them afloat until Spring, on the one hand, and a permanent 'Marshall Plan,' on the other. (It was this differentiation which I impressed upon Marshall last night as essential to any possibility of success.) We had a fairly harmonious time of it—with this discrimination in mind."[1]

Administration efforts to maintain Vandenberg's cooperation extended beyond the work day. Lovett, who both admired and liked Vandenberg, often visited his apartment at Washington's Wardman Park Hotel after work where, over cocktails, he briefed Vandenberg on developments overseas.

Lovett would carry "a sheaf of telegrams," he recalled years later, "and go over what had happened during the day with [Vandenberg] if it was a thing in which he was interested. Some things he'd never talk with me about at all—China. 'No,' he said, 'that's not up to you. That's Secretary Marshall, the China problem. But everything else,' he said, 'you're in charge here and I'd just like to know what's going on.'"[2]

In the fall of 1947, Lovett and Vandenberg reportedly spent more time with one another than with their wives.

. . .

That fall, Vandenberg pulled himself in competing directions over the Marshall Plan—always supportive of the idea, always agonizing over the costs.

"The confidential reports from Europe are that the Commies are losing ground (even their satellites are restless)," he wrote in the letter to his wife cited above. "This seems to be the time for us 'to make hay.' But if our friends in Western Europe are allowed to starve and freeze to death this winter, the Commies will be completely back in the saddle. On the other hand, we must keep our own feet on the ground and avoid commitments that would disrupt our own economy. Where to draw the line!"

As he mulled it over, Vandenberg had the Soviet "Commies" uppermost in his mind. Speaking at the University of Michigan on November 4, he noted that Moscow was deploying the "most amazing anti-American vilification which ever belabored the ears of the world," labeling Americans "Fascists," "economic imperialists," and "warmongers." Frustrated by U.S.-Soviet gridlock over the final status of Germany, Vandenberg proposed that if the Council of Foreign Ministers could not resolve the issue by winter, then interested nations with jurisdiction over German territory (e.g., the United States) should hold a peace conference to write separate treaties to govern their territories.

After chiding the Soviets that day, Vandenberg made a pitch for the Marshall Plan. "If," he said, "self-help and self-sufficiency" by Europe's recipient nations "can be made to work, this objective may well be a bargain." Success was not guaranteed, Vandenberg acknowledged, "But let's be honest enough with American destiny not to ignore the calculated risk if we do not proceed. Secretary Marshall correctly says it involves, 'The danger of the actual disappearance of the characteristics of Western civilization on which our government and our manner of living are based.'"[3]

A month later, Vandenberg described the risks of inaction to Malcolm W. Bingay, a *Detroit Free Press* columnist, in typically dramatic language. To Bingay's concerns about the inherent uncertainties involved, he wrote, "I respectfully submit that we do 'know enough' to know what will happen if [the Marshall Plan], or something like it, doesn't work. We know that independent governments, whatever their character otherwise, will disappear from Western Europe; that aggressive communism will be spurred throughout the world; and that our concept of free men, free government and a relatively free international economy will come up against accumulated hazards which can put our own, precious 'American way of life' in the greatest, kindred hazard since Pearl Harbor."[4]

. . .

While working privately with administration officials to craft the Marshall Plan legislation, Vandenberg was doing something else to boost its prospects: preemptively clearing away the obstacles on Capitol Hill.

At a Senate Foreign Relations Committee hearing of November 13 on the Krug report, Republicans Alexander Wiley of Wisconsin and Henry Cabot Lodge of Massachusetts expressed concern that, in dispensing Marshall Plan aid, the United States would repeat its mistake of the prior two years in not insisting that recipient nations provide something in return for the U.S. largesse. "In some of our international dealings in the past few years," said Wiley, a well-known isolationist, "we have been taken for a ride and it seems to [me] that we ought to start getting something for our money. I want to know if any effort has been made to obtain strategic bases or materials in return for our generosity. That doesn't mean we are being hard-hearted but it does mean we are through being 'Uncle Sap.'"

In response, Vandenberg told Wiley that, in implementing the Marshall Plan, the United States would craft bilateral agreements with each of the sixteen participating nations; that the agreements would come before the Senate Foreign Relations Committee for review; and that, as part of those agreements, reciprocal action would receive great attention. "Lest the Senator's remarks carry the implication that this program is being handled on the same old inadequate basis," Vandenberg told Wiley, U.S. actions to date on the Marshall Plan belied that suspicion. He reminded Wiley that U.S. officials had forced the sixteen nations to scale back their combined request for Marshall Plan aid. "The old idea that Europe can come to us and say what they want and when," Vandenberg said, "has been thoroughly dissipated in the past three months by reductions in their demands, in some cases of as much as 50 percent."

Lodge remained dissatisfied, and he proposed that Marshall Plan recipients provide the United States with, in particular, the strategic raw materials of which it was short. "There ought to be as much mutuality as possible about this program," Lodge said. "The more mutuality there is the more self-respecting the whole thing is going to be and the less we will be criticized afterward. It should be possible to have a very important percentage of the cost of this program met by this type of repayment."

Vandenberg now sought to assuage Lodge. When State Department official William T. Phillips, who was testifying that day before the committee, listed such strategic materials that the United States might acquire from the European nations as cobalt and industrial diamonds, Vandenberg asked about uranium. Phillips conceded that he didn't know enough about that topic to respond.

"You might indicate to some of the top [State Department] levels to which you referred," Vandenberg replied, "that some of us are going to want some information about uranium."[5]

. . .

"The United States," Truman wrote to Congress on December 19 as he sent his detailed Marshall Plan legislation to Capitol Hill,

> has taken the lead in world-wide efforts to promote industrial and agricultural reconstruction and a revival of world commerce, for we know that enduring peace must be based upon increased production and an expanding flow of goods and materials among nations for the benefit of all . . . We must now make a grave and significant decision relating to our further efforts to create the conditions of peace. We must decide whether or not we will com-

"Very Serious"

plete the job of helping the free nations of Europe to recover from the devastation of the war. Our decision will determine in large part the future of the people of that continent. It will also determine in large part whether the free nations of the world can look forward with hope to a peaceful and prosperous future as independent states, or whether they must live in poverty and in fear of selfish totalitarian aggression.

Truman appealed to lawmakers on the basis of both high-minded American values and raw American self-interest. "It is of vital importance to the United States that European recovery be continued to ultimate success. The American tradition of extending a helping hand to people in distress, our concern for the building of a healthy world economy which can make possible ever-increasing standards of living for our people, and our overwhelming concern for the maintenance of a civilization of free men and free institutions, all combine to give us this great interest in European recovery."

Truman set the Marshall Plan at the center of the Cold War. "Our deepest concern with European recovery, however,

is that it is essential to the maintenance of the civilization in which the American way of life is rooted. It is the only assurance of the continued independence and integrity of a group of nations who constitute a bulwark for the principles of freedom, justice and the dignity of the individual . . . Political events in Europe and in the rest of the world cannot be accurately foreseen. We must not be blind to the fact that the communists have announced determined opposition to any effort to help Europe get back on its feet. There will unquestionably be further indictments to strike, not for the purpose of redressing the legitimate grievances of particular groups, but for the purpose of bringing chaos in the hope that it will pave the way for totalitarian control.

Truman requested that Congress authorize the government to spend up to $17 billion on the Marshall Plan from April 1, 1948, through June 30, 1952, and he estimated that the program would need $6.8 billion of it in its first fifteen months.

. . .

With the Marshall Plan on Capitol Hill, Vandenberg said, Congress would "determine whether there is to be a third World War and whether the United States is to be fatally isolated in an economically Communist-controlled world."[6]

Framing the issue starkly, Vandenberg nevertheless would face no easy task in rallying his Republican colleagues to the cause. The GOP was split over the Marshall Plan in a somewhat predictable fashion. The Republican establishment expressed support. In early November New York's Republican governor, Thomas Dewey, who ran unsuccessfully for president against FDR in 1944 and planned to run again in 1948, told a thousand business executives at a dinner at New York's Waldorf Astoria that the nation had no choice but to aid struggling European nations under the Marshall Plan. Also in November Minnesota's former Republican governor, Harold Stassen, who unsuccessfully sought the Republican nomination for president in 1940 and 1944 and was busily seeking support from Republicans around the country for a run in 1948, urged congressional party leaders to back the Marshall Plan and, in that way, strengthen bipartisan foreign policy. In December Alf Landon, the former Kansas governor who lost the presidential race to FDR in a landslide in 1936, visited Truman at the White House and emerged to express his support as well.[7]

Of his chat with Truman, Landon told reporters, "I did remark to him that I had said in several speeches recently that whatever is done to implement the Marshall Plan . . . ought not to be done on a yearly basis or on a temporary basis." "I told him," he said, "these people in Europe are sticking out their necks, that their very lives are at stake and they ought to know what they can count on."

On Capitol Hill, however, the Republican lawmakers whom Vandenberg needed to rally included a contingent of isolationists who had run for Congress on promises of reducing both government spending and America's global footprint. Consequently, they either opposed the Marshall Plan outright due to its cost and ambition, or they wanted to decide at the end of each year whether the program was worth continuing.

Their views reflected the "new isolationism," described by the *New*

York Times' Cabell Phillips as "an unwillingness (in greatly varying degree) to expend more of United States solicitude, effort or dollars in the redemption of Europe or the rest of the world. This attitude stems variously from frustration over the many failures at international cooperation which have occurred since the war; an abiding distrust of Russia, which is viewed as the ubiquitous stumbling-block to all efforts to date, or a deep-seated prejudice against the whole concept of our collaborating politically in European affairs." The new isolationism rested on "the pessimistic assumption that Europe probably can't be saved anyway, and that our efforts to do so are but a recrudescence of that futile and wasteful doctrine of 'do-goodism' which is distastefully identified in many Republican minds with the New Deal."[8]

That Robert Taft, known as "Mr. Republican," was leading the Republican opposition in Congress and also planned to run for the GOP presidential nomination in 1948 would only complicate Vandenberg's efforts.

17

"A Problem Which They Themselves Must Meet"

ON JANUARY 5, 1948, Vandenberg announced triumphantly that Truman had taken his advice and withdrawn his request for $17 billion up front for the Marshall Plan, opting instead to seek funding in annual increments.

At the time, Vandenberg was juggling multiple balls related to the Marshall Plan. He was preparing for his committee's hearings, which would begin on January 8, and, both on and off the committee, he was moving to clear away the major political hurdles to enactment, including the biggest one: funding.

For many lawmakers of both parties, $17 billion was not just a huge number. It also represented a long-term funding commitment that they were unwilling to make. Opponents noted that, as a practical matter, the Eightieth Congress of 1947–48 could not force any future Congress to provide funding—every two-year session of Congress was free to make its own decisions—so the Eightieth Congress didn't have to authorize $17 billion for four years anyway. Vandenberg, who had unsuccessfully advised Truman earlier in 1947 not to propose the $17 billion figure in the first place, had more luck when he raised the issue again in a December 31 letter to Marshall. This time, Lovett wrote back to say that Truman would relent; the only specific amount he would seek at that moment was $6.8 billion for the first fifteen months. A proud Vandenberg released his letter and Lovett's response at a news conference. While significantly addressing the funding issue, however, Vandenberg's triumph didn't fully eliminate it.

Another big hurdle loomed as well. Truman had proposed to create a new agency to run the Marshall Plan and to have its administrator report to the secretary of state on all matters of foreign policy. Some influential Republicans, however, proposed that Congress create a new government corporation that would run the program and hold equal standing to the State Department. That's because Republicans didn't trust the State Department to run the program in a business-like manner. Marshall, however, opposed the GOP proposal because he feared competition from the administrator on foreign policy. "There cannot be two secretaries of state," Marshall complained. Hoping to defuse matters at least temporarily, Vandenberg in early January asked the Brookings Institution, a Washington think tank, to study the competing plans and provide its thoughts.

. . .

"The committee will come to order," Chairman Arthur Vandenberg declared on the morning of January 8, 1948, as the Senate Foreign Relations Committee opened hearings on the Marshall Plan.

Along with the committee, Vandenberg had invited other senators to attend the hearings and, on the first day, three did so. Also on hand that day was Marshall, the lead administration witness. In the coming days, he would be followed to the witness table by Lewis Douglas, U.S. ambassador to Great Britain; Commerce Secretary Averell Harriman; Agriculture Secretary Clinton P. Anderson; Interior Secretary Julius Albert Krug; Treasury Secretary John W. Snyder; William McChesney Martin, who chaired the Export-Import Bank's board of directors; Army Secretary Kenneth C. Royall; and Defense Secretary James Forrestal.

Vandenberg, however, didn't want to hear only from administration officials during the hearings, which occurred on most working days from January 8 until their completion on February 5. Nor, more brashly, did he want to let prominent Americans who might have something important to contribute—some of whom were voicing their opinions about the Marshall Plan in other venues—escape his clutches. He directed them to "offer to testify on the bill or be subpoenaed." Among those on his mind were such former top officials as President Herbert Hoover, Secretaries of State Henry Stimson and Jimmy Byrnes, Commerce Secretary Jesse Jones, Lend-Lease Administrator Leo Crowley, and the U.S. ambassador to Great Britain, Joseph Kennedy, as well as financier Bernard Baruch.[1]

For the most part, Vandenberg didn't use the hearings to deliver grand speeches and forcefully pitch the Marshall Plan to his colleagues. Instead, as with Greek-Turkish aid, he made his points more subtly by asking leading questions and, through that approach, addressing the concerns of other senators.

. . .

Vandenberg's deliberative approach began in his exchange with Marshall after the secretary delivered his prepared remarks on the opening day.

Walking Marshall through his Harvard speech and the subsequent discussions with Europe's participating nations, Vandenberg first sought to allay the fears of spendthrift senators who worried that Washington would pour more money down a rat hole. European nations, he noted, were forced to come together around a systemic and comprehensive plan before Washington would agree to finance it.

VANDENBERG: I assume that you were saying at [Harvard] that from here out the problem of European recovery, although constantly tinged with a powerful American self-interest, is essentially a problem which they themselves must meet, and you were saying that from here on our relationship to the problem must be on the basis of their own determination to help themselves, and to establish their own programs for their own recovery. Is that correct?

MARSHALL: That is correct.

Vandenberg next sought to address the complaints of liberal senators that the Marshall Plan would divide the continent more clearly into U.S. and Soviet spheres. The Soviets, Vandenberg noted with Marshall's assistance, had participated in early discussions with British and French officials but then decided to back away and prohibit any of their Eastern European satellites from participating.

VANDENBERG: How many [European nations] were invited in the first instance?

MARSHALL: All. All were invited. There was no limitation at all.

VANDENBERG: And the original response was from how many?

MARSHALL: It depends on what you mean by "response." In the first instance, the Soviet Union participated in the person of Molotov. There they were endeavoring to decide on the procedure to be followed. The others had not all come in . . .

VANDENBERG: I mean, how many in the first instance agreed tentatively to attend the conference?

MARSHALL: I think there were eighteen; this is, including Czechoslovakia and Poland, I believe. Czechoslovakia sent in the actual formal acceptance and later had to withdraw it. I think Poland indicated its intention to join in the affair, but never came forward with a formal acceptance. Czechoslovakia did accept and had to withdraw the acceptance . . .

Then, minutes later:

VANDENBERG: In the course of the subsequent weeks since the arrangement was tentatively perfected which we now have before us, has the Soviet Union officially categorically declared war—let's say declared cold war—on the success of this program?

MARSHALL: In effect, by the statement of a responsible official of the Soviet government . . . it made a declaration of antagonism and hostility to the program. Mr. Molotov has indicated very plainly his hostile attitude, the hostile attitude of the Soviet government to the program.

. . .

Douglas succeeded Marshall at the witness table on January 9, and Vandenberg returned to the issue of Europe's obligation under the Marshall Plan to make the necessary systemic changes to revive its economy.

When Vandenberg asked Douglas whether the legislation makes clear that European nations would have to make those systemic changes as a condition of receiving Marshall Plan aid, Douglas pointed to language stating that each participating nation would have to craft a formal agreement with the United States, specifying that it would take such steps to revive Europe's economy as the following:

> Promoting industrial and agricultural production in order to enable the participating country to become independent of abnormal outside assistance.
>
> Taking financial and monetary measures necessary to stabilize its currency, establish or maintain a proper rate of exchange, and generally to restore or maintain confidence in its monetary system.
>
> Cooperating with other participating countries in facilitating and stimulating an increasing interchange of goods and services among the participating countries and with other countries and cooperating to reduce barriers to trade among themselves and with other countries.

Vandenberg pressed on with his skeptical Republican colleagues in mind, suggesting that, as the legislation was then written, the obligation was more implicit than explicit. Douglas said he thought the obligation was clear, but he also offered to follow up with Vandenberg and other committee members.

. . .

A day later, Vandenberg again picked Douglas's brain to further allay cost fears.

As he understood it, Vandenberg told Douglas, Marshall Plan aid would be a combination of grants and loans, with the latter constituting 20 to 40 percent of the total. Correct, Douglas said. Using the $6.8 billion that Truman had requested for the first fifteen months as a "hypothetic figure for the purpose of this inquiry," Vandenberg asked whether the cost to the Treasury would be lower than $6.8 billion to the extent that some portion amounted to loans that were repaid. Correct again, Douglas said.

VANDENBERG: So that if 20 percent of the $6.8 billion went into loans that are repaid it would ultimately reduce the $6.8 billion by $1.3 billion or $1.4 billion.

DOUGLAS: That is right.

VANDENBERG: And if 40 percent goes into loans that are repaid it would reduce the $6.8 billion and its ultimate impact on the Treasury by about $2.75 billion.

DOUGLAS: That is right, sir.

VANDENBERG: So that the net burden of the $6.8 billion, assuming that the loans are repaid, would come down to about $5.5 billion under the low estimate, or down to about $4 billion under the high estimate?

DOUGLAS: That is correct, Senator.

. . .

Vandenberg worked to convince his colleagues that the choice was not simply whether to finance the Marshall Plan. The choice, instead, was whether to invest in economic aid under the Marshall Plan or in far more expensive military programs.

To make his points, Vandenberg grilled Army Secretary Kenneth Royall and Defense Secretary James Forrestal, who appeared one after the other on January 15.

VANDENBERG: I want to make one other point in your testimony inescapably clear. You said in your opening statement yesterday, and I quote, "I firmly believe that enlightened cooperative economic endeavor as visualized in the European recovery program can go a long way toward reducing the necessity for large-scale national armaments, and that without some such effort the army and its budget should be immediately and measurably increased." As I understand

"Very Serious"

you, what you were saying is that if it were not for the prospect of organized economic stabilization as a source of security you envision an alternative situation which would require immediate and measurable appropriations for larger-scale national armaments than have been thus far requested?

ROYALL: That is correct, sir.

VANDENBERG: Put still more bluntly, is it fair to say that your judgment offers us the choice, in part, between appropriations for economic cooperation on the one hand, or greater appropriations for military purposes in the interests of our ultimate national security?

ROYALL: That is my judgment.

Similarly, with Forrestal:

VANDENBERG: Mr. Secretary, in terms of the national security, for which you are primarily the responsible government agent, I want to ask you about the final sentence in your statement which reads as follows: "We need to maintain substantial military power, but I would rate the need for the restoration of the European community as equally strong." Without attempting to narrow the question to any specific bill, such as we have before us, I want to ask you whether it does not follow, from your final sentence, that we have a very definite and specific American defense self-interest in the economic restoration of Western Europe and western Germany, and whether the corollary of your final sentence would not be this: That except as the restoration of the European community, in the pattern to which you refer, occurs, there follows as an inevitable corollary that we must maintain a substantially larger military power than we would under the other circumstances?

FORRESTAL: I think there is a definite relation between the two. If what I have chosen to call the imbalance of Europe continues, there will be a rising necessity on our part to provide the only alternative balance to that imbalance, namely, greater military power for ourselves.

. . .

While steering the committee's discussions with administration officials, Vandenberg continued to read the tea leaves in Congress and adjust his position on the Marshall Plan legislation to address political problems. He sought to find the legislative sweet spot between Truman, who wasn't inclined toward much more compromise, and many Senate and House Republicans who were demanding it.

"The Senator from Michigan," the *New York Times*' Reston, who favored the Marshall Plan, wrote in early February, "has been walking the knife-edge for months between the broad objectives of the Administration's policy, which he approves, and the reluctant halfway policies of so many of his colleagues, who are neither isolationist nor internationalist but somewhere in between, at sea."[2]

Even with Truman's agreement to drop the $17 billion figure, funding remained the top hot-button issue. With groups of Republicans meeting to plot first-year cuts (anywhere from $1 billion to more than $2 billion), Vandenberg hinted at a January 13 hearing that he didn't view the $6.8 billion figure as "sacrosanct." On that, Truman and Vandenberg clashed publicly in early February when the president demanded the full $6.8 billion and the senator suggested he was open to a cut.

By mid-February Vandenberg had crafted a creative compromise to bridge the gap between Truman and congressional Republicans, giving each side the ammunition to declare victory. After five days of closed meetings that followed the public hearings, Vandenberg convinced his committee to set the initial funding at $5.3 billion. That funding, however, would cover only the first twelve months of the Marshall Plan, rather than fifteen, so it would give Truman about the same amount of monthly funding to launch the program. It also would give the person elected president that November—who, with Truman broadly unpopular, everybody assumed would be a Republican—an opportunity to put his own stamp on the Marshall Plan just a few months after taking office in early 1949. With a twelve-month duration, the funding would expire around then.

On the administrative front, the Brookings Institution gave Vandenberg the suggestion, which he endorsed, for another creative compromise. Under the proposal that it sent to Vandenberg in late January, Congress would create a new agency, with the rank of a cabinet department, to run the program. The secretary of state, however, could appeal its decisions that relate to foreign policy to the president. Republicans claimed victory because the agency would be free of State Department control, while Truman (and Marshall) claimed victory because there would not be "two secretaries of state."

After the Senate Foreign Relations Committee approved its version of the Marshall Plan unanimously on February 13, Vandenberg began to prepare for a contentious debate on the Senate floor.

18

"A Welcome Beacon in the World's Dark Night"

ON FEBRUARY 25, 1948, Harry Truman was five days into a two-week trip aboard the USS *Williamsburg* that would take him to Puerto Rico, the Virgin Islands, Cuba, and Key West, Florida. Heading for a short stop at Guantanamo Bay, he and his entourage hit rough waters. "Heavy weather (ground swells whipped up by a moderate gale—28 to 33 knots)," the official trip log recorded, "was encountered after we changed course at 6:45 a.m. and headed northward up and across the Windward Passage." The ship "rolled and tossed about making it somewhat uncomfortable for all hands."

Also on February 25 the geopolitical waters grew rougher for Truman as well. Events in Europe that culminated that day prompted new fears in the White House, the State Department, and Congress about Soviet aggressiveness and Western Europe's vulnerability. Those fears, in turn, provided a new burst of momentum behind the Marshall Plan just as Vandenberg was preparing to bring it to the Senate floor for debate.

The immediate flashpoint was Czechoslovakia, where a simmering conflict between Communist and non-Communist forces came to a head. President Eduard Benes, who returned from exile after World War II, had agreed to share power with the Communists after they won nearly 40 percent of the vote in elections in May of 1946. He invited Communist Party leader Klement Gottwald to serve as prime minister and gave the party various important government posts. Through 1947 and early 1948 Communist officials pushed their policy agenda on the nation while strong-arming non-Communists from power. When some non-Communist officials resigned in protest in early 1948, the Communists demanded that Benes give them full control of the government, and, on February 25, he reluctantly did so. In the coming weeks, the Communists would crack down on their opposition, firing or arresting hundreds and prompting thousands to flee the country. Foreign Minister Jan Masaryk died under mysterious circumstances on March 10—he either jumped to his death from a building or was pushed. The Communists held rigged elections in May to ratify their control, and a disheartened Benes resigned in June.

With, in late February, Czechoslovakia firmly in Communist hands—where it would stay until the Soviet crack-up forty years later—Moscow set its sights on Finland, seeking to bring it fully into the Soviet orbit. Two days after Benes turned Czechoslovakia over to the Communists, Stalin proposed a "Russian-Finnish treaty of mutual defense" that mirrored some of the treaties Moscow had inked with its Eastern European satellites. Though it gave Finland more independence than the Soviets had sought, it also called for military cooperation between the two nations if "Germany or its allies"—i.e., the United States—invaded the Soviet Union through Finland. Finland signed the treaty in early April.

"Events in Czechoslovakia and Finland," read a statement that Vandenberg's committee issued on February 28, "make it obvious that time is of the essence in doing whatever we are going to do."[1]

. . .

"With the unanimous approval of the Senate Foreign Relations Committee," Vandenberg told the Senate as he opened debate on the Marshall Plan on March 1,

> I report the Economic Cooperation Act of 1948 in its perfected text. In the name of peace, stability, and freedom, it deserves prompt passage. In the name of intelligent American self-interest it envisions a mighty undertaking worthy of our faith. It is an economic act—but economics usually control

national survivals these days. The act itself asserts that "disruption follow-ing in the wake of war is not contained by national frontiers." It asserts that "the existing situation in Europe endangers the establishment of a lasting peace, the general welfare and national interest of the United States, and the attainment of the objectives of the United Nations."

It was a classic Vandenberg moment, one for which he had prepared meticulously. The speech, which he rewrote seven times, ran 9,000 words and, for the hour and twenty minutes that he needed to deliver it, he asked the Senate to let him speak "without interruption." With Vanden-berg eager to make his case, others were equally eager to hear it. Almost every senator was in the chamber and some House members, who had walked over from the House side of the Capitol, lined the walls. The public gallery was packed, and those who couldn't get in stood in cor-ridors and on stairways.

"This act may well become a welcome beacon in the world's dark night," Vandenberg stated, adding a sense of urgency, "but if a beacon is to be lighted at all it had better be lighted before it is too late. Never-theless," he acknowledged, "the decision which here concerns the Sen-ate is the kind that tries men's souls." The Marshall Plan was hugely expensive and success was not guaranteed. So, with a nod to his spend-thrift and isolationist colleagues, he said, "I understand and share the anxieties involved. It would be a far happier circumstance if we could close our eyes to reality, comfortably retire within our bastions, and dream of an isolated and prosperous peace. But that which was once our luxury would now become our folly. This is too plain to be persua-sively denied in a foreshortened, atomic world. We must take things as they are."

"The greatest nation on earth either justifies or surrenders its lead-ership," Vandenberg declared, using one of his favorite lines. "We must choose. There are no blueprints to guarantee results. We are entirely surrounded by calculated risks. I profoundly believe that the pending program is the best of these risks. I have no quarrel with those who dis-agree, because we are dealing with imponderables. But I am bound to

say to those who disagree that they have not escaped to safety by rejecting or subverting this plan. They have simply fled to other risks, and
I fear far greater ones"—risks that might include Europe's economic
collapse, followed by Soviet-directed Communist insurrections from
within or even a Soviet invasion. "For myself, I can only say that I pre-
fer my choice of responsibilities."

Vandenberg made clear that the Marshall Plan was less about U.S.
generosity than self-interest. "This legislation," he said,

> seeks peace and stability for free men in a free world. It seeks them by eco-
> nomic rather than by military means. It proposes to help our friends to help
> themselves in the pursuit of sound and successful liberty in the democratic
> pattern. The quest can mean as much to us as it does to them. It aims to pre-
> serve the victory against aggression and dictatorship which we thought we
> won in World War II. It strives to help stop World War III before it starts.
> It fights the economic chaos which would precipitate far-flung disintegra-
> tion. It sustains Western civilization. It means to take Western Europe com-
> pletely off the American dole at the end of the adventure. It recognizes the
> grim truth—whether we like it or not—that American self-interest, national
> economy, and national security are inseverably linked with these objectives. It
> stops if changed conditions are no longer consistent with the national inter-
> est of the United States. It faces the naked facts of life.

"There is only one voice left in the world," Vandenberg declared, ending with a flourish, "which is competent to hearten the determination
of the other nations and other peoples in Western Europe to survive
in their own choice of their own way of life. It is our voice. It is in part
the Senate's voice. Surely we can all agree, whatever our shades of opinion, that the hour has struck for this voice to speak as soon as possible.
I pray it speaks for weal and not for woe." The Marshall Plan, he predicted, "can be the turning point in history for 100 years to come. If it
fails, we have done our final best. If it succeeds our children and our
children's children will call us blessed. May God grant His benediction
upon the ultimate event."

With that, the *New York Times* wrote, "Senators and spectators sprang to their feet in unrestrained applause."[2] No one sought to restore order, even though the outburst violated Senate rules. Virtually every senator in the chamber rushed to shake Vandenberg's hand or slap his back.

. . .

For the next two weeks, Vandenberg served as the Marshall Plan's lead champion in the Senate, defending the legislation against attack and mounting the opposition to amendments that would undermine it.

When Senator Kenneth Wherry, a Nebraska Republican, argued that Congress should reauthorize the plan itself (as opposed to its funding) one year at a time rather than for four years up front, Vandenberg said that would undermine the long-term U.S. commitment to Europe on which the plan was based, and that Congress was approving funding on an annual basis anyway. When Senator Homer Capehart, an Indiana Republican, proposed that Marshall Plan aid flow not from government to government but, instead, in business loans from the Reconstruction Finance Corporation, Vandenberg said that would undermine all of Europe's progress of the previous eight months.

The most serious challenge to Vandenberg, and to the Marshall Plan in general, came from Senator Robert Taft, the Ohio Republican whose influence among Senate Republicans on domestic issues rivaled that of Vandenberg on foreign affairs. On Friday, March 12, he proposed to cut first-year funding from $5.3 billion to $4 billion, explaining that he opposed funding beyond "specific programs clearly necessary for subsistence, or clearly helpful in increasing . . . production" by Western European nations. Vandenberg held his supporters in line and the Senate rejected Taft's amendment on a 56–31 vote.

Through two weeks of debate, Vandenberg's influence was overwhelming. When he voiced his support for an amendment by a colleague, the full Senate approved it. When he opposed one, the Senate rejected it.

The capstone of his efforts came shortly after midnight on March 14 when the Senate voted 69–17 for the Marshall Plan.

. . .

"There is an increasing threat to nations which are striving to maintain a form of government which grants freedom to its citizens," Truman told a joint session of Congress in a high-profile speech on March 17.

In addressing Congress, Truman had two goals in mind. First, he wanted to give the Marshall Plan, which the House still needed to approve, a final push. Second, he wanted to focus attention on other steps that Washington would have to take in response to rising Soviet aggressiveness on the world stage.

For Truman, as earlier for Vandenberg, the Czechoslovakian and Finnish developments would prove not only sobering but politically opportune; they would help push the Marshall Plan over the goal line by highlighting both ruthless Soviet expansionism and growing European vulnerability. So, too, would the looming national election in Italy in April, for which Communist forces were mounting a serious challenge. (In private discussions, the influential columnist Marquis Childs reported, Vandenberg was calling it perhaps the most important election of the past fifty years and the next one hundred.)[3]

"The tragic death of the Republic of Czechoslovakia has sent a shock throughout the civilized world," Truman said. "Now pressure is being brought to bear on Finland, to the hazard of the entire Scandinavian peninsula. Greece is under direct military attack from rebels actively supported by her Communist-dominated neighbors. In Italy, a determined and aggressive effort is being made by a Communist minority to take control of that country. The methods vary, but the pattern is all too clear.

"Faced with this growing menace," Truman continued, focusing on the Marshall Plan, "there have been encouraging signs that the free nations of Europe are drawing closer together for their economic well-being and for the common defense of their liberties. In the economic field, the movement for mutual self-help to restore conditions essential to the preservation of free institutions is well under way. In Paris, the sixteen nations which are cooperating in the European recovery program are meeting again to establish a joint organization to work for the economic restoration of Western Europe.

"The United States," he reminded lawmakers, "has strongly supported the efforts of these nations to repair the devastation of war and restore a sound world economy." Now, it was time for Congress to finish the job. "In presenting this program to the Congress last December, I emphasized the necessity for speedy action. Every event in Europe since that day has underlined the great urgency for the prompt adoption of this measure."

Two weeks later, Truman signed the Marshall Plan into law, calling the signing "a momentous occasion in the world's quest for peace."

. . .

The Marshall Plan remains one of America's most striking successes and perhaps its most generous global act.

The United States gave some $13 billion to sixteen nations of Western Europe from 1948 to 1951, providing the strategic guidance and financial wherewithal that enabled them to come together, rebuild their economies, and again provide the goods and services of a working society. By dramatically raising living standards for Europe's once-hopeless masses, the plan halted Communist advances in France, Italy, and elsewhere, saving freedom and democracy from the threat of domestic insurrection.

One year in, the Marshall Plan was already reaping huge rewards far beyond Europe's significant advances in economic production. It "gave us hope and help when we most needed it," Britain's prime minister, Clement Attlee, wrote to Truman on its one-year anniversary in April of 1949. "During the last year the whole economic scene in Western Europe has been transformed to a degree which must astonish all of us when we recall the uncertainties and perils of the immediate preceding years." By 1951, production far surpassed prewar levels. The plan also set the stage for long-term prosperity, with Western Europe enjoying its strongest growth ever in the quarter century after 1948.[4]

Truman called the Marshall Plan "perhaps the greatest venture in constructive statesmanship that any nation has undertaken," and it was hard to argue otherwise.

. . .

"At the very moment I am addressing you," Truman also told Congress on March 17, "five nations of the European community, in Brussels, are signing a fifty-year agreement for economic cooperation and common defense against aggression."

It was the Brussels Pact, a panicked response by Britain, France, Belgium, Luxembourg, and the Netherlands to the latest sign of Soviet aggressiveness. Even as the five nations were signing their treaty, however, they knew that, by itself, it could not hope to prevent the Soviet Union from sending its troops across the continent. Only a treaty that included the United States would force the Soviets to hesitate.

Truman acknowledged the point in words that thrilled Europe's leaders. "This development deserves our full support," he said of the Brussels Pact. Foreshadowing the need for more, he added, "I am confident that the United States will, by appropriate means, extend to the free nations the support which the situation requires. I am sure that the determination of the free countries of Europe to protect themselves will be matched by an equal determination on our part to help them to protect themselves."

The North Atlantic Treaty was the kind of regional security agreement that Truman foreshadowed on March 17, and the kind that Vandenberg had envisioned three years earlier when he helped fashion the United Nations Charter. And it was where Truman and Vandenberg would turn next.

PART 4

"An Attack against Them All"

"FREE MEN IN EVERY land are asking, 'Where is this leading? When will it end?'" a worried Harry Truman mused in a March 1948 speech at New York's Hotel Astor to commemorate Saint Patrick's Day.

It was the evening of March 17—the same day on which, ten hours earlier, Truman had spoken to Congress in a push for both congressional approval of the Marshall Plan and U.S. support for the Brussels Pact. His afternoon speech to Congress was strong and effective, but his evening speech in New York better reflected the panic and bewilderment that was then gripping Washington. Along with the ominous developments in Czechoslovakia and Soviet threats to Finland, U.S.-Soviet tensions were growing over Berlin, where Moscow was imposing new restrictions on movement in the city's western section—which was located in the Soviet's eastern zone in Germany but which was under Western control. In a letter to his daughter in early March, Truman likened the U.S. situation to what Britain and France faced with Germany in the late 1930s. Around the same time, General Lucius Clay, military commander of the U.S. zone in Germany, cabled with the ominous observation that "within the last few weeks, I have felt a subtle change in Soviet attitude which I cannot define but which now gives me a feeling that [war] may come with dramatic suddenness." Later in March, *Time* wrote, "All last week in the halls of Congress [and] on the street corners, U.S. citizens had begun to talk of the possibility of war between the U.S. and USSR."[1]

"I can bring you tonight no simple or easy answer," Truman continued that evening in New York. "But I can express my firm conviction
that, at this moment in history, the faith and strength of the United
States are mighty forces for the prevention of war and the establishment
of peace. Our faith and our strength must be made unmistakably [clear]
to the world. So long as democracy is threatened in the world, and during the period in which the free nations of Europe are regaining their
strength, this country must remain strong in order to give support to
those countries of Europe whose freedom is endangered."

"We will have to take risks during the coming year—risks perhaps
greater than any this country has been called upon to assume," Truman
concluded. "But they are not risks of our own making, and we cannot
make the danger vanish by pretending that it does not exist. We must
be prepared to meet that danger with sober self-restraint and calm and
judicious action if we are to be successful in our leadership for peace.
The people of the United States have learned that peace will not come in
response to soft words and vague wishes. We know that we can achieve
the peace we seek only through firm resolution and hard work."

Vandenberg shared Truman's concerns. Responding to an inquiry
about prospects for Soviet aggression against the United States, he wrote
in early April, "I have no doubt that Soviet Russia would be very glad
to scrupulously avoid direct aggression upon the United States if we
are content to let her go without challenge in direct aggression upon
everybody else. But I am sure you will agree that our own self-interest
could not permit us to complacently await our isolation in a Communist world. On the other hand, I would entirely agree that we must proceed with extreme prudence in assessing indirect aggression."[2]

Just as Congress was preparing to approve a plan to spend untold
billions to restore Western Europe's economy, America's leaders were
coming to realize that dollars alone would not protect the West. The
United States would have to join with the besieged continent in a defense
pact that would send a clear warning to the Soviet Union that America
would go to war to protect its allies. If, for Europe, the Marshall Plan
would restore faith in free markets and democracy and prevent a Com-

munist insurrection from within, a U.S.-led defense pact would protect the continent from without.

. . .

The North Atlantic Treaty—the fourth and final element of America's revolutionary new foreign policy—created NATO and culminated nearly two years of efforts in the United States and Europe that showcased both Truman's continuing leadership and Vandenberg's unusually consequential role.

Throughout 1947 Truman and Vandenberg were increasingly hearing the pleas of Western European leaders for the United States to help arm and protect their nations. For one thing, the Soviets were on the march. For another, Moscow was using its veto aggressively at the UN Security Council to promote its interests and block Western initiatives. Both U.S. and European officials worried that, if the Soviets advanced farther west, Moscow could then use its veto to prevent a strong U.S.-led global response. By late 1947, however, the United States had devised and tested a formula to circumvent the problem. Due to Truman and Vandenberg's efforts in San Francisco in 1945, the UN Charter allowed nations to create regional defense pacts. In mid-1947 Truman and Vandenberg played leading roles as the United States joined with its Western Hemispheric neighbors to create the "Rio Pact," providing collective hemispheric defense. Thus, by late 1947, the president and the senator had reason, law, and precedent on their side as they faced the question of European security.

Though presidents normally spearhead major U.S. foreign policy initiatives, it was Vandenberg who gave U.S. participation in European regional security its most important public push. In this case, Vandenberg was eager to lead, and Truman found it useful to sit back and let him do so. With Truman applauding privately and updated by his aides regularly, Vandenberg worked closely with Undersecretary of State Robert Lovett in early 1948 on a resolution through which the Senate urged the president to pursue "regional and other collective arrangements for individual and collective self-defense in accordance with the purposes, principles, and provisions of the Charter." Vandenberg previewed the resolution in public remarks, shopped it to his Senate colleagues, and, with Lovett, built support for it among Truman's top diplomatic and military aides. With the Senate approving the "Vandenberg Resolution" on a 64–4 vote in June of 1948, Truman felt he had the requisite domestic support to pursue a regional pact for Europe.

Vandenberg and Lovett had grown close during their many hours together, however difficult Vandenberg could be and however much Lovett disliked lawmakers as a group. But by early 1949—as Truman worked to create the North Atlantic Treaty and Vandenberg sought to secure Senate ratification for it—their key intermediary was no longer Lovett but, once again, Acheson. Truman appointed Acheson as secretary of state in January of 1949 when both the ailing Marshall and the exhausted Lovett resigned. Though Truman was happy to have Acheson back, Vandenberg was less happy to see him; he knew that Acheson's condescending ways would again irritate Senate Republicans. Nevertheless, Vandenberg and Acheson picked up where they had left off. Acheson again proved a skillful global negotiator and U.S. political insider, crafting a pact that could satisfy Truman and the Europeans (who supported a robust U.S. role in the pact) as well as Vandenberg (who sought to downplay America's commitments in order to reassure worried senators).

In the end, the United States joined eleven European nations on a treaty in which they pledged, "an armed attack against one or more of them in Europe or North America shall be considered an attack against them all." After months of vigorous debate in Washington, the Senate Foreign Relations Committee approved it unanimously in early May of 1949 and the Senate voted 82–13 to ratify it in late July. It was America's first peacetime military alliance outside the Western Hemisphere and, as such, it drove another nail into the coffin of traditional U.S. isolationism. It also built upon the Truman Doctrine, applying it legalistically to the defense of Western Europe.

Truman and Vandenberg's two-year collaboration to craft the treaty reflected their growing reliance on one another on a host of foreign pol-

　　　　　　　　　　　"Attack against Them All"

icy challenges and their careful efforts to not let interparty politics derail their bipartisan progress. Truman and his team, for instance, brought Vandenberg into their inner circle as they decided how to respond to the Soviet decision to blockade Berlin in June of 1948. The president and the senator also refrained from attacking one another during the brutal elections of 1948. Truman paid homage to Vandenberg when he launched his campaign in, of all places, the senator's hometown of Grand Rapids. Vandenberg held his tongue and seethed quietly as Truman attacked the very same Republican Congress with which the president had worked so closely on the Truman Doctrine and Marshall Plan.

For U.S.-led European security, Truman and Vandenberg began their efforts not in Washington but, instead, in South America.

19

"Their Hope Must Lie in This New World of Ours"

IN THE LATE SUMMER of 1947, Truman and Vandenberg traveled to Petropolis, Brazil, just outside Rio de Janeiro, for the Inter-American Conference for the Maintenance of Continental Peace and Security.

In Petropolis, the United States joined eighteen of its Latin American neighbors to sign the so-called Rio Pact. In language that Washington and its European allies would adopt in modified form for their own purposes two years later, the Rio Pact declared that "an armed attack by any State against an American State shall be considered as an attack against all the American States and, consequently, each one of the said Contracting Parties undertakes to assist in meeting the attack in the exercise of the inherent right of individual or collective self-defense recognized by Article 51 of the Charter of the United Nations." The pact was the first fruit of Truman and Vandenberg's labors two years earlier in San Francisco over Article 51, enabling the United States and its allies to create regional defense pacts without undermining the United Nations or its Security Council. The Rio Pact replaced the more modest Act of Chapultepec which the United States and its Latin neighbors had inked just weeks before the San Francisco conference.

Truman appointed Vandenberg to the U.S. delegation to Petropolis, and Vandenberg thoroughly enjoyed the respite from Washington as well as the work related to his cherished Article 51. Vandenberg was a beloved figure in Latin America, where officials remembered his efforts in San Francisco, and his work in Petropolis further nourished those warm feelings. There, he played a key role in resolving several nettlesome matters. For instance, he alleviated Latin American concerns by helping to limit the geographic scope of the Rio Pact, convincing the other U.S. delegates that the United States could not reasonably expect Latin nations to come to America's aid if it were fighting thousands of miles from their region. For that work, the conference honored him with a resolution stating that it "recalls with gratitude the services rendered by Senator Arthur Vandenberg" in San Francisco over Article 51 and "applauds the cooperation which in a lofty and comprehensive spirit he has given the discussion" of the Rio Pact.[1]

With the work of the conference completed, Truman joined Vandenberg and the other U.S. delegates in Petropolis in early September and, speaking to the final session, put the Rio Pact in the context of a divided world—with Washington on one side, devoted to peace, human rights, and the United Nations; and Moscow on the other, undermining all of them. "The Western Hemisphere cannot alone assure world peace," Truman declared, "but without the Western Hemisphere no peace is possible. The Western Hemisphere cannot alone provide world prosperity, but without the Western Hemisphere no world prosperity is possible . . . This Western Hemisphere of ours is usually referred to as the New World. That it is the New World is clearer today than ever before. The Old World [i.e., Europe] is exhausted, its civilization imperiled. Its people are suffering. They are confused and filled with fears for the future. Their hope must lie in this New World of ours. . . . The United States seeks world peace—a peace of free men. I know that you stand with us. United, we can constitute the greatest single force in the world for the good of humanity."

In early December Vandenberg pushed the Rio Pact through the Senate Foreign Relations Committee and, four days later, the Senate on a 72–1 vote. "We have," he told the Senate, "reknit the effective solidarity of North, Central, and South America against all aggressors, foreign and domestic. We have sealed a New World pact of peace which possesses teeth . . . With scrupulous regard for the United Nations—acting strictly within Articles 51, 52, 53, and 54 of the United Nations Char-

"Attack against Them All"

ter—we have demonstrated how like-minded, peace-loving members of the United Nations can make so-called regional arrangements which build peace and security for themselves and for the world, regardless of confusion in higher UN councils. This is sunlight in a dark world."[2]

While the Rio Pact offered a useful precedent as Truman and Vandenberg focused on Europe in late 1947, the Petropolis meeting also enabled Vandenberg to spend more time with Secretary of State Marshall, drawing them closer together. Their wives played an important role in their warming relations.

"Just to illustrate how wonderful they are with each other," Mrs. Vandenberg wrote in her diary about the Marshalls, "I found them playing Chinese checkers on the porch here after having had a ride to an especially beautiful site. They are completely congenial and a simply grand pair. If nothing else comes out of this conference, it has been a rare privilege to know them better, and [the senator] feels the same way. There is nothing stuffy at all about [Marshall], in fact, he is a lot of fun, and so human."[3]

When they returned to Washington, Truman and Vandenberg turned their attention to bolstering Europe's security.

. . .

"I can fully understand the pessimism about the United Nations which has taken possession of many of our people," Vandenberg wrote to a friend from Michigan in September of 1947. "It would be both silly and dangerous to ignore the worsening relationships between Moscow and Washington. But there is a way to circumvent the deadly [Soviet] 'veto'—as we demonstrated at Rio."[4]

More than two years after San Francisco, Truman and Vandenberg remained devoted to the United Nations and hopeful about its prospects for success. They continued to believe that, for all of its faults, this new global body was the world's most important venue for reducing international tensions by enabling hostile forces to confront one another at a table rather than across a battlefield.

"We are giving, and will continue to give, our full support to the

United Nations," Truman told Congress in his State of the Union address in January of 1948. "While that organization has encountered unforeseen and unwelcome difficulties, I am confident of its ultimate success." Vandenberg was similarly supportive of the body and, in letters to constituents around that time, candid about its problems. "I agree with you that the United Nations must be used in every possible way to create collective security through peaceful means," he wrote in April of 1948. "The great fundamental difficulty is that practically all of our American efforts in these directions are aggressively opposed by Soviet Russia and her satellites. This is true in the United Nations where we are constantly met by a Russian veto."[5]

Indeed, by the end of 1947, Moscow had used its veto at the Security Council nearly two dozen times to protect Soviet interests or thwart U.S. objectives. Moscow, for instance, blocked a series of resolutions designed to pressure Albania, Bulgaria, and Yugoslavia to stop providing support to Communist guerillas who were working to topple Greece's government; blocked a resolution that tied Albania to a mine field in the Corfu Channel that destroyed two British ships; and blocked resolutions that proposed UN membership for Transjordan, Portugal, Ireland, Italy, Austria, and Finland.

Though hopeful about the United Nations, Truman and Vandenberg weren't naive. As they well recognized, they needed to create a mechanism through which to circumvent the Soviet veto and, in turn, safeguard Western Europe. By late 1947, meanwhile, European leaders were agitating for the United States to join them in collective defense.

. . .

That November Truman sent Marshall to London for the next meeting of the Council of Foreign Ministers, this one to secure agreement among the United States, Soviet Union, Britain, and France over Germany's future. Nobody was optimistic about chances for progress—not Truman, not Vandenberg, and surely not Marshall.

The secretary had spent nearly seven weeks in Moscow at the previous Council of Foreign Ministers meeting in the spring, and he didn't

"Attack against Them All"

want to again waste his time in fruitless, frustrating meetings. He turned to John Hickerson, director of the State Department's Office of European Affairs, who was with him in London, and said, "I just want to tell you here and now that I'm going to look to you, in consultation with your British and French opposite numbers, to make reviews from time to time, and if you conclude there's no hope, then we're just going to wind [the meeting] up."[6]

For three weeks, U.S. and Soviet negotiators remained sharply divided over the question of German reparations for World War II as tensions continued to build between them over the Marshall Plan and U.S.-led efforts to create a West German government. With the talks going nowhere, an exasperated Marshall finally called for their adjournment. (Interestingly, Hickerson had predicted that Marshall would reach his breaking point in about three weeks.) More important was what happened at a private dinner after the talks collapsed.

On December 15 as Marshall dined with Britain's foreign minister, Ernest Bevin, at Bevin's London flat before returning to Washington, Bevin proposed the idea of a Western pact among the United States, Canada, and Western Europe to protect the Europeans from Soviet aggression. In the coming days, Bevin would explain that, in fact, he envisioned two pacts—a small one that emerged three months later in the Brussels Pact and a larger one that included the United States and emerged more than a year later in the North Atlantic Treaty. Bevin promoted the idea in a landmark House of Commons speech on January 22, 1948, that drew broad praise—including from opposition party leader Winston Churchill.

By then, Europe's vulnerability had nourished Washington's interest in European regional security. Months earlier, Republican foreign policy adviser John Foster Dulles, who represented Vandenberg at the Council of Foreign Ministers meeting in London, proposed that Europe create a "federal union" of sorts and that the United States provide guidance from its own experience in creating a federal system of government. In addition, Senate Democrats J. William Fulbright of Arkansas and Elbert Thomas of Utah proposed a Senate resolution calling for "the creation of a United

States of Europe within the framework of the United Nations" while Democratic Rep. Hale Boggs of Louisiana proposed a companion resolution in the House. Then, with Marshall in London, Fulbright pushed further for European regional security, declaring in a speech at the University of Toronto, "The continent, in its present fragmentary form, is a large power vacuum which Russia is trying to fill. Let us be under no illusions. If Russia obtains control of Western Europe, the control of Africa, the Near East, and the Middle East will fall into her lap like a ripe plum."[7]

Nevertheless, despite Washington's growing enthusiasm for European regional security, and despite a clear understanding that U.S. participation was required to make it believable, Marshall reacted cautiously to Bevin's idea as they dined together on that December evening. For one thing, he couldn't relay official U.S. support for such a significant measure without first briefing Truman and obtaining his approval. For another, the administration had not yet secured congressional passage of the Marshall Plan, and Marshall didn't want to jeopardize it by putting another item on Washington's agenda. After his dinner, Marshall directed Hickerson to learn more from Bevin's team about his ideas. "You've got to go down and see what the guy has in mind," Marshall ordered. "I just told him that I'd be glad to have him elaborate on that and that we would consider it and so forth and so on."[8]

Privately, Hickerson and his top aide, Theodore Achilles, thought Marshall's response to Bevin had been too tepid, as Hickerson told Dulles while the two returned to Washington from London by ship. Hickerson and Achilles felt strongly that a Western pact was vital, and they pushed it hard with Marshall and Undersecretary Lovett in the ensuing weeks. At a holiday party on December 31 at Washington's Metropolitan Club, where Hickerson was "full of fishhouse punch and an idea for a North Atlantic Treaty," he told Achilles, "I don't care if entangling alliances have been considered worse than original sin since George Washington's time. We've got to have a peace time military alliance with Western Europe. And we've got to get it ratified. It's your baby. Get going."[9]

After New Year's Day the challenge of a "peace time military alliance with Western Europe" sat squarely with Truman and Vandenberg.

"Attack against Them All"

20

"A Sound Answer to Several Critical Necessities"

IN THE EARLY MONTHS of 1948, Truman and Vandenberg recognized that despite U.S. global leadership that had come to life in the UN Charter, Truman Doctrine, and Marshall Plan, Europe remained concerned about America's staying power.

"Our European friends," Truman wrote later, "apparently remembered the League of Nations too; they were most anxious to have not only a presidential declaration of policy but also a congressional expression confirming it." The Senate's post–World War I rejection of the League of Nations had come just a generation earlier and, in London, Paris, and other Western European capitals, U.S. allies were seeking a sign that history wouldn't repeat itself at just the moment when Europe felt most besieged. Consequently, Truman wrote, Lovett "went to work" with Vandenberg "on a congressional declaration of policy which put the Senate on record as favoring regional arrangements 'based on continuous and effective self-help and mutual aid.'"[1]

With Dean Acheson's return to Wall Street in July of 1947, Truman appointed Lovett as undersecretary of state, and, by the spring of 1948, Lovett was spending lots of time consulting with Vandenberg. A Yale graduate and member of Phi Beta Kappa and the prestigious secret society Skull and Bones, Robert Abercrombie Lovett was another classic figure of the period, serving in government between stints as an investment banker. A registered Republican with a bald pate and heavy eyelids, Lovett had served as assistant secretary of war, receiving broad praise for directing America's heavy bomber program during World War II. He later served as deputy secretary and secretary of defense, guiding U.S. mobilization after war erupted in Korea. He was friendly and whimsical in demeanor, calm and cautious in judgment. He said that interacting with Congress was "like getting a shave and having your appendix taken out at the same time." Despite his mixed feelings about lawmakers, however, he and Vandenberg were good friends and, by early 1948, Lovett was visiting Vandenberg's apartment 500G at Washington's Wardman Park Hotel regularly to discuss pending matters.

At the time, Vandenberg was mulling how Congress could best express support for a U.S.-led security pact for Europe, which would reassure both Truman and the Europeans that the Senate would ratify it. Vandenberg and Lovett began meeting on a firmer schedule, with Lovett visiting him after work each day and often on Sunday for what they dubbed the "500G meetings." As they exchanged ideas, their staffs worked to turn them into written language, consulting with one another while putting pen to paper. From the State Department, Hickerson sketched out some verbiage. From the Senate Foreign Relations Committee, Chief of Staff Francis Wilcox did the same. Each produced drafts of several pages, which Vandenberg and Lovett agreed were too long.

Vandenberg, who insisted that he could say what he wanted in one page, then took over, floating his ideas with Lovett and pounding out the words on his manual typewriter. In between, they chatted by phone and met in Vandenberg's Senate office. Lovett briefed Marshall frequently on their progress. For Vandenberg, the issue was how best to balance his desire to strengthen the United Nations and also to allow for a European pact, akin to Rio, outside the control of the Security Council.

By the spring Vandenberg and Lovett were ready to begin floating their ideas with their key constituencies.

. . .

In late April of 1948 Vandenberg described the coming "Vandenberg Resolution" to a Michigan Chamber of Commerce meeting in Washing-

"Attack against Them All"

ton. "We would strengthen and revitalize the United Nations which is still the world's greatest peace potential despite the terrific strains which have been put upon it before it has even yet been allowed, thanks to Russian intransigence, to perfect its contemplated peace machinery," he told his state's business leaders, adding hopefully, "We have not yet scratched the surface of the possibilities of its regional arrangements, as exemplified by the Rio treaty. There can be vital progress in this procedure—and I venture to predict there will."[2]

Around that time, Vandenberg and Lovett brought their draft, which they had indeed sliced to a page, to a meeting at Blair House that included Marshall, Dulles, and military and congressional leaders—all of whom either offered their blessing or did not raise serious enough objections to derail the effort. Vandenberg also discussed his ideas with his Senate Foreign Relations Committee colleagues.

After completing the drafting, Vandenberg unveiled what he called his "working paper" to his committee on May 11. Lovett attended the meeting to provide the administration's official blessing. Over the next week, the committee examined the text in great detail during three long meetings before approving it unanimously on May 19. A day later, Truman heard Lovett tell the president's National Security Council that the resolution would "put us in a stronger position to discuss with the countries of western Europe measures to strengthen our national security as well as theirs."[3]

Through the resolution the Senate stated that "peace with justice and the defense of human rights and fundamental freedoms" require nations to work together more effectively through the United Nations, and it reaffirmed U.S. policy to achieve international peace and security through the global body. It advised Truman to seek changes to the Security Council veto; changes to the UN Charter if necessary; arms reductions by nations around the world; and troops for the United Nations. It also outlined three objectives for Truman that laid the groundwork for U.S. participation in the North Atlantic Treaty:

Progressive development of regional and other collective arrangements for individual and collective self-defense in accordance with the purposes, principles, and provisions of the Charter.

Association of the United States, by constitutional process, with such regional and other collective arrangements as are based on continuous and effective self-help and mutual aid, and as affect its national security.

Contributing to the maintenance of peace by making clear its determination to exercise the right of individual or collective self-defense under Article 51 should any armed attack occur affecting its national security.

All in all, the resolution reflected Vandenberg's top goals, making clear that the United States planned to strengthen the United Nations by working within its charter; that the Soviets need not fear regional pacts because they would be defensive in nature; that the United States would respect its own constitutional procedures (i.e., Senate ratification) in deciding whether to participate in such pacts; and that UN members should strengthen the United Nations by changing the charter, such as by scaling back the veto.

Vandenberg's resolution was, well, just a resolution—Senate Resolution 239, to be precise. It was not a law and, as such, didn't require House approval or Truman's signature. It merely expressed the Senate's sentiment. Nevertheless, for both Truman and Western European leaders, it addressed a vital need by putting the Senate on record in favor of U.S. participation in a regional defense pact and, in turn, further alleviating fears that the Republican-controlled body would revert to its post–World War I isolationist ways. Consequently, it proved hugely important.

. . .

"This resolution is a sound answer to several critical necessities in respect of foreign policy which America confronts," Vandenberg told the Senate on June 11 as he brought the measure before it.

"It is a plan for our practical American cooperation under specified circumstances, within the framework of the United Nations. It is an answer which encourages individual and collective self-defense against armed aggression within the charter and outside the veto. It asserts our interest in regional arrangements, specifically invited by the charter, as a means to renew its effectiveness for peace. It declares our willingness to consider by due constitutional process our own cooperation, in one way or another, with such regional arrangements, if and when we conclude that our own national interests are involved. But," he added, stressing that America wouldn't shoulder the burden of regional defense alone, "it warns that self-help and mutual aid are prerequisites. Our cooperation must be a supplement and not a substitute for the adequate and continuous defensive activities of others."

The Senate debated the resolution for eight hours that day before approving it on a 64–4 vote. The outcome was never in doubt—not in the aftermath of Soviet moves against Czechoslovakia and Finland, of European pleas for help, or of rising U.S.-Soviet tensions over Berlin. On his way to victory, however, Vandenberg was forced to fend off an amendment by the Soviet-sympathizing Florida Democrat, Claude Pepper, "to delete every reference to regional self-defense arrangements abroad."[4] Not surprisingly, Pepper was among the four "no" votes on final passage.

"In its size and in its substance," the *Washington Post* wrote afterward, "the vote was one of the most important Senate decisions in the field of foreign policy since the end of the war. News of it was promptly cabled to American embassies abroad, and was expected to give new confidence to the non-Soviet nations of Europe."[5] "It is a clear indication," the *Los Angeles Times* added, "by the House of Congress which exercises the closer control over U.S. foreign policy that it has cut the last cord of isolationism and that it is ready after 170 years of jealous and gingerly aloofness to endorse European alliances in peacetime.... Only one thing is certain: the Vandenberg Resolution has set a pattern for an American foreign policy, and that is something which the United States has not had in whole or even in coherent parts since the Monroe

Doctrine became too narrow a reference sheet for a country which has outgrown a hemisphere."[6]

The resolution did not escape Moscow's attention, either. It was, the Soviet newspaper *Izvestia* wrote, designed to enable the United States to use the United Nations as "cover" for U.S. imperialism.[7]

...

With the Senate—and, through it, the country—now on record in favor of U.S.-led regional security for Europe, Vandenberg's resolution gave Truman's top aides the political leeway to work openly for it.

Until then State Department officials had been working behind the scenes, fearful that a public campaign would backfire by reigniting isolationist sentiments and stirring opposition to the Marshall Plan. Starting in late March—just days after the Brussels Pact nations had inked their agreement and as Vandenberg was beginning to draft his resolution—Hickerson and Achilles met secretly for about ten days with their British and Canadian counterparts in the Pentagon offices of the Joint Chiefs of Staff. In their discussions Hickerson and Achilles tried to lay the groundwork for U.S. and Canadian participation in a wider European regional defense pact; Achilles even drafted a proposal for a North Atlantic security agreement.

Not all of Truman's State Department aides supported the idea, however. Marshall and Lovett weren't prepared to move as quickly as Hickerson and Achilles. In addition, the influential George Kennan, who had penned the "Long Telegram" of early 1946 and the "X" article in *Foreign Affairs* of mid-1947 to educate U.S. officials about Soviet psychology and explain Soviet behavior, now worried that a U.S.-led military alliance for Europe would provoke Stalin. "We are like a man who has let himself into a walled garden and finds himself alone with a dog with very big teeth," he said at the time. "The dog, for the moment, shows no signs of aggressiveness. The best thing for us to do is surely to try to establish, as between the two of us, the assumption that teeth have nothing to do with our mutual relationship."[8]

By then, however, Truman and Vandenberg did not see the world

"Attack against Them All"

through Kennan's reassuring academic glasses. They were thrown by the events in Czechoslovakia, worried about the future of Finland, and concerned about rising U.S.-Soviet tensions over Berlin. Czechoslovakia, in particular, "scared the living bejesus out of everybody in Western Europe," Hickerson recalled later. In early March he wrote to Marshall, advising the secretary that "a general stiffening of morale in Free Europe is needed."[9]

Less than two weeks after the Senate passed the Vandenberg Resolution, Lovett capitalized on that event to bring Hickerson and Achilles's private talks into the open, announcing at a June 23 news conference that he would expand them to include other European nations. "These discussions," the New York Times explained, "will be based on the Vandenberg resolution, adopted by the Senate, which proposes strengthening the United Nations and developing regional defense organizations within the world organization, and includes the possibility of military support by the United States."[10]

. . .

On Truman's behalf Lovett began his diplomatic discussions with the Brussels Pact nations in Washington on July 6. Separately in July U.S. and Canadian military officials joined the ongoing discussions among Brussels Pact nations about creating a Permanent Military Commission. For weeks by then, the Brussels Pact nations had been meeting privately to assess their military needs in hopes of later convincing the United States to help fill their gaps. U.S. surplus military supplies were not robust, however, and, for some items, the United States didn't even have what it needed for itself. With its current supplies and Europe's needs in mind, U.S. officials concluded that the cost of assisting Europe could be high.[11]

For Truman and Vandenberg, burdens were mounting at a relentless pace. Just three months earlier, they had steered the massive Marshall Plan through Congress, imposing enormous new financial burdens on the United States in the hopes of resurrecting the economy of a flattened continent. Now, they were recognizing that economic aid was but one side of Europe's urgent and expensive needs. The Marshall Plan could help rebuild Europe, revive living standards, and resurrect the normal flow of goods and services—all of which presumably would restore faith in U.S.-led capitalism and democracy and dampen interest in Communist alternatives—but it couldn't reasonably protect Western Europe from the cold reality of an aggressive Soviet Union if Moscow chose to attack westward. For military aid, U.S. officials told the Brussels Pact nations to follow the Marshall Plan formula—come together, assess their collective needs, and present an overall request to Washington.

"Everything in Washington has slowed down except the pace of great events," the *New York Times'* Reston wrote in early July. "The feverish Potomac summer is on us, and a lot of weary officials are looking to the Blue Ridge and the sea, but the hurry of fundamental issues will not subside." Reston posed a series of questions for his readers, the answers to which were complicated by the messiness of American democracy and the reality of Truman's growing political problems at the time. "How long can this go on? Does the United States have the will and the patience to proceed with this extraordinary adventure for world peace? Will the representatives of the people, now disbursed across the continent, in their various constituencies, support the efforts of a declining administration in its attempts to produce some kind of a decent world order?"

In the face of Soviet aggressiveness, Vandenberg argued for U.S. sturdiness of the kind that U.S.-led regional security would exemplify. "The Senate Foreign Relations Committee is convinced," he said that summer, "that the horrors of another world war can be avoided with certainty only by preventing war from starting. The experience of World War I and World War II suggest that the best deterrent to aggression is the certainty that immediate and effective counter-measures will be taken against those who violate the peace."[12]

. . .

As U.S. and European officials were beginning their formal discussions, a bone-tired Vandenberg fantasized about rest.

By July he had steered his resolution through the Senate and he had

"Attack against Them All"

returned from the Republican National Convention in Philadelphia, which nominated New York's governor, Thomas Dewey, to run for president against Truman in November. With the *Times'* Reston visiting his apartment, Vandenberg sat at the window, "stripped to the waist trying to get a breath of fresh air."

"I'm finally going to take a vacation, my first real vacation in four years," he told Reston. "I'm going to get on a boat and go to England; then I'm going to take a little ship into the Scandinavian waters. And, boy, am I looking forward to it!"[13]

Vandenberg was not much for leisurely travel, so he may not have followed through under any circumstance. But, as it turned out, the press of business swept away any hopes for a respite that he may have harbored. What kept Vandenberg in Washington, rather than sailing the Atlantic, was the crisis that erupted over Berlin. The administration's consultations with him showed just how much Harry Truman had come to rely on Arthur Vandenberg.

21

"Nothing Will Be Done without Consultation with You"

"UNDERSECRETARY LOVETT CAME TO my apartment five times in connection with this note," Vandenberg wrote in an undated diary entry that, events suggest, he penned in early July of 1948.

"This note," as he called it, was what Marshall handed to Alexander Panyushkin, Moscow's ambassador to the United States, on July 6 while the two were in Marshall's office. It noted the "extremely serious international situation" that the Soviets had created by blockading Berlin starting on June 24; labeled the move a "clear violation of existing agreements"; declared that the United States "will not be induced by threats, pressures or other actions to abandon their rights"; and demanded that "the movement of freight and passenger traffic between the western zones [of Germany] and Berlin be fully restored." The blockade—which followed months of rising U.S.-Soviet tensions over Germany's future—prompted Truman to launch a massive airlift of food and other goods into the besieged city that lasted until Stalin backed down and reopened the gates eleven months later.

The Soviet blockade provided considerable momentum to the burgeoning talks between the United States, Brussels Pact nations, and other European countries over a defense alliance because it raised concerns that the Soviets would build upon their brazen actions in Berlin to attack Western Europe more frontally. Truman and his team brought Vandenberg into the decision-making process over how Washington would respond. After Truman decided that the United States would deliver a stiff note of protest to the Soviets, Vandenberg played a central role in shaping its tone and its demands. At the time, U.S., British, and French officials were meeting in London to coordinate strategy in response to the blockade. After Marshall and Vandenberg would consult with one another in Washington, Marshall would relay his instructions to America's ambassador to London, Lewis Douglas, who was meeting with the British and French officials.

Of "this note," Vandenberg wrote in that same diary entry of early July, Lovett "brought me an original and partial draft. After much consideration I drew the final form on my own Corona [typewriter] one midnight." It was not really "final," however, for two reasons: Truman's top aides wanted to put their own stamp on it, and British and French officials thought that some of Vandenberg's language was "provocative." Vandenberg reportedly wanted the note to include an ultimatum, while U.S. and European officials settled on a protest.[1]

As Vandenberg described it, "the subsequent changes were very few—although some of it was toned down. However my own language was not belligerent. It explicitly disowned any trends toward war. But it made unmistakably plain that the United States intends to stand upon its rights in Berlin—making it equally plain that, if the siege and blockade first be lifted, we stand eagerly ready to 'talk things over.'"[2]

. . .

"The 'calculated risk' evidently is becoming more 'risky'—and probably deliberately so," Vandenberg wrote to Lovett on July 19 as he pondered the costs and benefits of America's stance over Berlin.

"I do not see how we can yield our basic position without total sacrifice of every chance we have for peace in Europe, or in the world," he continued. "But let's always keep in mind that our 'basic position' is that we cannot be *forced* out of Berlin by duress. It is *not* that we will not *get* out of Berlin voluntarily under satisfactory circumstances. Our aim, I take it, continues to be the latter."

Though he had pushed for a U.S. ultimatum in its note to Moscow, Vandenberg clearly was worried that the Berlin conflict could evolve

"Attack against Them All"

into something far more serious. Through Lovett, he advised Truman to walk a fine line, making clear to the Soviets that the United States would not back down but, at the same time, avoiding provocative public steps that would invite Soviet aggression. As much as anything, he worried about how the crisis would affect America's global standing.

"Unless there are more imminent reasons than I know, I hope we shall not resort to any sort of unilateral force which, in effect, asks for war," he wrote. "If war comes, it must be plain to the world that it is Soviet Russia which has 'asked' for it. On the other hand we cannot indulge the luxury of interminable 'notes' at a time when the rapidly complicating conditions in the Berlin air can precipitate a miscalculated accident almost any time . . . I am simply saying in essence that I would stand fast; but I would *stand fast* for peaceful settlement before ever voluntarily accepting *any* overt responsibility for a needless war."[3]

A month later Vandenberg responded to a *Detroit Free Press* editorial that blasted "'statesmen,' past and present, who inflict these needless and ghastly wars on helpless humans whose souls cry for peace" with a letter to publisher John S. Knight that reflected the full range of his character—vainglorious and self-righteous for sure, but also statesmanlike and vulnerable. Acknowledging he was "among the 'present' so-called 'statesmen' unavoidably responsible for the decisions of today and tomorrow," he wrote, "I can painfully testify that it is a *horrible* responsibility fraught with harrowed days and sleepless nights. It is a *tragic* obligation which sometimes makes life itself all but unbearable. The 'blood of our sons' has driven me to subordinate every other objective, in my public service, to the pursuit of honorable peace and to the organization of a global conscience and a global force to stop 'the infliction of needless wars on helpless humans whose souls cry for peace.' Relatively, nothing else matters.

"But how?" he continued, writing in a strikingly anguished tone. "*How? How?* Everything depends on our poor, fallible human judgments. The next war *should be* 'needless' (your word). Worse; it would be the crime of the ages. But, as you yourself have so often said, we do not escape it by running away from it. Appeasement merely precipitates the jeopardy it seeks to avoid. It takes two to keep the peace. We must forever choose between calculated risks. But *how*?"[4]

In late 1948 Truman, too, was anguished about the state of U.S.-Soviet relations and the risks to peace that it engendered. Rather than pour out this thoughts on paper, however, he pursued a more dramatic step—one that not only angered Marshall but that left Vandenberg more than a little befuddled.

. . .

"Following the premature publication of the proposed Vinson mission to Moscow, a number of complications set in that compelled me to reconsider the advisability of this mission," Truman wrote later.[5]

On Sunday, October 3, Truman called Supreme Court Chief Justice Fred Vinson and asked him to come to the White House on an urgent matter. When Vinson arrived, Truman explained that he wanted him to travel to Moscow on his behalf to tell Stalin that Truman sincerely wanted better U.S.-Soviet relations. Truman had not discussed the idea with either Marshall, his chief diplomat, or Vandenberg, his most important congressional ally on foreign affairs. Truman and Vinson were friends from when Truman was a senator and Vinson was a House member in the 1930s, and Truman had appointed him Treasury secretary and then chief justice. Nevertheless, Vinson was reluctant to go, telling Truman it was inappropriate for a chief justice to represent the president in what would surely be a politically controversial matter, especially in the midst of a presidential campaign. After Truman finally convinced Vinson to go, he told Press Secretary Charlie Ross to ask the radio networks for thirty minutes of time on the evening of Tuesday, October 5, so he could announce some important news.

But when Truman revealed his plans to Marshall on the morning of October 5, the secretary reacted angrily. At the time Marshall was meeting with British and French officials in Paris to discuss whether to bring the Berlin crisis before the United Nations. In essence, Truman was proposing to appeal unilaterally to Stalin at a time when Marshall was rallying key U.S. allies to maintain a united Western front

"Attack against Them All"

against Stalin over Berlin, and also when the United States was trying to strengthen the United Nations as the appropriate vehicle to settle global disputes. That Truman was bypassing Marshall for such a sensitive diplomatic assignment naturally outraged the secretary as well. In the face of Marshall's logic and unhappiness, Truman backed down and withdrew the idea.

Vandenberg didn't know anything about it when the White House called on the afternoon of October 5 to ask him to meet with Truman at 3:00 p.m. for an off-the-record chat. The White House called minutes later to cancel, but Truman phoned Vandenberg at his apartment that evening and asked him to "please slip in the back door [of the White House] at eight" for a private chat that also would include Senator Connally, the Foreign Relations Committee's top Democrat. Truman didn't mention the scrapped Vinson trip during his meeting with Vandenberg and Connally, but he did suggest that he might call Stalin to try to improve relations. Vandenberg didn't react other than to tell Truman that he wasn't sure a bilingual phone chat would work well. "It was quite evident," Vandenberg reflected in his diary days later, after news of the scrapped Vinson trip broke publicly, "that the President was earnestly anxious to 'do something.'" Nevertheless, he chalked up Truman's search for a dramatic step to improve U.S.-Soviet relations to the presidential campaign. "The way in which he was groping for some substitute idea [to Vinson] to spectacularly associate himself with the peace crisis abroad left me with the impression that he at least was not 'overlooking' the fact that he was coming down the home stretch in a political campaign which sadly needed a 'shot in the arm.'"[6]

Two weeks later Truman and Vandenberg were forced to address the issue of a Vinson-type mission one more time. While Vandenberg was at home in Grand Rapids, Reston called to say that Arthur Krock, an influential *Times'* foreign affairs columnist, heard that Truman planned to try another such mission and that Vandenberg had approved it. Vandenberg, who had approved no such thing, relayed his concern to Truman's secretary, Matt Connolly. From the campaign trail, Truman wired the senator with a message: "Nothing will be done without consultation with you."[7]

...

Truman and Vandenberg, of course, were not surprised when the five Brussels Pact nations decided in late October to formally ask the United States (and Canada) to join them in a broader North Atlantic pact.

U.S. officials had been laying the groundwork for that request for many months, both publicly and privately. Meanwhile, the Berlin crisis heightened the fears of Brussels Pact nations about Soviet aggressiveness, fueling their progress in September and October in meeting U.S. demands for greater coordination. As those nations catalogued their collective defense needs, U.S. officials monitored their efforts, offering a U.S. perspective on how much military aid Congress would likely approve. In that way, those officials played the same role that the State Department's Will Clayton had played a year earlier on the Marshall Plan. By early October the Brussels Pact nations had appointed leaders of a joint military staff to plan their collective defense.

Nobody in Washington or anywhere else, however, thought the task of negotiating a North Atlantic pact, which would take months to complete, would fall to Truman. That's because everybody expected Truman to lose the presidency that fall to Thomas Dewey—the pollsters, the pundits, the reporters, most of Truman's aides, even his wife. After all, Republicans were energized and united; Democrats were dispirited and split after Truman's former commerce secretary, Henry Wallace, bolted the party to run for president as a progressive and South Carolina's governor, Strom Thurmond, bolted to run as a states-rights conservative. Earlier in the year many leading Democrats sought to deny Truman the party's nomination and worked relentlessly to entice Dwight Eisenhower to seek it.

"It is now plain," Joseph and Stewart Alsop wrote strikingly on October 31, "that Gov. Thomas E. Dewey, long before he is officially installed in the White House, will be faced with a great and crucial decision. He can decide to approve a fundamental—and expensive—departure in

"Attack against Them All"

American foreign policy by negotiating a formal defensive pact with a number of European nations. Or he can decide to attempt to shove the whole painful business under the rug. Either way, it will not be an easy decision."[8]

Still, Truman and Vandenberg were each careful not to let the campaign skirmishing complicate their relationship.

. . .

Truman expected to win—conventional wisdom notwithstanding—so he assumed that he'd keep working with Vandenberg after the election. That's why, in officially launching his campaign on Labor Day in Vandenberg's hometown of Grand Rapids, he took time out from his incessant Republican-bashing to call Vandenberg his "good friend," say he's "intellectually honest," and add, "I like him."

Like everyone else, Vandenberg assumed Truman would lose, and he anticipated the moment when Dewey's triumph would give Republicans, who controlled both houses of Congress, all the levers of power in Washington. He didn't want to attack Truman or the Democrats with reckless abandon during the campaign, however, because he feared that would destroy the bipartisan approach to foreign policy that he had worked so hard to nourish. He viewed bipartisan foreign policy as a concept that should endure beyond any particular Democratic president or Republican senator because, he believed, unity at home over foreign policy would strengthen America on the world stage.

To ensure that bipartisanship would endure under Dewey, Vandenberg sought help from Dulles, the Dewey adviser who, Vandenberg assumed, Dewey would appoint as secretary of state. Vandenberg hoped Dulles would prevent Dewey from saying anything that would undermine the bipartisan foreign policy that was in place and, as a result, anger congressional Democrats. "It is peculiarly our job—yours and mine—to see that bipartisan liaison in the next Congress does not become impossible," Vandenberg wrote to Dulles in July. "Otherwise November will represent a pyrrhic victory."[9]

Despite Vandenberg's high-mindedness, Truman tried his patience badly that summer and fall when he derided the "do nothing, good for nothing" Eightieth Congress—the very one that funded the Truman Doctrine with aid to Greece and Turkey, enacted the Marshall Plan, began work on the North Atlantic Treaty, and supported Truman's foreign policy in a host of other ways. Finally at wit's end, Vandenberg delivered a nationwide radio address on October 4 to answer Truman. He promoted bipartisan foreign policy, reviewed the accomplishments of the Republican Congress, and "respectfully" suggested that "this record makes the 80th Congress, in all that relates to our foreign affairs, not 'the second worst in history' as we sometimes hear in general attack, but the best."

As noted in connection with the Vinson mission, Truman invited Vandenberg to the White House for a private chat on the evening of October 5—that is, a day after Vandenberg's radio address. During that chat Truman told Vandenberg that "it was a 'grand speech'; that he deeply appreciated the judicial way in which I had been able to keep my 'partisanship' on an unpartisan basis; and that he thought it was more important to retain the 'bipartisan foreign policy' than who was elected president.

"If that isn't a strange reaction to a campaign speech," Vandenberg mused, "I never heard one. It almost makes me wonder whether it did the GOP any good."[10]

. . .

Three days after Truman's startling victory, the *Detroit Times* ran what Vandenberg called a "streamer headline" announcing that the president would ask Vandenberg to serve as secretary of state.

The story seemed plausible. Marshall planned to retire for health reasons, and Lovett, who Truman might otherwise have promoted to replace him, also wanted to return to private life. Naturally, Truman would want to replace Marshall with someone who would face no serious Senate confirmation battle. Besides, Truman would surmise, Vandenberg might welcome the offer for two reasons: the position is prestigious, and Vandenberg was losing his committee chairmanship and headed

"Attack against Them All"

to the Senate minority because Democrats had regained control of the Senate on Election Day.

Vandenberg, who was in Michigan and saw the story there, dismissed it as "pure conjecture." When he returned to Washington, however, he learned otherwise. A "well-known Philadelphia newsman" told him by phone that the Democratic National Committee's chairman, J. Howard McGrath, was pushing the idea along with Leslie Biddle, secretary to Senate Democrats and, more importantly, "Truman's close buddy." Vandenberg didn't want the job, however, and he moved quickly to quash the scheme.

"I felt it was necessary to do something about the matter at once," Vandenberg wrote that day, "even though I had heard no word and had no reason to believe the President would consider any such idea." Truman, he noted, "does so many impetuous things 'off the cuff' that I feared he might announce it without talking to me about it." Vandenberg worried that if Truman offered him the job and he turned it down, that would send a signal around the world of U.S. disunity on foreign affairs.

As a result, Vandenberg "sent for Biddle," who was about to join Truman on his post-election vacation in Key West, Florida. When Biddle confirmed that he had recommended him for the position, Vandenberg expressed his "profound appreciation" but explained—for Biddle to tell Truman—why the idea was a bad one. If Republicans resented his move, particularly when they were suffering post-election shock and needed all the clear heads they could find, "it might well be that I would actually lose my best chance to be helpful in supporting 'bi-partisan foreign policy.'" Besides, Vandenberg explained that, as secretary of state, he'd want the flexibility to set his own agenda and make decisions independent of the president, and he recognized that, realistically, no secretary could do that.[11]

Instead, Vandenberg would return to the Senate and, on bipartisan foreign policy, he hoped to pick up where he and Truman had left off. In the heady aftermath of their unlikely electoral victories, however, neither Truman nor the new Senate Democratic majority made Vandenberg's job any easier.

22

"Politics Shall Stop at the Water's Edge"

ON JANUARY 7, 1949, Truman announced that he was appointing Acheson to replace the ailing Marshall as secretary of state, adding to the mounting challenges that Vandenberg faced in maintaining bipartisan foreign policy.

Earlier in January the new Senate Democratic majority had decided to alter the majority-minority ratio on the Senate Foreign Relations Committee for the Eighty-First Congress, angering Vandenberg and his colleagues. In the Republican-run Eightieth Congress, Vandenberg had convinced his GOP colleagues on the thirteen-member committee to maintain the narrowest possible split, 7–6, between Republicans and Democrats. By doing so Vandenberg sent an important signal that he respected the Democratic minority, welcoming its assistance and helping to strengthen the bipartisan collaboration that he felt was so important on foreign policy. Now that Democrats were in charge, they were sending a far different signal, insisting on an 8–5 party advantage.

Speaking to the Senate on January 5, Vandenberg expressed "very great disappointment" that Democrats had "seen fit . . . to take the first partisan action in opposition to the theory and spirit of bipartisan cooperation in foreign affairs which has prevailed in the past two years." He questioned "the wisdom of an act which is implicit with hostility, as it will be interpreted by the country." The implication, which he said "disillusioned" Republicans had already drawn, was that "in connection with the administration's foreign program for this year, Republican Senators are not quite trustworthy, and that there must be faithful partisan Democrats, to the maximum, put upon the committee for the sake of the national welfare." Vandenberg knew that he would now find it harder to rally Republican support for Truman's foreign policy initiatives for the purpose of showcasing America's unity to the world.

Truman's nomination of Acheson poured more salt in Vandenberg's wound because he didn't learn of it from the White House until an hour before the president's announcement at a morning news conference. Truman's pick was hardly surprising. For all their differences in background and personality, the plainspoken, often-earthy Truman and the arrogant, often-condescending Acheson had built a strong bond over the years. Truman was disappointed when Acheson left the State Department in July of 1947 to revive his law practice, and he tried to coax him back to government to run the Marshall Plan in 1948.

"I am frank to say," Vandenberg wrote to Clyde M. Reed, a Senate Republican from Kansas, five days after Truman's announcement, "that Mr. Acheson would *not* have been my choice for Secretary of State." That Lovett had resigned along with Marshall only left Vandenberg unhappier. Reflecting the close bonds between Lovett and Vandenberg, the undersecretary wrote to the senator upon his departure, "If a man is very lucky he has an opportunity once in his life to serve a good cause with men of singleness of purpose, integrity and complete understanding, and with friends whom he both admires and loves. I have had that experience with you and the General [Marshall]."[1]

Although Vandenberg felt slighted by the Democrats' committee action and the president's behavior, he quickly swallowed his pride and recovered his grace. Regarding Acheson, he suggested that a president should enjoy a "wider right of personal choice" with cabinet members than other appointees, and he praised Acheson's knowledge of foreign policy as well as his administrative abilities.[2] Moreover, he worked behind the scenes to ensure Acheson's confirmation, crafting the strategy to make it happen.

As the Senate Foreign Relations Committee held hearings in January on Acheson's nomination, Republicans were questioning his anti-

"Attack against Them All"

Communist bona fides and trying to tie him to then-suspected Soviet spy Alger Hiss, a former State Department official. When the committee met in "executive session" with Acheson on January 14, Vandenberg suggested that Acheson issue a statement to make clear that he strongly opposed Communism, giving wavering senators the political ammunition they needed to support him. When Acheson agreed, Vandenberg drafted it for him. "It is my view," Acheson declared in the statement, "that communism as a doctrine is economically fatal to a free society and to human rights and fundamental freedom. Communism as an aggressive factor in world conquest is fatal to independent governments and to free peoples."[3]

With work looming on the emerging North Atlantic Treaty, Vandenberg remained committed to bipartisanship because he continued to see it as a prerequisite for a strong U.S. foreign policy. "The form of things, to be sure, has changed, and responsibilities and initiatives have shifted," he said in a Lincoln Day speech in Detroit. "But the basic need remains. It will be a sad hour for the Republic if we ever desert the fundamental concept that politics shall stop at the water's edge. It will be a triumphant day for those who would divide and conquer us if we abandon the quest for a united voice when America demands peace with honor in the world. In my view nothing has happened to absolve either Democrats or Republicans from continuing to put their country first. Those who don't will serve neither their country nor their party nor themselves."[4]

. . .

"We are now working out with a number of countries a joint agreement designed to strengthen the security of the North Atlantic area," Truman announced on January 20, 1949, after taking the oath of office for the first time as an elected president.

"Such an agreement," he said, delivering his inaugural address from the Capitol's West Front on a brisk and sunny day,

> would take the form of a collective defense arrangement within the terms of the United Nations Charter. We have already established such a defense

pact for the Western Hemisphere by the treaty of Rio de Janeiro. The primary purpose of these agreements is to provide unmistakable proof of the joint determination of the free countries to resist armed attack from any quarter. Every country participating in these arrangements must contribute all it can to the common defense. If we can make it sufficiently clear, in advance, that any armed attack affecting our national security would be met with overwhelming force, the armed attack might never occur. I hope soon to send to the Senate a treaty respecting the North Atlantic security plan.

The behind-the-scenes work among top U.S. and European officials that began over the summer at Lovett's direction, and that had recessed in the fall, resumed after Truman's reelection. By late November the five Brussels Pact nations had delivered their proposed draft of the treaty to U.S. officials for their consideration. By December Lovett had resumed his in-person negotiations with his European counterparts to discuss treaty details, hosting the meetings in his State Department office. Through the course of those months, Lovett kept Vandenberg well-apprised of developments.

Though Truman had just won another term as president, giving him a public mandate to pursue his own policies, his top aides nevertheless tied their efforts to craft a North Atlantic Treaty more closely to Vandenberg. A policy statement on the treaty that the State Department issued on January 14 began this way: "The Vandenberg Resolution adopted by the Senate on June 11, 1948, by a vote of 64 to 4, marks a new departure in American foreign policy. The resolution proposes that for the first time in the nation's history the United States associate itself in peace-time with countries outside the Western Hemisphere in collective security arrangements designed to safeguard peace and to strengthen our own security."[5]

That the administration, in promoting its own foreign policy, began by discussing a Senate resolution speaks to the historical role that *this* resolution, in particular, played in creating the necessary conditions for U.S. participation in the treaty. In the coming weeks Vandenberg would find opportunities to put his stamp on the treaty itself.

. . .

"Attack against Them All"

Truman didn't break any new ground in discussing the emerging treaty briefly in his inaugural address.

Thus, Truman's words that day could not have surprised Vandenberg. Nor, as a general matter, could he have been unhappy with them. He strongly supported the notion of regional defense pacts under Article 51, and this pact, in particular, arose directly from his landmark Senate resolution. So, he was greatly predisposed to support the treaty when it emerged in final form, and he shared Truman's view of how it would greatly improve prospects for peace with the Soviets. Still, in the early months of 1949, Vandenberg refused to make a firm commitment to support whatever emerged from U.S.-European negotiations. Instead, in public comments and private letters, he pondered the benefits and costs of a treaty—particularly the assumption that, after signing it, the United States would be obligated to provide military aid to help the Europeans defend themselves.

In the weeks immediately after Truman's speech, Vandenberg returned to his practice of thinking out loud, rehearsing his arguments, and testing his conclusions for anyone who wanted to hear them. In doing so, the senator wrestled with several of the dicey issues that he would have to address with his Senate colleagues that spring if he hoped to gather the votes for Senate ratification.

"There is no doubt about the fact that it is a 'calculated risk' for us to even partially arm the countries of Western Europe," he wrote to a constituent in late January. "It is also very much of a 'calculated risk' if we do *not*. One risk will have to be weighed against the other." Yes, U.S. military aid would tie the United States more openly to Europe's security, raising chances that America would have to come to its defense. But a U.S. refusal to provide the arms would leave Europe more vulnerable and perhaps tempt the Soviets to launch a quick strike, which would almost certainly force a U.S. response anyway.

Vandenberg was weighing the timing of U.S.-led European defense as much as its merits. Should it come before or after the Marshall Plan had presumably revived Europe's economy? Did Europe need security first to achieve prosperity? "You suggest that it will be a safe thing to do

'when the economic stability of these countries shall have improved,'"
he wrote in the same letter. "The basic question we have to settle is
whether 'economic stability' can precede the creation of a greater sense
of physical security. I am inclined to think that 'physical security' is a
prerequisite to the kind of long-range economic planning which Western Europe requires. The fact remains that the problem is fraught with
many hazardous imponderables. I am withholding my own final judgment until I see the precise terms of the treaty under which this new
cooperation will be proposed."

To Truman's point that the treaty might prevent a Soviet attack in
Western Europe, Vandenberg wrote to another constituent, "in my opinion, when Mr. Hitler was contemplating World War Two, I believe he
would have never launched it if he had had any serious reasons to believe
that it might bring him into armed collision with the United States. I
think he was sure it would not do so because of our then existing neutrality laws. If an appropriate North Atlantic Pact is written, I think it
will exactly reverse this psychology so far as Mr. Stalin is concerned if,
as and when he contemplates World War Three. Under such circumstances, I very much doubt that World War Three happens."

A day later, he repeated the point in another letter but cautioned
that, in the event of a Soviet attack, the United States must reserve the
right to decide its response rather than "automatically" rush to war. "I
can think of no greater tragedy than to permit our friends in Western Europe to interpret the Pact beyond its actual realities. One reality is that we cannot commit ourselves to automatic war in the future."
Congress would have to approve a declaration of war and the funds
to support a military operation. "We are recognizing facts of life as
established in the Constitution of the United States. I will go as far as
I can within the Constitution. I will not go farther because it would
be an imposition upon our own good faith and a false reliance for our
friends abroad."[6]

Vandenberg's letter writing proved useful, for it prepared him for
similar questions from Senate skeptics in the weeks ahead.

. . .

"Attack against Them All"

In the spring of 1949 Truman and Vandenberg were forced to maneuver carefully among their varied constituencies, each with its own agenda, as they sought to build support for the emerging treaty.

Western Europe's leaders wanted to ensure that the treaty provided a strong guarantee that the United States would defend them in the event of Soviet attack. Vandenberg and his congressional colleagues, however, wanted to ensure that the treaty did *not* obligate America to defend Europe militarily in the absence of congressional approval. Moreover, congressional pacifists wanted to ensure that it didn't obligate America to military action at all as opposed to other steps to restore peace. Truman wanted to convince European nations beyond the Brussels Pact five, including Sweden, Denmark, and Norway, to join the treaty—but he didn't want to further inflame U.S. tensions with the Soviets, who charged that the treaty was an aggressive anti-Soviet measure. UN backers wanted to ensure that the treaty didn't undercut the global body. Finally, both Truman and Vandenberg wanted to ensure that the congressional debate over what the treaty meant for the United States would not hamper their efforts to secure continued funding for the Marshall Plan.

Because the draft treaty was the handiwork of both U.S. and European officials, it included particular provisions that could satisfy particular constituencies but that, in total, seemed to contradict one another. One provision—which became Article 5—stated that member nations would regard an attack on one as an attack on all, thus implying a robust response by the group as a whole. Another provision, however, stated that each member nation would decide whether an attack had occurred, and still another one stated that each nation could decide whether to respond to such an attack and how to do so. Ideally, the first of those provisions would satisfy the Europeans and deter the Soviets; the second and third provisions would protect America's independent authority and reassure Congress.

Truman's maneuvering involved lots of evasion and obfuscation because he didn't want to complicate the delicate work that Acheson and Vandenberg were doing. In early January he sidestepped a reporter's request to further explain language in his "budget request" to Congress that he expected to seek funds for military supplies to Brussels Pact nations and "certain other countries where the provision of such assistance is important to our national security." In early February he declined to comment on a report that Norway told the Soviets that while it would explore participation in the Western defense pact, it would never grant bases for foreign powers unless Norway was attacked or threatened with attack. When, two weeks later, a reporter asked Truman about congressional deliberations over the treaty, he largely avoided the issue and deferred to Acheson for further comment.

As for Vandenberg, he and his committee's chairman, Democrat Tom Connally, met with Acheson on February 5 to discuss the treaty's fine print. Vandenberg sought to tweak the language in ways that would garner more support in the Senate. European leaders, however, were startled to learn that Acheson was discussing wording changes with Vandenberg; they had assumed that U.S. officials who negotiated with them had already cleared the draft language with Congress.

Though Truman and Vandenberg were working in close concert with one another (albeit largely through Acheson), the senator's efforts to build support among his colleagues put him on an unavoidable collision course with the president.

. . .

"I am scarcely in a position to speak for the secretary of state on this subject," Vandenberg told the Senate on February 14.

"This subject" was a front-page *Kansas City Times* story that put Vandenberg in a tough spot. It asserted that a few days earlier, Acheson had told Norway's foreign minister, Halvard Lange, that while the emerging North Atlantic Treaty could not obligate the United States to use military force, "in joining the Alliance the American Government would subscribe to the principle that an attack on one member nation was an attack on all, and this would be interpreted as a moral commitment to fight." At the time Acheson was working to reassure European governments that, in joining the pact, the United States was committing tangibly to their defense. The firmer that commitment, however, the more it would ruffle the feathers of senators who were not about to relinquish Congress's power to declare war and provide the funds to finance it. That's why Senator Forrest C. Donnell, a Missouri Republican who opposed the pact, brought the article to the Senate's attention—and why the article complicated Vandenberg's efforts to gather Senate support for the pact.

"I am in position to speak for myself," Vandenberg continued on the Senate floor, directing his comments to Donnell, "I think the senator will find when the pact is available for specific study that that North Atlantic community agreement . . . is based essentially on the theory of the Rio Pact." Under Rio, he went on, "each signatory power retains unto itself the entire right of decision respecting the implementation of its obligations both as to its individual contribution and as to its collective contribution in respect to an ultimate armed attack." In other words, if the Soviets attacked a North Atlantic Treaty member nation, the United States would retain all of its independent authority to decide whether to respond and, if so, how—including the authority to decide whether to use force.

Donnell pressed the point, exploiting Acheson's language to highlight the gap between him and Vandenberg. He asked whether he was "correct in understanding, or in assuming, that the senator would not favor including in the North Atlantic pact anything which constitutes a moral commitment to fight on the part of the United States of America?" "If the senator means an automatic commitment," Vandenberg replied, "my answer is yes." In other words, Vandenberg acknowledged that he disagreed with Acheson's notion of a moral commitment. Donnell then asked whether, as Vandenberg had said before, he still believed the Vandenberg Resolution, which laid the foundation for U.S. participation in regional pacts, did not obligate the United States to "further commitments." Vandenberg said that he still did.

Acheson was now the one in a tough spot, with Truman and the Europeans on one side and Vandenberg and the Senate on the other. As noted earlier, Truman had already declared, in his inaugural address of the previous month, that "the primary purpose" of regional defense pacts "is to provide unmistakable proof of the joint determination of the free countries to resist armed attack from any quarter. Every country participating in these arrangements must contribute all it can to the common defense." That seemed pretty definitive on the subject of military force, and it was the firm commitment on which the Europeans were banking. Now, Vandenberg (strongly backed by Connally) had undercut the president. With that, Europe feared that "a new breeze of isolationism had blown . . . through the Senate."[7]

After Vandenberg's blast, Acheson reacted like many public officials who find themselves in a tough spot—he tried to rewrite the truth; he pleaded for forbearance; and he refused to make matters worse by commenting further. Specifically, Acheson directed State Department spokesman Lincoln White to tell reporters that there were "no differences on objectives" between Acheson and Vandenberg—which was true, but which wasn't the point. Acheson then asked reporters in particular, and the country in general, to exercise "restraint" when observing Senate deliberations and weighing their impact on the treaty. In effect, the secretary was urging reporters to paper over the conflicts between the administration and Congress so as not to upset the Europeans or weaken Senate support. Finally, when reporters asked Acheson whether European leaders were seeking the very "moral commitment" that Vandenberg refused to concede, an exasperated Acheson blurted, "I don't want to talk about those things—all they can do is cause trouble."[8]

For Truman and Acheson, the dance would grow only more complicated as Vandenberg sought wording changes to the draft treaty.

. . .

By February Vandenberg had already convinced Acheson to negotiate wording changes with the Europeans over Article 5 (that member nations would regard an attack on one as an attack on all).

Originally, the Europeans wanted the treaty to read that all members would "afford" an attacked nation "all military and other aid and assistance in their power." When U.S. negotiators refused, recognizing the problems that language would create with Congress, the Euro-

"Attack against Them All"

peans sought a commitment for members to "take military and other action forthwith." U.S. negotiators watered it down further by converting military action into an option rather than a requirement, making the language "military or other action forthwith." When Vandenberg saw that language, he and Connally convinced U.S. officials to water it down still more by deleting the military reference and replacing it with "take action forthwith."[9]

Not surprisingly, as Vandenberg made progress in reassuring the Senate that the treaty would not dilute Congress's power, Truman and his team lost ground with Europe. Acheson met privately for two and a half hours with the Senate Foreign Relations Committee on February 18, and he worked hard to keep the discussion a secret, fearing that disclosures would complicate matters with his constituencies. That's why he distributed copies of the draft to the senators but took them back when the meeting ended. Acheson and the committee might just as well have met publicly, however, because the *New York Times'* Reston told his U.S. and European readers what happened in a front-page story the next day. The "sense of the meeting," he wrote, was that the treaty should not automatically obligate the United States to take military action against aggression and should not necessarily raise the possibility of military action.[10] That was precisely what the Europeans did *not* want to hear.

In the end U.S. and European negotiators crafted language that included the requisite specificity and ambiguity to satisfy all parties. For the all-important Article 5, they wrote, "The Parties agree that an armed attack against one or more of them in Europe or North America shall be considered an attack against them all and consequently they agree that, if such an armed attack occurs, each of them, in exercise of the right of individual or collective self-defence recognized by Article 51 of the Charter of the United Nations, will assist the Party or Parties so attacked by taking forthwith, individually and in concert with the other Parties, such action as it deems necessary, including the use of armed force, to restore and maintain the security of the North Atlantic area."

Vandenberg announced his support for the treaty in stages, endorsing the draft as it stood on February 27 as "satisfactory and adequate," telling State Department officials a day later that he anticipated Senate approval, and announcing on March 19 (the day after negotiators finalized the draft) that he considered it a "major link in our own national security and . . . a powerful insurance policy against World War III." A few days later, in a speech that the *New York Times* reprinted in full, Vandenberg told the U.S. Conference of Mayors that the treaty would "tell any aggressor in 1949 that from the very moment he launched his conquest in this area he will face whatever united opposition, including that of the United States, is necessary to beat him to his knees." Thus, he called it "the greatest war deterrent ever devised."

By then, negotiators had submitted the treaty to the governments of all twelve member nations for their approval.

. . .

"This treaty is a simple document," Truman told Europe's foreign ministers who had gathered in Washington on April 4 to sign it for their governments.

"The nations which sign it," Truman declared at the late afternoon ceremony, "agree to abide by the peaceful principles of the United Nations, to maintain friendly relations and economic cooperation with one another, to consult together whenever the territory or independence of any of them is threatened, and to come to the aid of any one of them who may be attacked. It is a simple document, but if it had existed in 1914 and in 1939, supported by the nations who are represented here today, I believe it would have prevented the acts of aggression which led to two world wars."

With Truman and Vice President Alben Barkley standing to his right, a seated Acheson signed the treaty on behalf of the United States, and the eleven foreign ministers did the same for their governments—Britain's Ernest Bevin, France's Robert Schuman, Italy's Count Carlo Sforza, Denmark's Gustav Rasmussen, and so on. The United States was not finished, of course, because the Senate still needed to ratify the treaty. But by the time Acheson affixed his signature to the landmark

"Attack against Them All"

document, he had helped Truman and Vandenberg clear the major obstacles to ratification.

"In this treaty," Truman continued, "we seek to establish freedom from aggression and from the use of force in the North Atlantic community. This is the area which has been at [the root] of the last two world conflicts. To protect this area against war will be a long step toward permanent peace in the whole world." He dismissed Soviet charges that the pact was an "aggressive act" aimed at Moscow, asserting that such charges "slander our institutions and defame our ideals and our aspirations." Instead, Truman said, the treaty will be "a positive, not a negative, influence for peace" and he said it should "reassure peace-loving peoples everywhere" as a precedent-setting measure to "pave the way for the worldwide stability and peaceful development which we all seek . . . We are determined to work together to provide better lives for our people without sacrificing our common ideals of justice and human worth. But we cannot succeed if our people are haunted by the constant fear of aggression, and burdened by the cost of preparing their nations individually against attack."

Truman officially transmitted the treaty to the Senate on April 12, four years to the day he took over for FDR and began to craft the revolutionary new U.S. foreign policy that culminated in the North Atlantic Treaty itself.

23

"The Most Sensible, Powerful, Practicable, and Economical Step"

WHEN, ON WEDNESDAY, APRIL 27, 1949, the Senate Foreign Relations Committee began sixteen days of hearings on the North Atlantic Treaty, with Acheson as its first witness, Vandenberg assumed his customary role.

As he was during hearings on the Truman Doctrine and Marshall Plan, Vandenberg was less a grand orator than a cajoler-in-chief—asking leading questions to better enable administration officials to make their case; offering qualifying points to address the concerns of other senators; and, in this way, addressing the treaty's political vulnerabilities in the committee and the Senate as a whole. He sought to assure his colleagues that the treaty was limited in scope, U.S. obligations were clearly defined, and the Senate would have additional opportunities to weigh in before the president took any action under it, such as launching a military strike to aid an attacked nation.

When, for instance, Acheson suggested in a response to Connally that the treaty's obligations come into effect when an aggressor "contemplates or undertakes an attack," Vandenberg jumped in to clarify.

VANDENBERG: It is not my understanding that it would come into effect on the basis of a contemplation. The armed attack has to occur. Am I wrong on that?

ACHESON: You are right, senator. If I gave the other impression, it was inadvertence on my part.

Moreover, Vandenberg noted, "even the cooperative effort which is made under the North Atlantic Treaty" would end if the UN Security Council took steps to restore international peace and security. Vandenberg wasn't naive, of course. If Soviet aggression was the issue at hand, the Security Council clearly wasn't going to step in because Moscow could veto any action that other council members were envisioning. Nevertheless, in his back-and-forth with Acheson, Vandenberg sought to reassure those who feared that the treaty extended U.S. obligations too greatly or weakened the United Nations as an institution.

VANDENBERG: So we confront, then, this series of limitations. In the first place, no nation is the target of this treaty unless it nominates itself as an armed aggressor by its own armed aggression. Is that right?

ACHESON: Yes, sir, that is correct.

VANDENBERG: Secondly, it is effective only so long as the Security Council fails to take measures necessary to maintain international peace and security.

ACHESON: That is made repeatedly clear in the treaty itself, senator.

. . .

Vandenberg next sought to ease concerns over the administration's stated plans to ask Congress for $1.13 billion in 1950, and undetermined amounts in later years, in military aid for treaty member nations once the Senate had ratified the treaty—concerns that threatened to undermine support for the treaty.

Previously, Vandenberg had hoped the administration would not propose military aid at all because he thought it was both unnecessary and problematic: the treaty itself would sufficiently warn the Soviets against attacking Europe, and military aid would complicate Senate prospects for treaty ratification by reigniting the fears of wavering senators that such aid would tie America too closely to Europe. "I really think," he wrote in a letter two weeks before the hearings, "I would have preferred to have the Pact stand by itself as an all-out warning sustained by our general pledge but since the State Department has taken

"Attack against Them All"

this other route (supplementary arms aid) I am not disposed to enter into any *public* argument lest it be misconstrued."[1] Pressured by European leaders, the administration was preparing to formally ask Congress for the aid.

At the hearings Vandenberg conceded that the treaty and military aid were now inextricably linked, so he sought to assure his more tight-fisted and isolationist colleagues that the aid amounts would not necessarily grow significantly after 1950.

> VANDENBERG: Of course, in contemplating future budgets on this score, the greater the success of the program in increasing pacific and reliable security, the less will be the need, and the need may entirely disappear.

> ACHESON: This is entirely correct, senator. Of course, the outstanding purpose of both the treaty and of the military assistance program is the prevention of war. These two are complementary. If they prevent war from starting, and if that creates a stable situation in which you can look forward to the fact that war is not going to start, then the whole outlook is changed and greatly eased.

Here, too, Vandenberg was less predicting the future—nobody could honestly believe that U.S. aid obligations would end in 1950—than providing reassurances to convince other senators to support the treaty.

. . .

By the time of the hearings, Truman and Vandenberg had long recognized that U.S. military aid for Europe was perhaps the biggest obstacle to treaty ratification because, some senators feared, it signaled that America would invariably take military action to defend Europe.

Truman had repeatedly dodged reporters' questions about U.S. intentions for such aid over the course of 1948. In early 1949 Acheson did the same. Dodging a question in quintessentially Achesonian fashion in March, he quoted Supreme Court Justice Oliver Wendell Holmes's notion that people sometimes need to speak obscurely before they can speak clearly. (Privately, however, administration officials closely linked military aid to the treaty, arguing that it was essential to convince the Soviets to take the treaty seriously. Not surprisingly, European officials felt the same way.)

By early 1949 Truman had revealed his intentions publicly, making Acheson's linguistic games of the time appear childish. In his inaugural address of January, he followed his discussion of the treaty with a pledge to "provide military advice and equipment to free nations which will cooperate with us in the maintenance of peace and security." Besides, the Vandenberg Resolution, which Truman and his team cited often in the context of their treaty deliberations, raised the possibility of U.S. military aid in connection with regional pacts. In addition, a State Department paper of February 1949 about the North Atlantic security challenge asserted, "It seems clear that the United States must supply much of the military equipment which the countries working for recovery cannot produce themselves."[2]

Vandenberg, though, talked to other senators as he walked the halls of Congress, and he saw clearly that military aid complicated treaty ratification. After negotiators put the treaty in final form, Senator Bourke Hickenlooper, an Iowa Republican who served on the Senate Foreign Relations Committee, said he wanted to see "a general outline of what we are expected to contribute in money, equipment and other resources." Senator Harry F. Byrd, a Virginia Democrat, said he was "favorably inclined" toward the treaty "but with the understanding that it is not a commitment to arm Europe."[3]

Neither the Europeans nor the State Department made Vandenberg's job any easier in early April. Just days after Acheson signed the treaty—but before Truman had even submitted it to the Senate—eight of Europe's member nations sent an urgent request to Washington for U.S. military aid. The State Department released publicly not only the request but also its "guarded but favorable reply."[4]

. . .

"The critical habit is growing in the country of labeling the North Atlantic Treaty as a 'military alliance,' with all the connotations which his-

"Attack against Them All"

torically condemn either the morals or the utility of military alliances," Vandenberg told Warren Austin, America's ambassador to the United Nations.

It was April 28, the second day of hearings, and Vandenberg began an effort to reassure his colleagues that the pact was less military than diplomatic, and less offensive than defensive in nature. In the spring of 1949, many senators remained concerned about the military obligations that such a pact would engender.

VANDENBERG: I ask you whether this North Atlantic Pact is not in essence the precise opposite of the term "military alliance" in its traditional sense.

AUSTIN: Oh, absolutely. I agree completely with that characterization.

VANDENBERG: Is it not true that the North Atlantic Pact operates in its ultimate action only under two conditions: (1) That an armed aggressor has identified himself as an international criminal; (2) the pact operates only so long as the Security Council has failed to take the measures necessary to maintain international peace and security? Therefore, so long as the United Nations is able, under its procedures, to function, the North Atlantic Pact does not function in action, and it only functions within the completely limited area of action which I have described?

AUSTIN: Exactly.

In the coming days Vandenberg would engineer similar exchanges with other high-profile witnesses, all designed to alleviate fears that the United States was launching a great military adventure that it would later regret. Averell Harriman, then-U.S. special representative in Europe for the Marshall Plan, and Robert Lovett, the former undersecretary, both confirmed that, in the course of drafting the treaty, the United States had made no firm promises to its European allies about what military supplies it would then provide them. Omar Bradley, the army's chief of staff, agreed that the treaty didn't assume that member nations would establish joint forces of the size needed to win another world war. John

Foster Dulles, then a U.S. delegate to the United Nations, said the treaty did not obligate the United States to anything at all beyond the North Atlantic region.

When the committee voted unanimously on June 6 to support the treaty, the debate moved to the full Senate.

. . .

"This treaty," Vandenberg told the Senate on July 6, "is the most sensible, powerful, practicable, and economical step the United States can now take in the realistic interest of its own security; in the effective discouragement of aggressive conquest which would touch off World War Three; in the stabilization of western Germany; and, as described by its own preamble, in peacefully safeguarding the freedoms and the civilization founded on the principles of democracy, individual liberty, and the rule of law . . .

"Only those without eyes to see and ears to hear," Vandenberg went on, "can deny that these precious values—far dearer than life itself—are in jeopardy in today's tortured world. It is the overriding fact of life. Sooner or later every other problem is overshadowed by it. It is a condition, not a theory. It must be met as such. That is what this pending treaty undertakes to do."

With the Capitol undergoing repairs, senators were gathered in an old chamber that the Senate had used a century earlier. When the senators began their deliberations over the treaty on July 5, Connally, the committee's chairman, spoke first. Vandenberg spoke a day later with his usual flair and with enough emotion that, at the end, Republicans and more than a few Democrats stood to cheer.

By then, however, the result was a foregone conclusion. In the months leading up to Senate action, Truman and Vandenberg had addressed the major concerns and crafted the necessary phrases, sweeping away the opposition and building support for the treaty. The Senate debated the pact until July 21 but, with the votes for ratification assuredly in hand, Vandenberg felt little need to engage in much of the rhetorical sparring. When compelled, he repeated key points to reassure senators—on July

"Attack against Them All"

11, that the treaty and military aid were separate matters; on July 11 and 13, that Article 51 laid the legal groundwork for the treaty; and on July 21, that America retained its sole authority to decide whether to provide arms to other member nations.

The Senate ratified the treaty on an 82–13 vote, and Truman called it "an historic step toward a world of peace, a free world, free from fear."

. . .

With regard to its most immediate goal, the North Atlantic Treaty was a clear-cut and undeniable success.

Born in the midst of panic over Soviet threats to Western Europe, the treaty was designed to convince the Soviets that America would come to the aid of its allies in response to an attack—and that attack never came. Whether Moscow would have mounted one in the absence of that treaty, of course, remains an open question. By 1949 Truman had demonstrated more than once that the United States would confront Soviet aggression far from home. He sent warships to the Mediterranean in 1946 and aid to Greece and Turkey in 1947, and he spearheaded the Marshall Plan in 1947 and 1948. So, in the years leading up to 1949, Stalin had good reason to hesitate before sending his forces across the continent. Nevertheless, the treaty surely helped remove any doubt in his mind and, for the next four decades, it also dissuaded all future Soviet leaders from attacking Western Europe.

With the Soviet Union crack-up in 1991, NATO's members debated the organization's future scope and direction. President Clinton led efforts in the 1990s to expand NATO to the east—adding countries that were once in the Soviet sphere (and ruffling feathers in Moscow). Meanwhile, with the treaty's very raison d'etre—the Cold War—over, NATO greatly expanded the scope of its operations. It conducted its first military operations in 1994 in the former Yugoslavia; it invoked Article V for the first time after the September 11, 2001, terrorist attacks against America; and it conducted its first combat operations outside Europe in Afghanistan in 2003. In early 2015 NATO operations included peacekeeping in Kosovo, anti-terrorism in the Mediterranean, anti-piracy near

Africa, support for the African Union in Somalia, security assistance in Afghanistan, and sky patrols over Eastern Europe.

Whether confronting the Soviets during the Cold War or pursuing far-flung missions after it, the treaty has often been an uneasy one. "Burden sharing" has been a subject of incessant debate, with U.S. officials often complaining that America was assuming too much of NATO's military and financial costs. The United States spent more than 70 percent of what NATO's members spent in total on defense in 2014, up from about half during the Cold War. Nor have most NATO members met their commitment of 2006 to invest at least 2 percent of their gross domestic product on defense. NATO's military resources have become an issue of growing concern in recent years as the alliance has returned to its historical roots—focused once more on a hostile government in Moscow.[5]

"This is the gravest threat to European security and stability since the end of the Cold War," NATO Secretary-General Anders Fogh Rasmussen said of Russian expansionism in March of 2014.[6] Vladimir Putin had called the Soviet crack-up the "greatest geopolitical catastrophe of the century,"[7] and he now seemed determined to resurrect as much of the former Soviet empire as he could get away with. By the time Rasmussen spoke, Russia had annexed Crimea, was expanding into Ukraine by supporting pro-Russian rebel forces in their battles with Ukraine's government, and was sending hostile signals toward the Baltic states of Estonia, Latvia, and Lithuania.

Whether, in 2015 and beyond, NATO would muster the military forces and political will to stop Putin was open to question.

24

"The Senate Has Lost a Pillar of Strength"

"THIS HAS BEEN A tough day for the 'old man,'" Vandenberg wrote to his wife in September of 1949, two months after the Senate ratified the North Atlantic Treaty.

At the time, Vandenberg was suffering from lung cancer, walking with a limp, losing weight, and enduring severe headaches, but he refused his doctor's request to enter a hospital in Ann Arbor so that doctors could study a lesion in his left lung. He opted instead to maintain his work as best he could. After promoting Truman's request for military aid and debating the matter for two-and-a-half hours on the Senate floor, he told his wife, "I went straight to my hideout and lay down for two hours. This is the last of my really big efforts. I shall be 'sliding down hill' from now until I leave." He hoped Congress would soon pass the measure, at which point he planned to "take off for Ann Arbor" to address his health.[1] Two weeks later, doctors at the University of Michigan removed half of his left lung.

With Vandenberg gravely ill, neither he nor Truman could do much to protect their cherished bipartisan foreign policy from the increasingly vitriolic politics of Washington. Vandenberg ignored his doctors' warnings by flying from Michigan to Washington in December to tamp down isolationist sentiments among Senate Republicans. By then, Mao Tse-tung's Communist forces had established the People's Republic of China and Chiang Kai-shek had fled with his Nationalist forces to the island of Taiwan—unleashing a torrent of Republican rage at Truman for letting it all happen.

After his heroic trip to Washington in December, Vandenberg was too ill to attend Truman's State of the Union address in January of 1950. That month, he resigned from the Joint Congressional Atomic Energy Committee because he couldn't fully participate in its work. In April doctors at Georgetown University removed a tumor near his spine. In May he made his last appearance in the Senate, this one to help break a Southern filibuster on a fair employment measure. Upon seeing him, Vice President Alben Barkley interrupted the roll call to greet him and let other senators do the same.

. . .

Distressed in early 1950 that bipartisan foreign policy was collapsing in the face of McCarthyism, which fueled Republican charges that Democrats were "soft" on Communism, Vandenberg tried to do something from afar.

In a March 24 letter to Paul G. Hoffman, the former Studebaker chieftain who was running the Marshall Plan, he praised the bipartisan cooperation that had brought it to fruition, trumpeted its success in saving "Western Civilization," urged Congress to continue funding it at necessary levels, and declared, "United, we stand. Divided, we fall."

Truman thanked him in a letter three days later, noting, "I have been very much disturbed about the situation as it has been developing in the Congress with regard to the whole bipartisan foreign policy . . . I sincerely hope that the Lord will be good to the country and hurry along your physical recovery, so that you can come back and take your proper place as the Minority Leader of the Program."[2]

Vandenberg could not do so, however. By September of 1950, he was back in the hospital in Grand Rapids and then home to rest, increasingly confined to bed and left to exchange letters with friends and colleagues.

. . .

As Vandenberg lay dying in early 1951, foreign policy became the subject of even more partisan recriminations.

"Attack against Them All"

On the evening of April 10, Truman fired the legendary General Douglas MacArthur, who was commanding U N forces in Korea, after MacArthur repeatedly disobeyed his orders. The next day, "one of the bitterest" on Capitol Hill "in modern times," Republicans exploded in anger. Senator Robert Taft, House Minority Leader Joseph W. Martin, and other top Republicans talked openly of impeaching the president.

At Martin's invitation, MacArthur delivered a defiant address to a joint session of Congress on April 19, defending his record and calling himself "an old soldier who tried to do his duty as God gave him the light to see that duty." Truman ignored the speech, choosing to keep an appointment with Acheson. Later, he privately called MacArthur's remarks "a bunch of damn bullshit."[3]

. . .

A day before MacArthur spoke, Vandenberg died of cancer at home, prompting Truman to hail him as "a patriot who always subordinated partisan advantage and personal interest to the welfare of the Nation.

"In his passing," Truman continued, "the Senate has lost a pillar of strength in whom integrity was implicit in every decision he made and in every vote he cast during a long tenure. The Nation mourns a leader who had wisdom, fortitude, and courage. A grateful country will hold his memory in lasting remembrance."

By then, the bipartisan spirit that Truman and Vandenberg had brought to America's foreign policy had succumbed fully to increasingly bitter politics. Their landmark achievements, however, would long endure.

Epilogue

A Look Ahead

FROM APRIL OF 1945 to July of 1949, Harry Truman and Arthur Vandenberg crafted the policies and built the architecture of a revolutionary new U.S. foreign policy, transforming their nation from a reluctant world presence to a proud global leader. At a time of bitter partisanship, the Democratic president and Republican Senate leader worked closely with one another to build the needed bipartisan coalitions in Washington and nourish support for their policies around the country.

The United Nations, the Truman Doctrine, the Marshall Plan, and the North Atlantic Treaty—these were the four pillars of their foreign policy. Though they crafted their policy in response to contemporary events, it has proved remarkably enduring, guiding America's global presence for nearly three-quarters of a century. The United Nations brought to life the hopeful vision that adversarial nations could resolve their differences without resorting to war, which has proved true to some extent over the years; the Truman Doctrine provided the philosophical underpinning not just for America to assist Greece and Turkey, but for U.S. efforts to help many other nations that found themselves in a similar position; the Marshall Plan lifted a continent that remained economically prostrate from the devastation of World War II and laid the foundation for a permanent program of U.S. foreign aid; and the North Atlantic Treaty created NATO, ensuring that Moscow wouldn't try to overrun Europe and paving the way for other U.S.-led regional defense pacts.

After Truman and Vandenberg created this new foreign policy, the ramifications quickly became clear. By 1950 U.S. troops were seeking to repel a Communist advance far from home—in the remote Asian nation of South Korea—and they received a global blessing to do so when the Soviets boycotted the UN sessions that sanctioned the effort. In ensuing decades the United States (among many ventures) fought the Cold War through a mix of military strength, tough diplomacy, and covert aid to democratic activists behind the Iron Curtain; helped Israel win the 1973 Yom Kippur War; overthrew a corrupt dictator in Panama in 1989; forced Iraq out of Kuwait in 1991; launched bombing campaigns in the 1990s that helped end genocide in the Balkans; and worked with its NATO partners in 2011 to empower rebel forces to topple Libya's Muammar Gaddafi.

Nevertheless, the role of global leader is inherently a difficult one. America has a far greater capacity to do good—end war, stop slaughter, deliver aid—than any other nation, and a much greater willingness to do it. But, even the world's richest, most powerful nation cannot be everywhere and do everything; it cannot choose wisely every time it decides whether to act and what to do; and, even when it chooses wisely, it cannot always perform well. It could not assist the popular uprisings in East Germany in 1953, Hungary in 1956, and Czechoslovakia in 1968 without risking a military confrontation with Moscow; it could not deliver clear-cut victory in Korea in the 1950s, Vietnam in the 1960s and 1970s, and Afghanistan and Iraq in the early years of this century; and it chose not to stop horrific slaughter in Cambodia, Rwanda, Sudan, Syria, and elsewhere.

On balance, the foreign policy that Truman and Vandenberg crafted has served America well, defending our interests and promoting peace in ways that isolationism could not have done. We can fairly declare it a success as long as we acknowledge that, in a complicated world, it has not been an unqualified one.

. . .

As America gazes into the future, however, the key question is what shall become of this successful policy.

Currently, the United States is suffering from a crisis of confidence on foreign affairs. In Washington and across the country, policymakers, opinion leaders, and average Americans are increasingly asking two questions: First, facing huge budget deficits and a growing social welfare state, *can* the United States afford to continue underwriting this policy? Second, after recent ventures like the wars in Afghanistan and Iraq that provided no satisfying conclusion, *should* it continue to do so?

America is reconsidering its post–World War II role, reducing its footprint around the world, promoting more burden sharing with allies, and focusing on what President Obama calls "nation building here at home." In both political parties, growing isolationist wings are exerting more influence on their mainstreams, expressing doubt that America can do much good in the world and skepticism that its efforts would be worth the cost. In the fall of 2013, the Pew Research Center found that "for the first time since it began polling the question in 1964, a majority of Americans—52 percent—agree with the view that the United States 'should mind its own business internationally.'"[1]

As a practical matter, the United States may soon be minding its own business because it has no realistic option to do otherwise. Years of budget cutting are leaving the world's best-trained, best-equipped military without enough troops, planes, and ships to play its traditional role around the world or respond effectively to threats to U.S. interests far from home. "By 2017," *Wall Street Journal* foreign affairs columnist Bret Stephens wrote, "the U.S. military will be an increasingly hollow force, with the Army as small as it was in 1940, before conscription; a Navy the size it was in 1917, before our entry into World War I; an Air Force flying the oldest—and smallest—fleet of planes in its history; and a nuclear arsenal no larger than it was during the Truman administration."[2]

. . .

Rather than promote the policy and defend the global order that has served America well, President Obama envisions a different world—of different principles, different human relations, and different economies.

"People are anxious," he said in July of 2014. "Now, some of that has to do with some big challenges overseas. I am very proud that we have ended one war, and by the end of this year we will have ended both wars that I inherited before I came into office. But," he went on,

> whether people see what's happening in Ukraine, and Russia's aggression towards its neighbors in the manner in which it's financing and arming separatists; to what's happened in Syria—the devastation that Assad has wrought on his own people; to the failure in Iraq for Sunni and Shia and Kurd to compromise—although we're trying to see if we can put together a government that actually can function; to ongoing terrorist threats; to what's happening in Israel and Gaza—part of people's concern is just the sense that around the world the old order isn't holding and we're not quite yet to where we need to be in terms of a new order that's based on a different set of principles, that's based on a sense of common humanity, that's based on economies that work for all people.

The new mood in Washington and around the country has raised alarms across the foreign policy community, with liberals and conservatives alike warning that America's retrenchment, if not retreat, will create a dangerous vacuum on the world stage for hostile, aggressive, anti-American, anti-Western forces to fill. That, in turn, will make the world not only less stable but also less hospitable to the democratic, free-market values from which the United States and its allies benefit.

Not surprisingly, with less U.S. leadership and with China, Russia, Turkey, and other regional powers promoting alternative models of governance to U.S.-led capitalism and democracy, freedom and democracy are declining around the world. In early 2015 the watchdog group Freedom House reported that freedom—i.e., political rights and civil liberties—had declined for the ninth straight year. That freedom's decline began as President George W. Bush lost interest in promoting freedom in the messy aftermath of the Iraq War, and that it has picked up steam through the Obama years, is no coincidence.

"Many Americans and their political leaders in both parties, including President Obama, have either forgotten or rejected the assumptions that undergirded American foreign policy for the past seven decades,"

Brookings Institution scholar Robert Kagan wrote in a landmark essay in the *New Republic* in May of 2014.

In particular, American foreign policy may be moving away from the sense of global responsibility that equated American interests with the interests of many others around the world and back toward the defense of narrower, more parochial national interests . . . At the core of American unease is a desire to shed the unusual burdens of responsibility that previous generations of Americans took on in World War II and throughout the cold war and to return to being a more normal kind of nation, more attuned to its own needs and less to those of the wider world. If this is indeed what a majority of Americans seek today, then the current period of retrenchment will not be a temporary pause before an inevitable return to global activism. It will mark a new phase in the evolution of America's foreign policy. And because America's role in shaping the world order has been so unusually powerful and pervasive, it will also begin a new phase in the international system, one that promises not to be marginally different but radically different from what we have known these past 70 years. Unless Americans can be led back to an understanding of their enlightened self-interest, to see again how their fate is entangled with that of the world, then the prospects for a peaceful twenty-first century in which Americans and American principles can thrive will be bleak.[3]

. . .

All over the world, America's uncertainty is shaking the tectonic plates on which global security has long rested.

A rising China and a resurgent Russia are each testing America's staying power around the world. China is staking claims to the South China Sea and disputed territories, worrying Japan, the Philippines, and other longtime U.S. allies. Russia has annexed Crimea, helped Russian-backed rebels seize parts of Ukraine, and threatened the Baltic states of Latvia, Estonia, and Lithuania. America's response to Vladimir Putin's territorial demands bears an eerie similarity to Europe's response to Hitler at Munich.

Across the Greater Middle East, U.S. friends and adversaries alike wonder how long the United States will play its traditional role, ensuring regional stability while supporting Israel, Saudi Arabia, and other longtime allies. Obama largely ignored calls at home and abroad to help stop strongman Bashar al-Assad from slaughtering his own people during Syria's horrific civil war, and he stepped back from what seemed certain military action after al-Assad crossed his "red line" against using chemical weapons. His standoffishness toward Syria and his full-scale withdrawal of U.S. forces from Iraq left a vacuum on the ground that was filled by the alarming rise of ISIS, the brutal terrorist group that, by mid-2015, was seizing more and more territory in those two countries. Also by mid-2015 and at Obama's behest, U.S. negotiators had spearheaded a global nuclear agreement with Iran that will leave its nuclear program in place, likely speeding its rise to regional hegemon and launching a regional nuclear arms race that will undercut the global nonproliferation regime.

For the Western Hemisphere, Secretary of State John Kerry declared in a speech in late 2013 at the Organization of American States in Washington DC, "The era of the Monroe Doctrine is over. . . . That's worth applauding. That's not a bad thing." Perhaps, but as in the Greater Middle East, U.S. friends and adversaries in our hemisphere wonder about America's commitment to the region. In South America a coalition of nations that was spearheaded by Cuba and Venezuela and now includes Bolivia, Nicaragua, Ecuador, and a few smaller nations—which they dubbed the Bolivarian Alliance for the Americas—presented a growing socialist challenge to the U.S. model of freedom and democracy as the coalition sought new members in the region and alliances well beyond it. Meanwhile, Iran and its terrorist proxy, Hezbollah, expanded their presence across South America.

The seeds of global breakdown are planted thousands of miles from one another, but they reinforce one another: Beijing observes Putin's conquests and feels emboldened in its own region; Putin notes Obama's red-line reversal in Syria and assumes America lacks the stomach for a fight; Tehran pockets nuclear concessions and relief from sanctions and digs in further, insisting on more concessions that Obama then approves in what seems like a desperate quest for a nuclear deal; and America's Middle East allies study the U.S.-Iran nuclear talks and Obama's hands-off approach to Syria and make plans to defend themselves in an increasingly turbulent, post–Arab Spring region.

. . .

To chart the future, we return to the two questions with which Americans are increasingly grappling: Can we afford to underwrite the policy that Truman and Vandenberg crafted? Should we do so?

First, even with the long-term fiscal challenge that an aging population will present for federal retirement and health programs, we *can* well afford that policy. In fact, though it has not received nearly the notice it deserves, the nation's leaders have made enormous progress on the fiscal challenge in recent years through budget cutting and tax raising. A relatively modest bit more of both will enable them to address the remaining piece of that challenge, restoring the budget to health in the coming years.

Years after the financial crisis and deep recession that assured Obama's election in 2008 and raised doubts about the future of U.S.-led capitalism, the United States is once again well-placed to drive the future. Its economy remains the world's most dynamic, with more potential to nourish leading-edge discoveries that will propel growth. It remains both the leading destination point for people across the world who are seeking better lives and the nation that can best assimilate immigrants into its society. Its universities remain the world's envy, attracting more and more of the world's best students.

Second, and more importantly, we *should* do so—for we have no luxury to do otherwise. When a bankrupt Great Britain revealed in early 1947 that it could no longer play its traditional role of promoting world order, America was well-positioned to fill the void and enlightened enough to do so. By then, the United States had already signaled, through its role in creating the United Nations, that it would remain engaged internationally. After Britain's announcement, the United States grabbed the reins of global leadership through the Truman Doctrine, Marshall Plan, and North Atlantic Treaty.

Today, however, no great nation sits in the wings, ready to defend freedom if we bow out for the long run. No single European power can do so, and Europe as a whole has shown no capacity to act robustly in the face of threats both near and far. The same goes for Asia, where Japan struggles economically while it seeks U.S. help to contain an increasingly aggressive China.

If, then, the United States will not defend freedom and secure global order in the face of rising threats, who will?

NOTES

Prologue

1. "United States Strategic Bombing Survey," *Over-All Report (European War)* (Washington: Government Printing Office, 1945).

2. Behrman, *Most Noble Adventure*, 23–24; James M. Long, "Famine Treads Heels of Peace in Europe," *Washington Post*, May 6, 1945, M 4; Cabell Phillips, "Millions to Be Hungry in Europe This Winter," *New York Times*, July 22, 1945, 67.

3. Bernard Wasserstein, "European Refugee Movements after World War Two," BBC, http://www.bbc.co.uk/history/worldwars/wwtwo/refugees_01.shtml.

4. Raymond Daniell, "Europe Faces a Black Winter," *New York Times*, August 19, 1945, SM8.

5. C. L. Sulzberger, "Europe Faces Dread Winter; Food, Fuel and Hope Scarce," *New York Times*, November 13, 1945, 1.

6. Margaret MacMillan, "Rebuilding the World after the Second World War," *The Guardian*, http://www.theguardian.com/world/2009/sep/11/second-world-war-rebuilding.

7. Unger and Unger, *George Marshall*, 392.

8. Drew Middleton, "Influence of Moscow Is Strong in Western Europe," *New York Times*, June 3, 1945, E5.

9. Behrman, *Most Noble Adventure*, 15.

10. Goldman, *Crucial Decade—And After*, 28.

11. Bohlen, *Transformation of American Foreign Policy*, 96.

12. Donovan, *Conflict and Crisis*, 164.

13. Beinart, *Good Fight*, 3–4.

Introduction

1. Vandenberg, *Private Papers*, 577–79.

2. Donald, *Citizen Soldier*, 8.

3. Vandenberg, *Private Papers*, 5.

4. Vandenberg, *Private Papers*, 165–66.

5. McCullough, *Truman*, 46.

6. Donald, *Citizen Soldier*, 11.

7. Miller, *Plain Speaking*, 12.

8. Tompkins, *Senator Arthur H. Vandenberg*, 2.

9. Tompkins, *Senator Arthur H. Vandenberg*, 2.

10. Ferrell, *Harry S. Truman*, 57.

11. Donald, *Citizen Soldier*, 41.

12. Ferrell, *Harry S. Truman*, 70–71.

13. Tompkins, *Senator Arthur H. Vandenberg*, 16.

14. "Foreign Relations: To the World," *Time*, April 30, 1945, http://content.time.com/time/subscriber/article/0,33009,797388,00.html.

15. "National Affairs: Big Michigander," *Time*, October 2, 1939, http://content.time.com/time/subscriber/article/0,33009,788994,00.html.

16. Vandenberg, *Private Papers*, 10.

17. Tompkins, *Senator Arthur H. Vandenberg*, 34.

18. "Foreign Relations," *Time*.

19. Tompkins, *Senator Arthur H. Vandenberg*, 39.

20. Truman, *Volume One*, 142.

21. Dallek, *Harry S. Truman*, 11.

22. McCullough, *Truman*, 215–16.

23. Ferrell, *Harry S. Truman*, 134.

24. Vandenberg, *Private Papers*, xviii.

25. James B. Reston, "The Case for Vandenberg," *Life*, May 24, 1948, 111.

26. "Billion-Dollar Watchdog," *Time*, March 8, 1943, http://content.time.com/time/subscriber/article/0,33009,774390,00.html.

27. Vandenberg, *Private Papers*, 1.

28. Hill, "Senator Arthur H. Vandenberg, the Politics of Bipartisanship, and the Origins of Anti-Soviet Consensus, 1941–1946," 225.

29. Vandenberg, *Private Papers*, 59.

30. McCullough, *Truman*, 314.

31. McCullough, *Truman*, 327; Donald, *Citizen Soldier*, 126; Donovan, *Conflict and Crisis*, 9, 15; Truman, *Volume One*, 2, 19.

32. Truman, *Volume One*, 21.

33. Vandenberg, *Private Papers*, 165.

34. Truman, *Volume Two*, 244.

35. Truman, *Volume One*, 331.

36. Truman, *Volume One*, 338.

37. Ferrell, *Off the Record*, 96.

38. Wilcox, "Arthur Vandenberg," 2; Vandenberg, *Private Papers*, 325–30.

39. Reston, "Case," 104.

40. Donovan, *Conflict and Crisis*, 24.

41. Ferrell, *Off the Record*, 47.

42. Ferrell, *Off the Record*, 40.

43. McCullough, *Truman*, 500–501.

44. Hernon, *Profiles in Character*, 180.

45. Vandenberg, *Private Papers*, xv.

46. "Big Michigander," *Time*.

47. Vandenberg, *Private Papers*, 305–8.

48. Acheson, *Sketches from Life*, 145.

Part 1. "Victory against War"

1. Truman, *Volume One*, 271.
2. Vandenberg, *Private Papers*, 168.
3. Truman, *Volume One*, 29.

1. "President Wilson"

1. Hersey, *Aspects of the Presidency*, 46–47.
2. Truman, *Volume One*, 271.
3. Truman, *Volume One*, 323.
4. Tompkins, *Senator Arthur H. Vandenberg*, 191.
5. Gazell, "Arthur H. Vandenberg, Internationalism, and the United Nations," 380.
6. Vandenberg, *Private Papers*, 41.
7. Vandenberg, *Private Papers*, 160.
8. Vandenberg, *Private Papers*, 172.

2. "Perfect This Charter"

1. James B. Reston, "Security Plan Poses a Basic U.S. Decision," *New York Times*, August 27, 1944, http://select.nytimes.com/gst/abstract.html?res=F1071EFB3B59147B93C5AB1783 D85F408485F9.
2. Kaplan, *Conversion of Senator Arthur H. Vandenberg*, 16, 88.
3. International News Service, "Vandenberg 'Cagey' about Parley Bid," *Washington Post*, February 15, 1945, 1.
4. Vandenberg, *Private Papers*, 147.
5. Vandenberg, *Private Papers*, 149.
6. Vandenberg, *Private Papers*, 151–52.
7. Vandenberg, *Private Papers*, 152–53.
8. Vandenberg, *Private Papers*, 153–54.
9. Donovan, *Conflict and Crisis*, 18.
10. Vandenberg, *Private Papers*, 159–60.
11. Vandenberg, *Private Papers*, 160–61.
12. Schlesinger, *Act of Creation*, 33–35.
13. Vandenberg, *Private Papers*, 158.
14. Richard Holbrooke, "Last Best Hope," *New York Times*, September 28, 2003, http://www.nytimes.com/2003/09/28/books/last-best-hope.html?pagewanted=all&src=pm.
15. Vandenberg, *Private Papers*, 158.
16. "Grew Says World Must Bar Anarchy," *New York Times*, March 4, 1945, http://select.nytimes.com/gst/abstract.html?res=F10717FE345416738FDDAD0894DB405B8588F1D3.
17. Schlesinger, *Act of Creation*, 53–55, 67.
18. Vandenberg, *Private Papers*, 171.
19. "Foreign Relations," *Time*.

3. "Dumb as They Come"

1. Vandenberg, *Private Papers*, 167–68.
2. Schlesinger, *Act of Creation*, 74.
3. Acheson, *Present at the Creation*, 88–89; Schlesinger, *Act of Creation,* 74–75.

4. Ferrell, *Harry S. Truman*, 186.

5. Steinberg, *Man from Missouri*, 239.

6. Vandenberg, *Private Papers*, 168.

7. Vandenberg, *Private Papers*, 169.

8. Truman, *Volume One*, 272.

9. Truman, *Volume One*, 279.

10. Vandenberg, *Private Papers*, 170–71.

11. Truman, *Volume One*, 15.

12. Donovan, *Conflict and Crisis*, 36–37.

13. Alan S. Oser, "Ex-Gov. Averell Harriman, Advisor to Four Presidents, Dies," *New York Times*, July 27, 1986.

14. Isaacson and Thomas, *Wise Men*, 262.

15. Isaacson and Thomas, *Wise Men*, 258–67.

16. Donovan, *Conflict and Crisis*, 42.

17. Vandenberg, *Private Papers*, 175–76.

4. "Sensible Machinery"

1. "At a soiree given by Patricia Bosworth's father," one historian wrote, "Paul Robeson, the famous African American singer, entertained notables such as I. F. Stone, Adlai Stevenson, Alger Hiss, Hollywood producer Walter Wanger, movie star Joan Bennett, screenwriter Dalton Trumbo, opera singer Lily Pons, and columnist Herb Caen." At "another festive occasion," the *New York Times'* Arthur Krock saw "the youthful journalist John Fitzgerald Kennedy 'cutting in on Anthony Eden, who was dancing with the beautiful lady who became Viscountess Harcourt—and getting promptly cut in on again by Eden himself.'" Schlesinger, *Act of Creation*, 118–19, 155.

2. Vandenberg, *Private Papers*, 156.

3. Vandenberg, *Private Papers*, 181.

4. Vandenberg, *Private Papers*, 180.

5. Schlesinger, *Act of Creation*, 134–35.

6. Vandenberg, *Private Papers*, 182.

7. Vandenberg, *Private Papers*, 184–85.

5. *"America Wins!"*

1. Truman, *Volume One*, 286.

2. Vandenberg, *Private Papers*, 191–92.

3. Truman, *Volume One*, 285.

4. Vandenberg, *Private Papers*, 196.

5. Vandenberg, *Private Papers*, 197.

6. Vandenberg, *Private Papers*, 199–200.

7. Vandenberg, *Private Papers*, 201.

8. Truman, *Volume One*, 258.

9. Truman, *Volume One*, 287.

10. Schlesinger, *Act of Creation*, 205.

11. Vandenberg, *Private Papers*, 203–4.

12. Truman, *Volume One*, 287.

13. Vandenberg, *Private Papers*, 208.

14. Vandenberg, *Private Papers*, 187.

15. They did so two years later, adopting the "Rio Treaty" in September of 1947.

16. Schlesinger, *Act of Creation*, 177–79.

17. Vandenberg, *Private Papers*, 189.

18. Vandenberg, *Private Papers*, 190.

19. Vandenberg, *Private Papers*, 192–93.

6. "Solid Structure"

1. Bert Andrews, "Truman in San Francisco to Close Parley Today; Vandenberg for Charter," *New York Herald Tribune*, June 26, 1945, 1; "Vandenberg Statement," *New York Herald Tribune*, June 26, 1945, 8.

2. Vandenberg, *Private Papers*, 218.

3. Abba Eban, "The UN Idea Revisited," *Foreign Affairs*, September/October 1995, http://www.foreignaffairs.com/articles/51397/abba-eban/the-un-idea-revisited; Paul Kennedy and Bruce Russett, "Reforming the United Nations," *Foreign Affairs*, September/October 1995; Robert McMahon, ed., "UN Sanctions: A Mixed Record," Council on Foreign Relations, http://www.cfr.org/international-organizations-and-alliances/un-sanctions-mixed-record/p12045.

4. Vandenberg, *Private Papers*, 218–19.

Part 2. "Support Free Peoples"

1. Jones, *Fifteen Weeks*, 138–41; memo from Joseph Marion Jones to Loy Henderson, February 28, 1947, from J. M. Jones Papers, Harry S. Truman Library & Museum, http://www.trumanlibrary.org/whistlestop/study_collections/doctrine/large/documents/index.php?documentdate=1947–02–00&documentid=8–4&pagenumber=1.

2. Acheson, *Sketches from Life*, 128; Acheson, *Present at the Creation*, 219. Mythology surrounds Vandenberg's reaction, with numerous accounts stating that, after hearing Marshall and Acheson make the case for U.S. aid to Greece and Turkey, the senator suggested that Truman deliver a speech and "scare hell out of the country." Apparently, historian Eric F. Goldman put the story in play on page 59 of his *The Crucial Decade—And After: America, 1945–1960* (New York: Vintage Books, 1960). In the years since, pundits sometimes point to Vandenberg's purported comment and suggest that the presidents of their day do the same thing to rally public support around this policy or that. The evidence suggests, however, that Vandenberg said no such thing in that important meeting of early 1947. Vandenberg never mentioned that he used such language and Truman never mentioned hearing it. Nor did anyone else who was reportedly there. Most likely, someone later paraphrased Vandenberg's comments this way and the tale assumed a life of its own.

7. "What Is Russia Up To?"

1. Truman, *Volume One*, 546–52.

2. Vandenberg, *Private Papers*, 220–29; Truman, *Volume One*, 547–48.

3. Vandenberg, *Private Papers*, 232–36.

4. Isaacson and Thomas, *Wise Men*, 350.

5. Truman, *Volume One*, 552.

6. Isaacson and Thomas, *Wise Men*, 352.

7. Gaddis, *George F. Kennan*, 215–19.

8. Vandenberg, *Private Papers*, 245–51; individual newspapers.

9. Vandenberg, *Private Papers*, 225.

10. Vandenberg, *Private Papers*, 243–45.

11. Vandenberg, *Private Papers*, 251.

8. "Trying to Chisel Away"

1. Isaacson and Thomas, *Wise Men*, 367.

2. Jones, *Fifteen Weeks*, 54–55.

3. Dobbs, *Six Months*, 248–50.

4. Hamby, "Harry S. Truman," 21.

5. Isaacson and Thomas, *Wise Men*, 371.

6. Vandenberg, *Private Papers*, 266–67.

7. Vandenberg, *Private Papers*, 286.

8. Vandenberg, *Private Papers*, 297–98.

9. Clifford, *Counsel to the President*, 109–13 and 123–29. See also "Oral History Interview with Clark Clifford," Interview by Jerry N. Hess, Washington DC, March 23 and April 13, 1971, and March 16, 1972; "Interview with George Else, 4/12/95," The National Security Archive, George Washington University, http://www2.gwu.edu/~nsarchiv/coldwar/interviews/episode-1/elsey1.html.

9. "Halfbright"

1. Vandenberg, *Private Papers*, 304.

2. Vandenberg, *Private Papers*, 309–17.

3. Dallek, *Harry S. Truman*, 50.

4. Vandenberg, *Private Papers*, 311.

5. Truman, *Volume Two*, 103.

10. "Complete Agreement"

1. Vandenberg, *Private Papers*, 342.

2. Vandenberg, *Private Papers*, 339.

3. Walter Lippmann, "Freedom at Stake," *New York Herald Tribune*, March 1, 1947.

4. Jones, *Fifteen Weeks*, 79–80.

5. Truman, *Volume Two*, 100.

6. Jones, *Fifteen Weeks*, 84.

7. Acheson, *Present at the Creation*, 90.

8. Acheson, *Sketches from Life*, 2–3.

9. Clifford, *Counsel to the President*, 140.

10. Acheson, *Present at the Creation*, 71, 223.

11. Isaacson and Thomas, *Wise Men*, 389.

12. Steel, *Walter Lippmann*, 439–40.

13. Acheson, *Present at the Creation*, 218.

14. Truman, *Volume Two*, 101.

15. James Reston, "Truman Asks Aid to Greece; British Unable to Bear Costs," *New York Times*, February 28, 1947, 1.

16. Vandenberg, *Private Papers*, 340–41.

17. Joseph Alsop, "The President and American Foreign Policy," *New York Herald Tribune*, March 3, 1947.

18. Walter Lippmann, "The Nettle of the Middle East," *New York Herald Tribune*, March 11, 1947.

19. Truman, *Volume Two*, 105.

20. Jones, *Fifteen Weeks*, 169.

21. Alsop, "President and American Foreign Policy."

22. Truman, *Volume Two*, 102.

23. "Drafting of the President's Message of March 12, 1947," from J. M. Jones Papers, Harry S. Truman Library & Museum, http://www.trumanlibrary.org/whistlestop/study_collections/doctrine/large/documents/index.php?documentdate=1947–03–00&documentid=7–3&pagenumber=1; Clifford, *Counsel to the President*, 133–37.

24. Isaacson and Thomas, *Wise Men*, 396–98; Elsey, "Impressions of a Speechwriter," 57.

25. Truman, *Volume Two*, 105.

11. "Message Faces Facts"

1. Jones, *Fifteen Weeks*, 172–73.

2. Harold Callender, "Europe Is Amazed by Blunt Warning," *New York Times*, March 13, 1947, 3; Vandenberg, *Private Papers*, 343.

3. C. P. Trussell, "Congress Is Solemn: Prepares to Consider Bills after Hearing the President Gravely," *New York Times*, March 13, 1947, 1.

4. James Reston, "Acheson Is Slated to Quit This Week; Lovett to Get Post," *New York Times*, May 12, 1947, 1.

5. Trussell, "Congress Is Solemn," 1.

6. Vandenberg, *Private Papers*, 343–44.

12. "Colossal Blunder"

1. Vandenberg, *Private Papers*, 339.

2. C. P. Trussell, "Mid-East Policy Faces Fight; Bipartisan Unity in Balance," *New York Times*, March 18, 1947, 1.

3. Robert C. Albright, "House Bill Would Okay Greek-Turk Loan, Grant," *Washington Post*, March 19, 1947, 1.

4. C. P. Trussell, "Pepper Denounces Truman Doctrine," *New York Times*, March 26, 1947, 4; Edwards, "Congress and the Origins of the Cold War," 134.

5. Vandenberg, *Private Papers*, 344–46; Acheson, *Present at the Creation*, 223–24.

Part 3. "Very Serious"

1. George C. Marshall, letter to James B. Conant, May 28, 1947, "How the Marshall Plan Came About," National Endowment for the Humanities, http://www.neh.gov/humanities/1998/novemberdecember/feature/how-the-marshall-plan-came-about.

2. Vandenberg, *Private Papers*, 373.

13. "Desperate Men"

1. Tom Williams, "Tuberculosis Reverses 100-Year Ebb, Becomes Europe's No. 1 Killer," *Washington Post*, April 6, 1947, B2.

2. White, *Fire in the Ashes*, 53.

3. Churchill, *Never Give In!*, 437–38.

4. Vandenberg, *Private Papers*, 231.

5. Truman, *Volume Two*, 110; Behrman, *Most Noble Adventure*, 136.

6. Larry I. Bland, "Marshall and the 'Plan,'" The George C. Marshall Foundation, http://marshallfoundation.org/marshall/essays-interviews/marshall-and-the-plan-bland/; Gaddis, *George F. Kennan*, 265.

7. Fossedal and Mikhail, "Modest Magician"; Behrman, *Most Noble Adventure*, 45–50.

8. "Memorandum by the Undersecretary for Economic Affairs (W. L. Clayton)," May 27, 1947, http://www.neh.gov/humanities/1998/novemberdecember/feature/how-the-marshall-plan-came-about.

9. Acheson, *Present at the Creation*, 227–30; Jones, *Fifteen Weeks*, 27; Behrman, *Most Noble Adventure*, 57–59; Clifford, *Counsel to the President*, 143–44; Isaacson and Thomas, *Wise Men*, 409–10.

10. Isaacson and Thomas, *Wise Men*, 410.

14. "No Illusions"

1. Truman, *Volume Two*, 112; Donovan, *Conflict and Crisis*, 267; Drew Pearson, "Truman Letting Down Marshall, Some Fear," *Washington Post*, October 3, 1947, B10.

2. James Reston, "The Man Who Will Speak for Us at Moscow," *New York Times*, March 9, 1947, SM7.

3. Isaacson and Thomas, *Wise Men*, 424.

4. Clifford, *Counsel to the President*, 144.

5. Vandenberg, *Private Papers*, 376.

6. Vandenberg, *Private Papers*, 380.

7. Behrman, *Most Noble Adventure*, 133.

8. Vandenberg, *Private Papers*, 381.

9. Joseph Alsop and Stewart Alsop, "'Problem Here,' Says Vandenberg," *Washington Post*, August 3, 1947, M13.

10. Marquis Childs, "Working Partnership," *Washington Post*, August 14, 1947, 9.

11. Acheson, *Present at the Creation*, 234.

12. George F. Kennan (writing as "X"), "The Sources of Soviet Conduct," *Foreign Affairs*, July 1947, http://www.foreignaffairs.com/articles/23331/x/the-sources-of-soviet-conduct.

13. Donovan, *Conflict and Crisis*, 291.

15. "Hunger and Cold"

1. Joseph Alsop and Stewart Alsop, "Timetable of a Tourniquet," *Los Angeles Times*, July 24, 1947, A4.

2. Robert C. Albright, "Congress Wants Facts on European Aid, He Warns, and Won't Write Blank Checks," *Washington Post*, September 6, 1947, 1.

3. Pearson, "Truman Letting Down Marshall."

4. James Reston, "Democrats Let Vandenberg Carry Load in Aid Debate," *New York Times*, November 25, 1947, 15.

16. "Back in the Saddle"

1. Vandenberg, *Private Papers*, 378.
2. "Oral History Interview with Robert A. Lovett," Interview by Richard D. McKinzie and Theodore A. Wilson, New York N Y, July 7, 1971.
3. "Text of Senator Vandenberg's Call for Speed on Peace Treaties," *New York Times*, November 4, 1947, 7.
4. Vandenberg, *Private Papers*, 382.
5. Felix Belair Jr., "Current Taxes Must Finance Marshall Plan, Says Truman," *New York Times*, November 14, 1947, 1; Ferdinand Kuhn Jr., "U.S. to Seek Rare Minerals from Europe," *Washington Post*, November 14, 1947, 1.
6. Marshall Andrews, "Rough Going Is Forecast for Four-Year Aid Proposal," *Washington Post*, December 21, 1947, M1.
7. Will Lissner, "Dewey Favors Aid in Europe and Asia on Business Basis," *New York Times*, November 6, 1947, 1; Warren Moscow, "Foreign Aid Plea Made by Stassen," *New York Times*, November 19, 1947, 2; Ferdinand Kuhn Jr., "Truman Gives Landon View on Europe," *Washington Post*, December 13, 1947, 7.
8. Cabell Phillips, "Isolationism Endangers Marshall Plan," *The Globe and Mail*, July 22, 1947, 6.

17. "They Themselves"

1. James Reston, "Vandenberg Wants a National Debate on Marshall Plan," *New York Times*, December 22, 1947, 1.
2. James B. Reston, "Politics Affect E R P, But Not Its Basic Aims," *New York Times*, February 8, 1948, E3.

18. "Welcome Beacon"

1. "Russian Tide," *New York Times*, February 29, 1948, E1.
2. Felix Belair Jr., "Says Peril Near: He Urges Counter-Action to Stop Communism's Westward March," *New York Times*, March 2, 1948, 1.
3. Marquis Childs, "Republican Sniping at E R P," *Washington Post*, March 10, 1948, 11.
4. Behrman, *Most Noble Adventure*, 252; Diane B. Kunz, "The Marshall Plan Reconsidered: A Complex of Motives," *Foreign Affairs*, May/June 1997, http://www.foreign affairs.com/articles/53056/diane-b-kunz/marshall-plan-commemorative-section -the-marshall-plan-reconsider.

Part 4. "Attack against Them All"

1. Isaacson and Thomas, *Wise Men*, 439–40; Kaplan, *NATO*, 57–58.
2. Vandenberg, *Private Papers*, 401.

19. "Their Hope Must Lie"

1. Vandenberg, *Private Papers*, 370–71.
2. Vandenberg, *Private Papers*, 371.

3. Vandenberg, *Private Papers*, 372.

4. Vandenberg, *Private Papers*, 400–401.

5. Vandenberg, *Private Papers*, 401.

6. "Oral History Interview with John D. Hickerson," Interviewed by Richard D. McKinzie, Washington DC, November 10, 1972.

7. Kaplan, *NATO*, 18–19, 63.

8. "Hickerson," Interviewed by McKinzie.

9. Kaplan, *NATO*, 20.

20. "Sound Answer"

1. Truman, *Volume Two*, 243–44.

2. Vandenberg, *Private Papers*, 405–6.

3. Truman, *Volume Two*, 245.

4. Ferdinand Kuhn Jr., "'Historic' Vote, 64–4, Paves Way for U.S. Military Help to Western European Union," *Washington Post*, June 12, 1948, 1.

5. Kuhn Jr., "'Historic' Vote, 64–4."

6. "A Pattern for Foreign Policy," *Los Angeles Times*, June 18, 1948, A4.

7. "Assails Vandenberg Resolution," *New York Times*, May 22, 1948, 3.

8. Isaacson and Thomas, *Wise Men*, 447.

9. "Second Oral History Interview with John D. Hickerson," Interviewed by Richard D. McKinzie, Washington DC, January 26, 1973; Isaacson and Thomas, *Wise Men*, 448.

10. Bertram D. Hulen, "U.S. to Open Talks on Western Pact," *New York Times*, June 24, 1948, 20.

11. Hanson W. Baldwin, "Rearming West Europe: U.S. Lacks a Balanced Surplus—Its Own Needs, Cost, and Time Factors Evaluated," *New York Times*, July 7, 1948, 3.

12. James Reston, "Military Aid to Europe Is Big Question for U.S.," *New York Times*, July 11, 1948, E3.

13. James Reston, "Capital Keeps Hopes for a Soviet Agreement," *New York Times*, July 18, 1948, E3.

21. "Consultation with You"

1. Marquis Childs, "Vandenberg's Handiwork," *Washington Post*, July 10, 1948, 5; "Soviet Reply," *Washington Post*, July 16, 1948, 20.

2. Vandenberg, *Private Papers*, 453.

3. Vandenberg, *Private Papers*, 453.

4. Vandenberg, *Private Papers*, 454–55.

5. Truman, *Volume Two*, 216.

6. Vandenberg, *Private Papers*, 458.

7. Vandenberg, *Private Papers*, 456–60.

8. Joseph Alsop and Stewart Alsop, "Dewey Faces Decision before He's Installed," *Los Angeles Times*, October 31, 1948, A5.

9. Vandenberg, *Private Papers*, 447.

10. Vandenberg, *Private Papers*, 448–52.

11. Vandenberg, *Private Papers*, 462–64.

22. "At the Water's Edge"

1. Vandenberg, *Private Papers*, 405.
2. Vandenberg, *Private Papers*, 467–70.
3. Acheson, *Present at the Creation*, 250–53.
4. Vandenberg, *Private Papers*, 472–73.
5. "Text of U.S. Policy Statement on the North Atlantic Defense Pact," *New York Times*, January 15, 1949, 7.
6. Vandenberg, *Private Papers*, 475–80.
7. Harold Callender, "French Cabinet Informed," *New York Times*, February 17, 1949, 4.
8. W. H. Lawrence, "State Department Sees No Division on Atlantic Pact," *New York Times*, February 16, 1949, 1.
9. James Reston, "Truman Denies Confusion in U.S. North Atlantic Policy," *New York Times*, February 18, 1949, 1.
10. James Reston, "Pact Compromise Aided as Acheson Informs Senators," *New York Times*, February 19, 1949, 1.

23. "The Most Sensible"

1. Vandenberg, *Private Papers*, 479.
2. James Reston, "Arms Tie to Atlantic Pact Being Debated in Capital," *New York Times*, March 3, 1949, 5.
3. "Atlantic Pact Wins Support of Capitol Hill," *Los Angeles Times*, March 19, 1949, 1.
4. Ferdinand Kuhn Jr., "Arming of Western Europe Faces High Hurdles," *Washington Post*, April 10, 1949, B1; Arthur Krock, "Storm Signals Up for the Atlantic Pact," *New York Times*, April 12, 1949, 28.
5. Jonathan Masters, "The North Atlantic Treaty Organization (NATO)," Council on Foreign Relations, http://www.cfr.org/nato/north-atlantic-treaty-organization-nato/p28287.
6. "Ukraine Crisis: NATO Chief Calls Tensions in Crimea Greatest Threat to European Security since the Cold War," *The Telegraph*, March 19, 2014, http://www.telegraph.co.uk/news /worldnews/europe/ukraine/10710044/Ukraine-crisis-Nato-chief-calls-tensions-in-Crimea -greatest-threat-to-European-security-since-the-Cold-War.html.
7. Associated Press, "Putin: Soviet Collapse a 'Genuine Tragedy,'" April 25, 2005, http:// www.nbcnews.com/id/7632057/ns/world_news/t/putin-soviet-collapse-genuine-tragedy /#.VQMx-U10zIU.

24. "Pillar of Strength"

1. Vandenberg, *Private Papers*, 515.
2. Vandenberg, *Private Papers*, 557–60.
3. McCullough, *Truman*, 841–52.

Epilogue

1. Stephens, *America in Retreat*, 15–16.
2. Bret Stephens, "The Meltdown," *Commentary*, September 2014, 25.
3. Robert Kagan, "Superpowers Don't Get to Retire," *New Republic*, May 26, 2014, http:// www.newrepublic.com/article/117859/allure-normalcy-what-america-still-owes-world.

BIBLIOGRAPHY

THIS BOOK RESTS HEAVILY on the rich and plentiful primary source materials by and about Truman, Vandenberg, the other major players in this narrative, and the landmark events of the late 1940s. Truman's speeches, press conferences, public statements, directives, appointment calendars, travel logs, and many private writings are available through the website of the Truman Library, at www.trumanlibrary.org. Other private writings from Truman are available through the collections of authors and editors (listed below). For Vandenberg, *The Private Papers of Senator Vandenberg* (also listed below), which his son masterfully edited, provides a treasure trove of speeches, media interviews, letters, and diary entries.

This book also rests heavily on news coverage from the period by the nation's leading newspapers, including the *New York Times*, *Washington Post*, *Los Angeles Times*, *Chicago Tribune*, *International Herald Tribune*, and *Detroit Free Press*; on commentary by such influential columnists as Walter Lippmann, Drew Pearson, and Joseph and Stewart Alsop; and on articles in such leading periodicals as *Time* and *Life*. Transcripts from Senate Foreign Relations Committee hearings are available online, is as the *Congressional Record*, which records all public activities of the Senate and House. So, too, are important government reports from the period as well as key memos from the major players in this story. Finally, oral history interviews with such important figures as Dean Acheson, Clark Clifford, Robert Lovett, Averell Harriman, George Elsey, John

D. Hickerson, and Francis O. Wilcox—many available through the Truman Library—provide important perspectives and details.

The following secondary sources on Truman, Vandenberg, other figures, and the events in question also proved very useful:

Acheson, Dean. *Present at the Creation: My Years in the State Department*. New York: W. W. Norton & Company, 1969.

———. *Sketches from Life of Men I Have Known*. New York: Harper & Brothers, 1959.

Applebaum, Anne. *Iron Curtain: The Crushing of Eastern Europe, 1944–1956*. New York: Doubleday, 2012.

Auchincloss, Louis. *Woodrow Wilson: A Life*. New York: Penguin Books, 2000.

Baylis, John. "Britain, the Brussels Pact, and the Continental Commitment." *International Affairs* 60, no. 4 (Autumn 1984): 615–29.

Behrman, Greg. *The Most Noble Adventure: The Marshall Plan and the Time When America Helped Save Europe*. New York: Free Press, 2007.

Beinart, Peter. *The Good Fight: Why Liberals—and Only Liberals—Can Win the War on Terror and Make America Great Again*. New York: HarperCollins, 2006.

Blum, John Morton. *Woodrow Wilson and the Politics of Morality*. Boston: Little Brown and Company, 1956.

Bohlen, Charles E. *The Transformation of American Foreign Policy*. New York: W. W. Norton & Company Inc., 1969.

———. *Witness to History: 1929–1969*. New York: W. W. Norton & Company Inc., 1973.

Bostdorff, Denise M. *Proclaiming the Truman Doctrine: The Cold War Call to Arms*. College Station: Texas A&M University Press, 2008.

Brookings Institution. *Administration of United States Aid for a European Recovery Program. Report to the Committee on Foreign Relations, United States Senate, January 22, 1948*. Washington DC: Government Printing Office, 1948.

Brown, Archie. *The Rise and Fall of Communism*. New York: HarperCollins, 2009.

Butterfield, Henry Ryan, Jr. "The American Intellectual Tradition Reflected in the Truman Doctrine." *The American Scholar* 42, no. 2 (Spring 1973): 294–307.

Chace, James. "An Extraordinary Partnership: Marshall and Acheson." *Foreign Affairs* (May/June 1997).

Cherny, Andrei. *The Candy Bombers: The Untold Story of the Berlin Airlift and America's Finest Hour*. New York: G. P. Putnam's Sons, 2008.

Churchill, Winston S., ed. *Never Give In! The Best of Winston Churchill's Speeches*. New York: Hyperion, 2003.

Clifford, Clark. *Counsel to the President: A Memoir*. New York: Random House, 1991.

Dallek, Robert. *Harry S. Truman*. New York: Times Books, 2008.

———. *The Lost Peace: Leadership in a Time of Horror and Hope, 1945–1953*. New York: HarperCollins Publishers, 2010.

Dobbs, Michael. *Six Months in 1945: FDR, Stalin, Churchill, and Truman—From World War to Cold War*. New York: Alfred A. Knopf, 2012.

Doenecke, Justus D. "American Isolationism, 1939–1941." *The Journal of Libertarian Studies* 4, nos. 3–4 (Summer/Fall 1982): 201–16.

Donald, Aida D. *Citizen Soldier: A Life of Harry S. Truman*. New York: Basic Books, 2012.

Donovan, Robert J. *Conflict and Crisis: The Presidency of Harry S. Truman, 1945–1948.* Columbia: University of Missouri Press, 1977.

———. *Tumultuous Years: The Presidency of Harry S. Truman, 1949–1953.* Columbia: University of Missouri Press, 1982.

Ebban, Abba. "The UN Idea Revisited." *Foreign Affairs* (September/October 1995). http://www.foreignaffairs.com/articles/51397/abba-eban/the-un-idea-revisited.

Edwards, Lee. "Congress and the Origins of the Cold War: The Truman Doctrine." *World Affairs* 151, no. 3 (Winter 1988–89): 131–41.

Elsey, George. "Impressions of a Speechwriter." In *The Truman Doctrine of Aid to Greece: A Fifty-Year Retrospective,* edited by Eugene T. Rossides, 55–59. New York: The Academy of Political Science and Washington: The American Hellenic Institute Foundation, 1998.

Ferrell, Robert H. *Harry S. Truman: A Life.* Columbia: University of Missouri Press, 1994.

———, ed. *Off the Record: The Private Papers of Harry S. Truman.* New York: Harper & Row, Publishers, 1980.

Fossedal, Gregory, and Bill Mikhail. "A Modest Magician: Will Clayton and the Rebuilding of Europe." *Foreign Affairs* (May/June 1947).

Fromkin, David. "Entangling Alliances." *Foreign Affairs* (July 1970).

Gaddis, John Lewis. *The Cold War: A New History.* New York: The Penguin Press, 2005.

———. *George F. Kennan: An American Life.* New York: Penguin Books, 2011.

———. "Was the Truman Doctrine a Real Turning Point?" *Foreign Affairs* (January 1974): 386–402.

Gazell, James A. "Arthur H. Vandenberg, Internationalism, and the United Nations." *Political Science Quarterly* 88, no. 3 (September 1973): 375–94.

Goldman, Eric F. *The Crucial Decade—And After: America, 1945–1960.* New York: Vintage Books, 1960.

Hamby, Alonzo L. "Harry S. Truman and the Origins of the Truman Doctrine." In *The Truman Doctrine of Aid to Greece: A Fifty-Year Retrospective,* edited by Eugene T. Rossides, 12–23. New York: The Academy of Political Science and Washington: The American Hellenic Institute Foundation, 1998.

Harrington, Daniel F. "The Berlin Blockade Revisited." *The International History Review* 6, no. 1 (February 1984): 88–112.

———. *Berlin on the Brink: The Blockade, the Airlift, and the Early Cold War.* Lexington: University Press of Kentucky, 2012.

Hartmann, Susan M. *Truman and the 80th Congress.* Columbia: University of Missouri Press, 1971.

Heindel, Richard H., Thorsten V. Kalijarvi, and Francis O. Wilcox. "The North Atlantic Treaty in the United States Senate." *The American Journal of International Law* 43, no. 4 (October 1949): 633–65.

Herken, Gregg. *The Georgetown Set: Friends and Rivals in Cold War Washington.* New York: Alfred A. Knopf, 2014.

Hernon, Joseph Martin. *Profiles in Character: Hubris and Heroism in the U.S. Senate, 1789–1990.* Armonk NY: M. E. Sharpe, 1997.

Hersey, John. *Aspects of the Presidency.* New Haven CT: Ticknor & Fields, 1980.

Hill, Thomas Michael. "Senator Arthur H. Vandenberg, the Politics of Bipartisanship, and the Origins of Anti-Soviet Consensus, 1941–1946." *World Affairs* 138, no. 3 (Winter 1975–76): 219–41.

Hindley, Meredith. "How the Marshall Plan Came About." *Humanities* 19, no. 6 (November/December 1998). http://www.neh.gov/humanities/1998/novemberdecember/feature/how-the-marshall-plan-came-about.

"The Hopkins Mission to Moscow." University of Wisconsin Digital Collections.

Hotz, Alfred J. "NATO: Myth or Reality." *Annals of the American Academy of Political and Social Science* 288 (July 1953): 126–33.

Isaacson, Walter, and Evan Thomas. *The Wise Men: Six Friends and the World They Made.* New York: Simon & Schuster, 1986.

Joffe, Josef. *The Myth of America's Decline: Politics, Economics, and a Half Century of False Prophecies.* New York: W. W. Norton & Company, 2014.

Jones, Joseph Marion. *The Fifteen Weeks (February 21–June 5, 1947): An Inside Account of the Genesis of the Marshall Plan.* San Diego: Harcourt Brace Jovanovich Publishers, 1955.

Kagan, Robert. *The World America Made.* New York: Alfred A. Knopf, 2012.

Kaplan, Lawrence S. *The Conversion of Senator Arthur H. Vandenberg: From Isolation to International Engagement.* Lexington: University Press of Kentucky, 2015.

———. *NATO 1948: The Birth of the Transatlantic Alliance.* Lanham MD: Rowman & Littlefield Publishers Inc., 2007.

Karabell, Zachary. *The Last Campaign: How Harry Truman Won the 1948 Election.* New York: Vintage Books, 2000.

Kennedy, Paul, and Bruce Russett. "Reforming the United Nations." *Foreign Affairs* (September/October 1995).

Kennan, George F. *American Diplomacy.* Chicago: University of Chicago Press, 1951.

———. "Long Telegram." February 22, 1946, National Security Archive, George Washington University. http://nsarchive.gwu.edu/coldwar/documents/episode-1/kennan.htm.

———. "The Sources of Soviet Conduct." *Foreign Affairs* (July 1947). http://www.foreignaffairs.com/articles/23331/x/the-sources-of-soviet-conduct.

Kindleberger, Charles P. "In the Halls of the Capitol: A Memoir." *Foreign Affairs* (May/June 1947).

Kunz, Diane B. "The Marshall Plan Reconsidered: A Complex of Motives." *Foreign Affairs* (May/June 1997). http://www.foreignaffairs.com/articles/53056/diane-b-kunz/marshall-plan-commemorative-section-the-marshall-plan-reconsider.

Kurlantzick, Joshua. *Democracy in Retreat: The Revolt of the Middle Class and the Worldwide Decline of Representative Government.* New Haven CT: Yale University Press, 2013.

Lieber, Robert J. *Power and Willpower in the American Future: Why the United States Is Not Destined to Decline.* New York: Cambridge University Press, 2012.

Mandelbaum, Michael. *The Case for Goliath: How America Acts as the World's Government in the 21st Century.* New York: Public Affairs, 2005.

Masters, Jonathan. "The North Atlantic Treaty Organization (NATO)." *Council on Foreign Relations.* http://www.cfr.org/nato/north-atlantic-treaty-organization-nato/p28287.

McCullough, David. *Truman.* New York: Simon & Schuster, 1992.

McMahon, Robert, ed. "UN Sanctions: A Mixed Record." *Council on Foreign Relations.* http://www.cfr.org/international-organizations-and-alliances/un-sanctions-mixed-record/p12045.

Meijer, Hank, "America's Senator: The Unexpected Odyssey of Arthur H. Vandenberg." The Hauenstein Center at Grand Valley State University. http://hauensteincenter.org/americas-senator-the-unexpected-odyssey-of-arthur-h-vandenberg/.

———. "Arthur Vandenberg and the Fight for Neutrality, 1939." *Michigan Historical Society* 16, no. 2 (Fall 1990): 1–21.

Merrill, Dennis. "The Truman Doctrine: Containing Communism and Modernity." *Presidential Studies Quarterly* 36, no. 1 (March 2006): 27–37.

Miller, Merle. *Plain Speaking: An Oral Biography of Harry S. Truman.* New York: Tess Press, 1974.

Miscamble, Wilson D. "Harry S. Truman, the Berlin Blockade, and the 1948 Election." *Presidential Studies Quarterly* 10, no. 3 (Summer 1980): 306–16.

Rayfield, Donald. *Stalin and His Hangmen: The Tyrant and Those Who Killed for Him.* New York: Random House, 2004.

Rostow, Walt W. "Lessons of the Plan: Looking Forward to the Next Century." *Foreign Affairs* (May/June 1947).

Satterthwaite, Joseph C. "The Truman Doctrine: Turkey." *Annals of the American Academy of Political and Social Science* 401 (May 1972): 74–84.

Schlesinger, Stephen C. *Act of Creation: The Founding of the United Nations.* Cambridge MA: Westview Press, 2003.

Spalding, Elizabeth Edwards. *The First Cold Warrior: Harry Truman, Containment, and the Remaking of Liberal Internationalism.* Lexington: University Press of Kentucky, 2006.

Spritzer, Neil. "Dividing a City." *Wilson Quarterly* 12, no. 3 (Summer 1988): 100–122.

Stalin, J. *Speeches Delivered at Meetings of Voters of the Stalin Electoral District, Moscow.* Moscow: Foreign Languages Publishing Group, 1954.

Steel, Ronald. *Walter Lippmann and the American Century.* Boston: Little, Brown and Company, 1980.

Steinberg, Alfred. *The Man from Missouri: The Life and Times of Harry S. Truman.* New York: G. P. Putnam's Sons, 1962.

Stephens, Bret. *America in Retreat: The New Isolationism and the Coming Global Disorder.* New York: Sentinel, 2014.

Stetzer, Susanne. "NATO: A Brief History of Expansion." *Congressional Research Service.* http://congressionalresearch.com/98-51/document.php?study=NATO+A+BRIEF+HISTORY+OF+EXPANSION.

Thompson, Nicholas. *The Hawk and the Dove: Paul Nitze, George Kennan, and the History of the Cold War.* New York: Henry Holt and Company, 2009.

Tompkins, C. David. *Senator Arthur H. Vandenberg: The Evolution of a Modern Republican, 1884–1945.* East Lansing: Michigan State University Press, 1970.

Truman, Harry S. *Memoirs by Harry S. Truman, Volume One: Year of Decisions.* Garden City NY: Doubleday & Company Inc., 1955.

———. *Memoirs by Harry S. Truman, Volume Two: Years of Trial and Hope.* Garden City NY: Doubleday & Company Inc., 1956.

Truman, Margaret, ed. *Where the Buck Stops: The Personal and Private Writings of Harry S. Truman.* New York: Warner Books, 1989.

Unger, Debi, and Irwin Unger. *George Marshall: A Biography.* New York: HarperCollins, 2014.

"United States Strategic Bombing Survey." In *Over-All Report (European War).* Washington DC: Government Printing Office, 1945.

Vandenberg, Arthur H. "The New Deal Must Be Salvaged." *The American Mercury* 49, no. 193 (January 1940): 1–10.

Vandenberg, Arthur H., Jr., ed. *The Private Papers of Senator Vandenberg*. Westport CT: Greenwood Press, Publishers, 1974.

White, Theodore H. *Fire in the Ashes: Europe in Mid-Century*. New York: William Sloane Associates, 1953.

Wilcox, Francis O. "Arthur Vandenberg and the Nonpartisan Approach to Foreign Policy." In *Arthur H. Vandenberg: His Career and Legacy*. Ann Arbor: University of Michigan, 1975.

Wilcox, Francis O., and Thorsten V. Kalijarvi. *Recent American Foreign Policy: Basic Documents, 1941–1951*. New York: Appleton-Century-Crofts Inc., 1952.

Wilson, Theodore W. "The Marshall Plan, 1947–1951." *Foreign Policy Association*, Headline Series, no. 236 (June 1977): 1–64.

Index

Bohlen, Charles, xvi, 65, 79, 105, 114, 134–35, 168, 181–83
Bolivarian Alliance for the Americas, 284
Bradley, Omar, 271
Britain. *See* Great Britain
Brookings Institution, 202, 208–9
Brussels Pact, 218, 231, 239–40, 248
Bunche, Ralph, 57–58
Bush, George H. W., 153
Bush, George W., 153, 282
Byrd, Harry F., 270
Byrnes, James "Jimmy," 20, 203; appointed secretary of state, 58; peace treaty work of, 112–14, 158; replaced by Marshall, 95, 173; role in foreign policy, xvii; and U.S.-Soviet tensions, 99, 107, 110

Callender, Harold, 140
Canada, 248
Capehart, Homer, 215
Carey, James B., 178–79
Carter, Jimmy, 153
Chandler, Zachariah, 14
Chapultepec, Act of, 81–85, 227
Chiang Kai-shek, 275–76
Chicago Times (newspaper), 146
Chicago Tribune (newspaper), 30, 117
Childs, Marquis, 25, 180, 216
China, 76–77, 158, 275–76, 283
Christian Science Monitor (newspaper), 140
Churchill, Winston: on the European crisis, 164; "iron curtain" speech, 109–10; and the North Atlantic Treaty, 231; praise for Marshall, 95; on Soviet aggression, xii, 63; at the Yalta conference, 46–47, 76–77
Civil War, 3
Clark, Tom, 114
Clay, Lucius, 221
Clayton, Will, xvii, 142, 168–69, 178, 183, 187
Clifford, Clark, 24, 26, 114–15, 134–35, 175, 186
Clifford-Elsey report, 114–15
Clinton, Bill, 153, 273
Cold War, 103, 197, 273, 280. *See also* U.S.-Soviet relations
Collier's (magazine), 9

Committee of Eight (SFRC), 50
Communism: Marshall Plan as counter to, 194–95, 197; threat of during Europe's crisis, 151, 154, 159, 164, 168; as a way of life, 138–39. *See also* Soviet Union
Conant, James B., 158
Congress (U.S.): approval of Greek-Turkish aid, 171; and the Marshall Plan, 196–97, 216–17; partisanship in, 253–54, 275–77; Republican control of, 119–20; special session on emergency aid, 185–86, 188–91; tax cut bills, 172; and the Truman Doctrine, 97, 137–39. *See also* House of Representatives (U.S.); Senate (U.S.)
Congress of Vienna (1814), 40
Connally, Tom, 28, 42, 79, 88, 247; and the Greek-Turkish crisis, 129, 147, 148; and the North Atlantic Treaty, 260, 263, 272; role in foreign policy, xvii; and the UN Charter conference, 35, 51, 55–56, 60, 67, 69; during World War II, 18
Connally Resolution, 18
Connolly, Matt, 247
Conway, Granville, 167
Council of Foreign Ministers: on Germany's future, 230–31; postwar treaties, 112–14; and Soviet aggressiveness, 99–102, 168
Crowley, Leo, 203
Curzon Line, 47–48
Czechoslovakia, 182, 204, 211–12, 216, 239

Daniell, Raymond, xiii
Davies, Joseph, 65
Davis, Chester C., 178–79
defense pacts. *See* regional defense pacts
Delta State Teachers College (Cleveland MS), 169–71
Denver Post (newspaper), 146
Detroit Free Press (newspaper), 106, 245
Detroit Times (newspaper), 250
Deupree, R. R., 178–79
Dewey, Thomas, 22, 55, 146, 198, 241, 248–49
domino theory, 139
Donnell, Forrest C., 261
Douglas, Lewis W., 189–90, 202, 205–6, 244
Douglas, William, 103

Dubinsky, David, 146

Dulles, John Foster, 157, 165; advising Vandenberg, 17, 48, 249; on the European crisis, 169, 231; and the North Atlantic Treaty, 272; and the UN Charter, 83; and the Vandenberg Resolution, 235

Dumbarton Oaks draft, 45–46, 55, 58, 59. *See also* UN Charter conference (San Francisco)

Dunn, Jimmy, 52, 79, 85

Early, Steve, 35

Eaton, Charles A., xvii, 51, 83, 120, 129, 187–89

Eden, Anthony, 61, 69, 70, 72, 290n1

Eichelberger, Clark M., 179

Eisenhower, Dwight, 63, 112, 129, 248

elections: of 1928, 14–15; of 1940, 22; of 1944, 20–21; of 1946, xviii, 117–21; of 1948, xviii, 3–4, 22, 225, 248–50

Elsey, George, 114–15, 134–35

Europe: early attempts at global peace in, 40; economic crises in, 154, 159, 163–69, 175–77, 185–91; impact of the Marshall Plan on, 217; and the Marshall Plan, 161, 239–40; and the North Atlantic Treaty, 231–32, 239–40, 256–59, 262–65, 270–71, 273; obligations under the Marshall Plan, 203, 205; postwar crises in, xiii–xiv; reaction to the Truman Doctrine, 140; Soviet aggressiveness in, xii, 96–97, 109–12, 125–26, 139, 151, 168; U.S.-Soviet divisions in, 182–83; and the Vandenberg Resolution, 233, 234, 236

Evatt, H. V., 61

Ferris, Woodbridge, 14

Finland, 212, 216, 230

Ford, Gerald, 153

Foreign Affairs (journal), 182

foreign aid programs: in the Clifford-Elsey report, 115; European food aid, 163–66; Greek-Turkish aid, 97, 120, 137–39, 141–43, 145–47, 157–59, 171; Lend-Lease aid, xii, 12; short-term relief programs, 158–59, 185–91

Forrestal, James V., 105, 114, 202, 206–7

France: during the Berlin crisis, 244; in the Brussels Pact, 218; emergency aid for, 187–91; and the Marshall Plan, 182; tensions over Germany's future, 230–31; and UN veto power, 76–77; during World War II, xi

Franklin D. Roosevelt (supercarrier), 111

Freedom House, 282

Fulbright, J. William, 119–20, 231–32

Gaddafi, Muammar, 153

General Assembly (UN), 37, 45, 51–53, 71–73, 105

George VI (king of Britain), 4

Germany: and the Berlin crisis, 221, 225, 243–45, 246–47, 248; economic crisis protests in, 163; postwar crisis in, xiii; U.S.-Soviet tensions regarding, 113, 194, 230–31; during World War II, xi

Gildersleeve, Virginia C., 51

Goldman, Eric F., xv, 291n2

Gottwald, Klement, 211

Grand Rapids Herald (newspaper), 9, 14

Great Britain: and atomic inspections, 101–2; during the Berlin crisis, 244; in the Brussels Pact, 218; decreasing global role of, 92, 95, 99–100, 128–31; economic crisis in, 123–26; and Germany's future, 230–31; Lend-Lease program, 12; and the Marshall Plan, 182; and the North Atlantic Treaty, 231–32, 238–39; and the UN Charter conference, 51–53, 69–70, 76–77; U.S. loans to, 165; during World War II, xi

Greece: Britain's withdrawal from, 92, 95, 123, 125; debate on proposed aid to, 147–53; gathering support for U.S. aid to, 141–43, 145–47; and the Marshall Plan, 182; proposed U.S. aid to, 120, 137–39; Soviet threats to, 92, 95–97, 111, 125–26; U.S. aid package to, 97, 157–59, 171; U.S. response to crisis in, 129–35

Green, Fred, 15

Grew, Joseph, 52, 55, 75

Griswold, Dwight, 157

Gromyko, Andrei, 52, 77–78, 80

Halifax, 1st Earl of (Edward Frederick Lindley Wood), 61

Hannegan, Bob, 20

Harriman, Averell, 157, 181; as ambassador to Great Britain, 110; on isolationism, xv; and the Marshall Plan, 178–79, 202; and North Atlantic Treaty, 271; political career of, 63–64; and presidential poker, 24; role in foreign policy creation, xvii; on Truman's style, 26; and the UN Charter, 79; on U.S.-Soviet relations, 63–65, 105

Harriman Committee, 178–79

Haswell, James M., 106

Hayden, Jay, 25

Henderson, Loy, 133

Henry IV (king of France), 40

Hickenlooper, Bourke, 270

Hickerson, John, 231–32, 234, 238–39

Hiss, Alger, 67, 255, 290n1

Hoffman, Paul G., 178–79, 276

Holbrooke, Richard, 53

Holmes, Oliver Wendell, 269

Hoover, Herbert, 203

Hopkins, Harry, 58, 79–80

House of Representatives (U.S.): and Greek-Turkish aid, 142, 148, 152, 171; and the Marshall Plan, 160; proposed budget cuts, 132; Republican control of, 119–20; Truman Doctrine speech in, 137–39

Houston Post (newspaper), 107

Hull, Cordell, 50, 58

Hungary, 112, 157–58

Inverchapel, 1st Baron (Archibald Clark Kerr), 125, 128

Iran, 99, 110, 284

Iraq, 282, 284

ISIS, 284

isolationism: changing views on, 18–19, 36–37; current trends in, 281–83; historic, xiv–xv; and the Marshall Plan, 198–99; postwar return of, xv, 120, 132–33

Italy, 113, 157–58, 182, 187–91, 216, 230

Izvestia (newspaper), 238

Jacobson, Eddie, 8

Januszewski, Frank, 69

Japan, xi

Johnson, Hiram, 89

Johnson, Lyndon B., 24

Jones, Jesse, 36, 203

Jones, Joseph Marion, 133–34

Kagan, Robert, 282–83

Kansas City Times (newspaper), 260

Kant, Immanuel, 40

Kennan, George F.: and the Marshall Plan, 168, 181; and the North Atlantic Treaty, 238–39; role in foreign policy creation, xvii; on Soviet expansionism, 103–5, 110, 114; and the Truman Doctrine speech, 134–35; on U.S.-Soviet relations, 103–5, 182

Kennedy, John F., 153, 290n1

Kennedy, Joseph, 203

Kerry, John, 284

Knighton, William, 25

Krock, Arthur, 115, 247, 290n1

Krug, Julius Albert, 178–79, 202

Kuhn, Ferdinand, 25

La Follette, Robert M., Jr., 178–79

LaGuardia, Fiorella H., 148

Landon, Alf, 146, 198

Lange, Halvard, 260

Langer, William, 89

Lapham, Roger, 67

Latin America, 81–85, 227–29

Lawrence, David, 47–48

League of Nations, 40–41, 60

Leahy, William D., 114

Lend-Lease aid, xii, 12

Life (magazine), 26

Lippmann, Walter, 128, 131

"Locksley Hall" (Tennyson), 39

Lodge, Henry Cabot, 41, 195–96

Los Angeles Times (newspaper), 237

Lovett, Robert Abercrombie, 181; and the Berlin crisis, 244–45; briefing Vandenberg, 193–94; and Europe's economic crisis, 186, 187; and the Marshall Plan, 201; and the North Atlantic Treaty, 232, 238–39, 256, 271; resignation of, 250, 254; role in foreign policy creation, xvii; and the Vandenberg Resolution, 223–24, 233–35

Lublin government (Poland), 47, 53, 65, 70

Luxembourg, 182, 218

MacArthur, Douglas, 22, 27, 277

Mackinac Charter, 18–19, 42

MacLeish, Archibald, 55, 57–58

MacMillan, Margaret, xiii

Mao Tse-tung, 275

Marshall, George C., xvii, 132; background of, 173–74; during the Berlin crisis, 243–44, 246–47; and Britain's withdrawal, 125, 128–29; collaborating with Vandenberg, 174; and Europe's economic crisis, 186, 187; and Greek-Turkish aid, 95–96, 134–35; Harvard luncheon speech, 158, 159, 175–77; on isolationism, 133; and the North Atlantic Treaty, 231–32, 238–39; relationship with the Vandenbergs, 229; retirement of, 250; secretary of state appointment, 173; as Senate witness, 202–4; on Soviet expansionism, 168–69; and the Vandenberg Resolution, 235; and the Vinson mission, 246–47

Marshall, Thomas R., 14

Marshall Plan, 160–61, 232; administration issue, 202, 208–9; assessing viability of, 177–79; background to, 158–59, 163–71, 175–77; congressional deliberation on, 160, 196–97, 202–9, 212–15; development of, 160, 168–69, 174–75, 177–83, 186–87, 193; enactment of, 217; Europe's obligations under, 205; funding issues, 160, 183, 196, 197, 201–2, 205–6, 208, 215; gathering support for, 179–80, 194–96, 198; impact on the North Atlantic Treaty, 257–58; implications of, 161; opposition to, 195–96, 198–99, 201, 208; responding to Soviet aggression, 161, 216–17, 239–40; results of, 217, 279–80; short-term aid preceding, 185–91, 193

Martin, Joseph W., 129, 137, 190, 277

Martin, William McChesney, 202

Masaryk, Jan, 70, 212

Mason, Edward S., 178–79

McCormick, Anne O'Hare, 126

McCormick, Robert, 30

McGrath, J. Howard, 251

McKim, Eddie, 21

Meany, George, 178–79

Mediterranean region, 111–12, 125–26. *See also* Greece; Turkey

Merriam, Gordon, 133

Metternich, Klemens Wenzel von, 40

Middle East, 139, 284. *See also* Turkey

Missouri (battleship), 110, 111

Molotov, Vyacheslav, 100; and the Marshall Plan, 181–82, 204; peace treaty work of, 112; return to Moscow, 78; Truman's confrontation with, 65–66; and the UN Charter conference, xii, 52, 63, 64, 69–73, 80

Monroe, James, 81, 141

Monroe Doctrine, 81, 141

Moody, Blair, 25

Myers, William I., 178–79

NATO. *See* North Atlantic Treaty Organization

the Netherlands, 182, 218

Neutrality Acts (1930s), 12

New Republic (magazine), 282–83

New York Herald Tribune (newspaper), 52, 87, 131, 140, 146

New York Times (newspaper), xiii, 140–41, 146, 174, 191, 199, 208, 214–15, 239, 240, 263, 264

Nixon, Richard, xviii, 153

North Atlantic Treaty, 81, 218, 224; background to, 222–23, 231–32, 235–38, 261; building support for, 256–64, 272–73; calculated risks in creation of, 257–58; development of, 238–40, 243, 248, 255–58; military obligations under, 257, 258, 259, 260–63, 267, 268–71, 274; results of, 273–74, 279–80; Senate debate on, 272–73; Senate ratification of, 273; SFRC hearings on, 267–69, 271–72; signing of, 264–65; Vandenberg Resolution's impact on, 256, 270

North Atlantic Treaty Organization (NATO), xvi, 223, 273–74, 280. *See also* North Atlantic Treaty

Norway, 182, 259, 260

Nye, Gerald, 12

Obama, Barack, 153, 281–82, 284–85

Omaha World-Herald (newspaper), 106–7

Truman, Harry S (continued)
Greek-Turkish aid, 128–35, 137–38, 152–53, 157, 291n2; role in the Rio Pact, 227–28; Senate tenure of, 14, 15, 16–17, 20–21; and short-term European aid, 158–59, 185–89, 190–91; on tax cuts, 171–72; Truman Doctrine of, 97, 115, 137–41, 153; UN Charter conference collaborations, 69–71, 75, 76–77, 78–82, 84, 87, 89; UN Charter conference opening speech, 68–69; UN Charter conference preparations, 52–53, 59–61; on U.S.'s increasing global role, 95–97, 125; and the Vandenberg Resolution, 223–24, 233, 235–36; as vice presidential candidate, 20–21; and the Vinson mission, 246–47
Truman, John Anderson, 3, 5, 7, 8, 9–10
Truman, John Vivian, 5
Truman, Martha Ellen Young, 3, 5
Truman Committee, 16–17
Truman Doctrine: gathering support for, 141–43, 150–51; impact on the North Atlantic Treaty, 224; importance of bipartisanship in, 146–47; as response to Soviet aggression, 97, 115, 139, 151–52; results of, 153, 279–80; Truman's speech outlining, 137–41
Turkey: Britain's withdrawal from, 92, 95, 123, 125; debate on proposed aid to, 147–53; gathering support for U.S. aid to, 141–43, 145–47; and the Marshall Plan, 182; proposed U.S. aid to, 137–39; Soviet threats to, 92, 95–96, 111–12, 126, 137–39; U.S. aid package to, 97, 157, 171; U.S. response to crisis in, 120, 129–35
Turkish Straits, 111–12

Ukraine, 70, 153, 274, 283
UN Charter conference (San Francisco): addressing past injustices, 71–73; delegation selection, 45–46, 48–56; opening session, 67–69; preparations for, 31, 48–56, 57, 59–61; public support for, 55–56; regional defense pact issue, 73, 81–85, 223; Senate ratification of, 87–90; Soviet challenges at, 69–71; Stettinius's role at, 58–59, 75–76; Truman's initial ignorance of, 50, 62; U.S.-Soviet tensions preceding, 62–66; veto power controversy, 73, 76–80

United Nations (UN): building support for creation of, 41–43, 54–56; importance of, 35–37; North Atlantic Treaty's impact on, 268; pessimism regarding, 229–30; results of, 90–91, 279–80; roots of, 37–38, 39–41; and the Truman Doctrine, 138, 143, 147–50; uncertainty following FDR's death, 35–36; and the Vandenberg Resolution, 235–37. See also UN Charter conference (San Francisco)
United Nations Relief and Rehabilitation Administration (UNRRA), 149
United States: changing views on isolationism, xiv–xv, 36–37; future global role of, 281–86; and Germany's future, 230–31; impact of UN on, 91, 138–39; increasing global role of, xvi, 95–97, 125–26, 128–31, 280; postwar stability of, xiv. See also foreign aid programs; Marshall Plan; North Atlantic Treaty; Truman Doctrine; UN Charter conference (San Francisco)
U.S. Congress. See Congress (U.S.)
U.S. House of Representatives. See House of Representatives (U.S.)
U.S. Senate. See Senate (U.S.)
U.S.-Soviet relations: during the Berlin crisis, 221, 237, 243–46; and the Marshall Plan, 180–83; North Atlantic Treaty's impact on, 259, 273; postwar rivalry, xii; and tensions over Germany, 113, 194, 230–31; and the Truman Doctrine, 97, 143; Truman's approach to, 62–66, 91–92, 99–103, 107, 109–12, 114–15, 273; during the UN Charter conference, 37; Vinson mission, 246–47

Vandenberg, Aaron, 3, 10
Vandenberg, Alpha, 3, 6
Vandenberg, Arthur Hendrick: during the 1946 election, 117–19; during the 1948 election, 22, 249–50; and Acheson, 127–28, 141–42, 224, 254–55; approach of, 23–26, 203, 267; assessment of Stettinius, 75–76; on atomic inspections, 101–2; background of, 2–3, 4, 6–7, 8–9; during the Berlin crisis, 225, 243–46; changing views on isolationism, 10, 11–13, 17–19,